Why this Cover?

The cover was designed by Baba Wade Nobles, and as I see it, depicts the workings of Black critical conscious mind. The Black critical conscious mind represents how we, as Africans, think consciously and unconsciously. The image of the brain with various African culture groups (Yoruba, Bantu, Dogon, Kongo, Luba/Bomba, or Ewe-Fon) reflects where we may have evolved from the culture of African people. The tribal/ethnicities (Fulani, Mandinka, Wolof, Asante, Jola, Temmie, Mande, Kwa-Zula, Bambara, Hausa, and Jalonke) demonstrate our lineage from whom we descend. The philosophical Ley lines are genealogical lines that are dotted, and represent how Africans in the diaspora ascended from Africa, like latitudinal and longitudinal lines, and carry mystical and natural energy.

When you look into advanced civilizations like the Ancient Egyptians, it is clear that they seemed to understand the energy and power of Ley Lines. Along these lines, the intersecting places shape our understanding of being **divine spirits housed in a physical body having a human experience.** Here we have divine energy that can be harnessed by us as individuals that define and explicate the human experience and shape our **humanity, personhood, and Being**; this is the pineal gland, Anja, or third eye, reflecting intuition, perception, knowledge, and open-mindedness.

The terminology within the brain gives us access to what the African-thinking mind looks like. Rising out of the recesses of our minds, we see what influences us via Cultural laws, Cultural Virtues, Cultural prerequisites, Cultural themes, and Cultural Customs. To connect the workings of the brain to our African mind, we know that the African mind uses more of the brain's right hemisphere and the midbrain, characterized by spiritual concepts such as love, affection, and sharing. The terminology within the frontal region of the brain reflects our perceptions of various sensations, including pain, as reflected in our belief in Higher Being, being in the light, dimensions of the spirit, destiny ordained by God, a person being divine, God in everything, theological hierarchy, ancestral veneration, and death as a transition.

The terminology also reflects how being social is highly valued, respect for elders, obligatory non-reciprocal sharing, harmony in opposites, complementary role performance, sense of oneness, family group centeredness, and shared responsibility. Rising out of our prefrontal cortex controlling decision-making, we can see proper conduct, self-control, content-dependent leadership, collective survival responsibility, freedom of personality, and personal contribution. Equal balances of rational thought characterize the midbrain, and creative thought reflects our desire to live in a just society, power of the word, respect for the land, harmonious circular time, and feminine as primary and paramount.

I like to say that "we are as African as we are." What do I mean by that? In our conscious and unconscious minds, we have an African way of being that begins with spirit and filters through how we think and see the world. This is the result of our ancestral lineage that lives within us. Ayi Kwei Armah's Two Thousand Seasons reminds us:

"Our way, the way, is not a random path. Our way begins from coherent understanding. It is a way that aims at preserving knowledge of who we are, knowledge the best way we have to relate to each other, each to all, ourselves to other people, and all to our surroundings. If our individual lives have a worthwhile aim, that aim should be a purpose inseparable from the way". We are as African as we are. The cover reflects "Our Way," the typology of an African mind that upholds a consciousness and love for the African way of thinking. Black Critical consciousness reflects the memetic mind mapping laid out by Baba Nobles and displays what makes sense in how we have been, how we should be, and what we should strive to achieve for having Black critical consciousness.

UBUNTU MUSINGS

The Need for Black Critical Consciousness

DR. DEREK J. WILSON

Foreword By Baba Dr. Wade W. Nobles

UBUNTU Publishing

Ubuntu Musings
The Need for Black Critical Consciousness

Published and Copyright © 2023 by Ubuntu Publishing & Dr. Derek J. Wilson. All rights reserved.

Volume I

Published by Ubuntu Publishing. Copyright © 2023 by Ubuntu Publishing. All rights reserved.

Printed in the United States of America.

This book is printed on acid-free paper.

ISBN: 979-8-218-20617-8

Library of Congress Cataloging-in-Publication Data
Registration Number/Date: TXu002373337 / 2023-05-04
Names: Wilson, Derek, Author
Title: Ubuntu Musings: The Need for Black Critical Consciousness / Dr. Derek Wilson
Description: Volume I. | Chapel Hill, NC: Ubuntu Publishing, 2023.
LC record available at https://cocatalog.loc.gov/

Contents

Acknowledgment

I want to acknowledge the one person who encouraged me to become more significant than I thought I could be. That is my Mother, known everywhere she goes as "Mother BJ" Bettye-Wilson. She is a respected elder in all the communities she has participated in. I have watched her fight to exist as a Black Woman in America and demonstrate a warrior attitude against racism and sexism in the military and the VA System. She was a Jegna to many women as evidenced by her excellence in Being, Becoming in her way of showing what other women can do and most notably by doing what great Black Women do, lead, care for, and Zola up on all who have come across her path. My Mother was the first African/Black woman to establish and lead a community mental health program in a neighborhood health center and an HIV Counseling, Testing and Referral Center. She culminated her 22-year military career as Colonel and Chief Nurse of a United States Army Hospital. She made history. ABPsi honored her in 2010 for the Community Service Award. That's My Momma! She was the first to teach me how to exhibit Ubuntu in our beingness and spirit.

I want acknowledge my wife, Dr. Paula Moore-Wilson for her unwavering support during this endeavor. I also want to acknowledge my daughters Akilah Jo Wilson and Onyeka Oluseyi Jo-Ann Wilson for their love and support. They have kept me honest in my being and have challenged me not to be a living spirit of (mis)Knowing, (non)Being, and (un)Doing in my existence. It is their spirit I carry with me

I want to thank ABPsi for providing the roadmap for Jegnaship & the countless many students who have allowed me to Jegna them. ABPsi has allowed me to bring my students on this journey, and they have changed lives. I need to recognize some special students that I am proud of knowing and serving as Jegna. Dr. Eryka Boyd was the first to come through my tutelage in ABPsi and obtain her doctorate. She set the standard and tone by which all of my students are judged. Aida Fall, who is always there when I need her and continues to demonstrate fire spirit in wanting to impact and change our community. Rozy Uzuh-Frances, M.S., who showed tenacity to say I want a graduate degree and went and got it! My young brother Oba, soon to be a doctor, Tsare Woodyard, M.A., is a doctor in knowing. The last two were past Student-Circle Presidents of ABPsi. I want to thank ABPsi for bringing out the best in all four of them. One with the utmost respect is iiiYansa T. Muse, a former student who became a Yoruba Priestess of Oya. I have watched them all become enlighteners in their own right! Without them, I wouldn't exist as a Jegna.

I want to say Abaraka Baki (Thank you! in Mandinka) to my editing team, Nancy Johnson-James, Mother BJ, and Dr. Nobles. Without your help and assistance, this project would not be what it turned out to be.

"ayanmo ni iwa pele, iwa pele ni ayanmo." destiny is good character, good character is destiny.

- yoruba proverb

Foreword

It is my honor to have read Dr. Derek Wilson's manuscript, *Ubuntu Musings: The Need for Black Critical Consciousness* and to see that he has respectfully utilized some of my own work and the best of many other African centered Black psychologists and intellectuals. It is, indeed, a special privilege to be asked to write the foreword to *Ubuntu Musings: The Need for Black Critical Consciousness*. Musing in the title of this book is appropriate. This manuscript is Derek's meditation. It is his ponder, reflection, introspection, reverie and dreaming about Black critical consciousness. It is, however, more than that. It is a special musing because it also provides the reader with insight and critical intelligence regarding African episteme and worldview. In a very special way, this book stimulates the reader's memory and imagination to be receptive of new/old African thinking.

As foreword, I invite the reader to remember that it is extremely important to recognize that in breaking out from the savage prism of colonialism and enslavement, African scholars/intellectuals must rescue, reclaim, and refine our authentic way of knowing, doing and being; and, in so doing, make essential contributions to the restoration of wellness for African people. Each of us must make our contribution. Derek Wilson's *Ubuntu Musings: The Need for Black Critical Consciousness* is a welcomed contribution.

Consciousness or Dr. Wilson's interest in critical consciousness is how one is aware of all else, and identity is how others see and define your meaning as an entity. African Consciousness and Black Identity are inextricably linked. As such, the shattering of African consciousness and the fracturing of Black identity have been and is the untreated barrier to African development and advancement worldwide. The reading of this text makes explicit the use of rituals in expanding Black critical consciousness and the need to enliven and illuminate the African Spirit. This is why Dr. Wilson's musing is timely and essential to our understanding and ability to reestablish ourselves as whole and well. Through the lens of UbuNtu, Dr. Wilson carries the reader along a detailed journey through the crossroads between Black Psychology and Liberation psychology. He shows us how the one is necessary for the other.

Dr. Wilson's musing helps the reader to find clarity in the muddy waters of conceptual incarceration, scientific colonialism and transubstantive errors. If read carefully and completely, this book can provide the reader with protection from the danger of defaulting back to Western (white) understandings of knowing. In fact, I would invite the reader to consider that in musing, Dr. Wilson's actual Muse is the recognition and honoring of "living Ancestors", Asa Hilliard, Kobi Kambon, Frances Cress Welsing, Amos Wilson, and Bobby Wright, who have taken him to places that his western training denies as a real and valuable resource.

Finally, *Ubuntu Musings: The Need for Black Critical Consciousness* seduces our imagination to ponder or wonder about decoloniality and African affirmation as the bridge or pathway to the recovery of our historical memory and the ability to restore the African way of thinking, being, and doing."

Dr. Derek Wilson's *Ubuntu Musings: The Need for Black Critical Consciousness* is an important contribution in the unfolding of our African science of human functioning.

Baba Dr. Wade W. Nobles

(Ifágbemì Sàngódáre, Nana Kwaku Berko I, Be-jana, Onebunne) *|Co-Founder and Past President (1994-1995) of The Association of Black Psychologists. | Chair, ABPsi Global Pan African Initiative Professor Emeritus, Black Psychology, and Africana Studies. San Francisco State University Founding. | Executive Director (retired), The Institute for the Advanced Study of Black Family Life & Culture, Inc.*

Preface

This book is a dedication to the men and women who helped shape me into a Black man. The works in this first book reflect (1) my exposure as a young Black male to Baba Asa Hilliard, who took time to teach the Black youth in our community about his travels to KMT and (2) my work at the Institute for the Advanced Study of Black Family Life and Culture (The Institute) under Baba Wade Nobles, Baba Lawford Goddard, and Baba William Cavil). The genius emanating from the Institute exposed me to what it meant to think great as a Black man. It was their dedication to impact the Black community in which we lived. I was honored by running the HAWK Federation Perfected Black Manhood program. HAWK stands for High Achievement of Wisdom and Knowledge. The greatest joy from this experience was recruiting and working beside some dynamic young brothers/men in the community (Yakan, Miles, Mike, Anthony, Daniel "Dakhari," Omar, Jabari, and Timothy). They served as Hersethas (Trainers) to young Black males called Herbaks (students) between 11-16 years old.

HAWK Program early years

I dedicate this work to those early years in my career that began at Club Arlington through my brotherhood with VSheridan, Yakan, Hunter, Douglas, Ethan, Rick, Hollywood and Tadd. We demonstrated the implementation of African knowledge, culture, and philosophy to the elevation of young Black males through jegnaship, guidance, and brotherhood. The techniques used within this program were instrumental in developing critical consciousness in the youth with whom we worked. Those same techniques are even more relevant today in teaching young black students, whether in middle school, high school, or college. It was my work at The Institute that propelled me toward a career in the field of Psychology. Still, most importantly, this work through the genius of The Institute taught me how to be dedicated to liberating the African mind, illuminating and elevating the African Spirit, and enlivening the African character. I was tutored, mentored, and taught by greatness, which is why I, as a Black man, will always be committed to African people in whatever I do in the Spirit of Ubuntu.

What is Ubuntu? The word *Ubuntu* comes from the Zulu and Xhola languages and can be roughly translated as "humanity to others." The following Zulu maxim, "Umuntu

Ngumuntu Ngabantu," literally means that a human is a human through other humans. Jahn and Mbiti educate us that **NTU** emanates from ancient African Bantu philosophy meaning *Being* itself and **universal cosmic** force. The African cosmology of NTU is the universal force that merges with its manifestations. For example, Kintu and Muntu. 'Muntu' is God, spirits, the deceased, persons, and present 'force.' 'Force' is the *Kintu* that acts under the command of the Muntu. Ubuntu is a philosophy, a way of understanding the composition of being. *Ubuntu* philosophy embodies the African notion of humaneness, where the social structure extols harmony and the Spirit of sharing among the members of society, NTU is the foundation of Kintu, Muntu and Ubuntu. We are people because of other people and recognize the need to connect with other humans and, in turn, structure all behavioral expressions of human functioning, mental functioning, and well-being. This first discourse will articulate the African Spirit of Ubuntu toward liberation through the development of critical consciousness. The African philosophy of Ubuntu allows us to understand and define liberatory functioning from an African worldview perspective, a perspective missing from the Western psychological discourse.

There has been a significant resurgence in the use, understanding, and ways of practicing Ubuntu. Scholars have discussed the conceptual framework of Ubuntu in discourse contextualizing psychological functioning. In elucidating African psychologies and practices of Ubuntu, its relations are characterized by the Spirit of interdependence and mutual trust as people rely on each other in everyday life. Within this Ubuntu spirit, this work sets the foundation for how this author discovered the need to know what makes African people African. My earlier collection of works will feature the importance of developing critical consciousness through the poly epistemic Spirit of African people. Black critical consciousness will serve as volume 1 of this work, demonstrating connections between Africans and Africans in the diaspora. I choose to identify both groups as African, thus linking African episteme, and cosmology to cognitive and mental functioning.

While Ubuntu helps define the function of humaneness, it also espouses a system of principles that seemingly contradict current Western values, episteme, and cosmogony. Ubuntu stands for "I Am Because We Are, and since We are, therefore I am." Essentially "there is no 'I' without the 'We.'" It places the community at the forefront while requiring us to understand our collective consciousness of self. Baba Kobi Kambon's African Self-extension Orientation reflects this Ubuntu consciousness that portrays a spirit of oneness and harmony. For example, an examination of the Baoulè universe states, "their thirst for unity, the desire for cohesion, seems to be the deepest aspiration of the Baoulè: to stick closely as possible to one another, be the other a deity, the universe, or the clan (p. 29)." Ubuntu is given to us because we are spirit beings. *Muntu* is God-consciousness thus creating our relational essence informing our identity, ethics, and Black liberated minds.

In essence, Ubuntu can be conceptualized as the ability to live and fulfill the highest, most authentic expression of ourselves as human beings. In other words, "one's humanity is made possible through the humanity of others" (consciousness). This African axiom recognizes every person and every life through connectedness, competency, and consciousness, emphasizing understanding, collaboration, and partnership. From the Akan culture, Gyekye (n.d.) states: "Because the human individual is not self-sufficient, he would necessarily require the assistance, goodwill and the relationships of others to satisfy his basic needs...the well-being of man depends upon his fellow man - *obi yiye firi obi.*" Ubuntu recognizes the humanity in us all. Discovering ourselves and resolving our human differences through our collective consciousness. Ubuntu, then, may prove to be a much more beneficial and enduring conceptual paradigmatic episteme when examining contemporary functioning as it has the potential to inform a broader, more inclusive understanding of our African well-being. Well-being in African Ghanian lexica involves:

● Good living (asetenopa in Akan and noyaa in Ga) (including moral living, material success, and proper relationality).

● Good health (alaafee in Dagbani and lamase in Ewe).

● Positive affective states (anigye in Akan and suhupielli in Dogbani).

● Peace of mind (toijorle in Ga and tomefafa in Ewe).

Black is an advantage, for if it were not, whites would not work so hard to destroy it as if Blacks had no value. From the African worldview, we see African psychological terms of purpose, appraisal, offering, achievements, and inheritance to help define reality, mental functioning, and intellectual processes of potentiality are Black, Whole, Land, Heritage, Poly, Even, Peace, Collective, Communal, Inherent, Circular, Reality, Diaspora, Qualitative, and Maternalistic. The terms of purpose that serve as a guide for empowerment, restoration, and repair are Spiritual, Development, Intuitive, Universal, Discrimination, Reparative, Flexible, Balance, Optimal, Restorative, Experiential, and Vital. Thus, I bring to you Ubuntu Musings Volume I: The Development of Black Critical Consciousness.

Dr. Derek Wilson

Ofamfa

Ofamfa is the Akan symbol of critical examination. It appropriately captures and symbolizes the aims and objectives of this exposition.

While "Musings" are most often thought of as meditations, ponderings, contemplations, deliberations, reflections, introspections, dreamings, or reveries. This book is designed for us to muse and critically examine, reflect, introspect and revere in the value and need for African/Black Psychology from a Black Critical consciousness. I further note that a "need" is something that is necessary; hence Black Critical Consciousness is necessary. Musing/thinking is work. It's key to our ability to examine the past and envision the future.

Introduction

He [African/Black social scientist] must seek his culture elsewhere, anywhere at all; and if he fails to find the substance of culture...the native intellectual will very often fall back upon emotional attitudes and will develop a psychology which is dominated by exceptional sensitivity and susceptibility. –Franz Fannon, The Wretched of the Earth (1963)

We, Black social scientists, must prevent creating a psychology that does not hold up Africans' integrity, intellect, and ingeniousness worldwide. 'African' in this book means Africans on/in the continent of Africa, the Americas, the diaspora, and all rich dark melanin Black people of African ancestry. This book is designed to capture and reflect the essence of African philosophy, wisdom, knowledge, and consciousness in treating others with humanity and as subjects of life and living.

Part one is the mainspring chapter of this manuscript. It is dedicated to discussing the need for critical consciousness. It sets the tone for needing to stop compromising our mental integrity. I discuss three branches of psychology in their potential formulation and underpinnings for critical consciousness. Liberation Psychology will be discussed as musing critical consciousness. Community Psychology will be addressed as an essential need of critical consciousness. And lastly, African/Black Psychology will be discussed as a basis for critical consciousness. In addition, this discourse discusses how compromised mental integrity is due to scientific colonialism, conceptual incarceration, and transsubstantive errors. Finally, a theoretical construct for constructing critical consciousness as an emancipatory practice alleviating the suffering from mental bondage is revealed.

Part two examines why we need our African Mind because that is the one that is free from the system of racialized capitalism that continues to dehumanize us. It is a system in which Black people and creation are reduced to being products for the marketplace. No matter what we do in the system / how much money we make doing it, if we don't engage with our African Mind we lose ourselves. This chapter emphasizes how Black critical consciousness is necessary in order to place our wellbeing at the center of our own thinking rather than societal norms and expectations. Important because we are only human within Black critical consciousness. This society was constructed on our dehumanization. It is not meant to nurture us. It was meant to use us. First, to conscientize is to understand the need for sociopolitical change. Critical consciousness requires the individual's capacity to think critically, reflect personally, and examine the sociopolitical system concerning oppression, colonization, and racism. The essential components of mainstream critical consciousness discussed are (a) critical reflection, (b) political advocacy, and (c) action. Black critical consciousness emanates from African/Black psychology and is a prerequisite for the liberation of the African mind. Black Critical consciousness is a crucial component of our framework for mental liberation. Consequently, ABPSi's liberation psychology set the means for addressing this challenge.

Part three illustrates what culture is and its constructs. Cultural Asili is discussed as that which determines how the cultural essence. The template, Utamawazo, identifies how self-conscious expressions explain the group's culturally patterned thought and framework. In addition, the cultural orientation of Utamaroho is presented as the unconscious level of collective behaviors and fundamental feelings of a particular group. Next, Authentic African cultural structure is articulated around these constructs and how culture influences critical consciousness. It is the conditions of a people's political and social factors that, when located within the culture, people "find the seed of opposition."

Part four rests on a fundamentally different basis of learning from the African perspective and how our learning style, knowledge acquisition, and cognitive style help shape our thinking and consciousness. I discuss inherent cultural values such as communalism, collective self-identity, and social relationships. Next, African Worldview vs. European worldview is delineated to demonstrate how consciousness creates our understanding of culture. When operating in consciousness, the goal is not to let other people be the determiners of African consciousness, personality, and culture. Deep and Elaborative Processes are identified as Knowing, Being, and Doing with fundamental core qualities of *"Being," "Belonging,"* and *"Becoming,"* as seen as critical markers for understanding African wisdom and knowledge to ward against (mis)Knowing, (non) Being, and (un)Doing.

Part five connects cognitive characteristics to critical consciousness. Depth of processing is a significant task of critical evaluation as situations are conceptualized within the context and content. Context is the feeling, sensing, perceiving, and thinking, while content is believed to be how black children instinctively learn. Culture's influence on Black consciousness, Empowerment Theory as Political

Falsehood for Africans, and Empowerment and critical consciousness are critically examined. Critical consciousness at the community level recognizes oppression on the group level through three psychological processes: group identity, group consciousness, and group efficacy. I identify how community healing, resistance, and advocacy emanate from Black consciousness.

Part six examines the work of reprogramming that in my opinion is dangerous. I say dangerous because if we recognize our power the world will change. Since our values are based on an African-centered consciousness, we become empowered as African people through the degree it is based on African-centered values. The hijacking of our consciousness occurs to the degree that other people determine those values and consciousness. Losing our way means that our culture will not be functional in a way that protects our interests. Our cultural authenticity and self-knowledge must develop a new African consciousness based on African history, African culture, and African values. If we are to be empowered and if our power is to work in our interests, our African consciousness must seize the power of our experience, African reprogramming is a dynamic process that happens in community rather than in isolation. In our circle of well-being we are actively holding and being held in community. Our community knows that we bring both our pain and our strength, our weariness and our passion, our cynicism, and our hope.

Part seven reveals how evaluating a Black Manhood training and development program proves the importance of a Culturally Consistent Curriculum.

Finally, in Part eight, I discuss ways to materialize our conceptions through specific practical applications and training techniques for developing African critical consciousness for creating social action and change.

In summary, this book highlights the challenge for Black critical conscious social scientists. Needed are the bravery, strength, and intellect of Africans in Africa, in the Americas, in the diaspora, and all rich melanin people with nappy hair, representing a culture of knowing, deep in wisdom, and high civilization. As spoken by Ayi Kwei Armah, "Our culture has a way of reciprocity, a form of creation, a knowing purpose, restoration, and revitalization [of] spiritness...We are caring, giving, and sharing with people whose spirit is itself life." We must also remember the words of Marcus Garvey:

"We are going to emancipate ourselves from mental slavery, for though others may free the body, none but ourselves can free the mind...The man who is not able to develop and use his mind is bound to be the slave of the other man." (1937)

UBUNTU MUSINGS

I

The Need for Black Critical Consciousness

The domination/oppression equation operates by certain rules and yields certain consequences in the behavior of oppressor and oppressed that are unrelated to abilities. (Hilliard, 1991, p. 11)

The American Psychological Association (APA) chose to reconcile to the community at large about its participation in historical atrocities, blatant disregard, and flat-out engagement of racist practices to all communities of color to develop psychological theories and practices. What is interesting about this public apology is that APA admitted to breaking the law and code of ethics. They acknowledged that this psychology, as we know it, operates from an evil ontological spirit and has no intention ever to serve Black people with care or to understand them psychologically. Even more egregious and a form of trickery is that the Black leadership of APA chose to engage in this endeavor to apologize to the Black community. But what percentage of white members have supported such a letter? Why has APA not overtly and boldly made public appearances and statements about how Black folks were treated and the disparities in the way they were served? Robert Guthrie charged white psychology with having a history of racism detailing especially American psychology's role and using psychological science to reinforce and perpetuate the myth of white supremacy. Guthrie noted that this science was always suspect while this analysis of what Guthrie called scientific racism was an important contribution to our understanding of psychology's history. White psychology in its arrogance of the present will have you forget the intelligence of the past. The writing of this letter serves the purpose to get Black psychologists to forget their past. I call this one of the greatest hoodwinking scam, fraud, and blatant disrespect to the black community by an organization that has been siphoning the will and Spirit of one of its constituents. APA has turned a blind and dirty eye to the atrocities it has committed since its inception. Yet, as a field, it would preach engaging in authentic relationships, genuine empathy, and "to do no harm." They admitted, in my eyes, acts of violence and psychological warfare. Reading their letter leaves you with a gut punch about a field that had lied for centuries regarding incorporating psychological knowledge of Black folk. APA has operated much like the dominant culture of this Western society which has a blatant history of dehumanizing African people. As a field and organization, APA has never had the interest of black people at heart–not even the Blacks who were trained in the field. What is the challenge for Black social scientists becoming social activists and advocating for change in psychology? It has been a practice of "Bad Blood"!

For the Black social scientists, when do they (we) wake up to this fact? Jacob Carruthers reminds us that this *dialogue among [the African] thinkers about getting out of the mess in which African peoples have been for the last "2000 seasons"... has been remarkably consistent...aptly captured the essence of the worldwide African debate...[as] integrationist and the nationalist streams [of thought] represented the most fundamental division among us."* We are now the most confused group to ever exist in contemporary times. The continental and diasporic Africans (especially the Africans in America) who were seen as a nationalist began to subsume the integrationist doctrine and beliefs, which can be seen as Europeanized Africans, and we see this as acceptable. While Africans no longer have to experience political colonialism (Democratic and Republican are the new form) and slavery (not valid for the many brothers and sisters in penitentiary systems), all disagreements regarding African humanity have been met with ignominious exploitation by European rule. The greatest significant menace to African self-worth is in the province of intellectual potentiality or power. Europeans have been demeaning and disrespecting the African intellect for the last 250 years and wonder what's wrong with the African mind. The natural critical conscious mind demonstrates the role of "power" in African psychology.

I need African social scientists to become psychological activists to challenge and change the field for the world! When examining the conditions of African people and recognizing the methods for explaining and rectifying these conditions, there exist contradictions. For example, how can you subscribe to a European value system with its fundamental ethos of exploitation, greed, domination, individualism, and superiority, yet its prescriptions directly contradict its actual values orientation? This contradiction exposes the field in its understanding for not knowing how to solve its problems. For instance, where in European culture do collective work and responsibility ideas benefit the tribal group without exploitation? In addition, we see European values manifesting when examining the precursors of some psychological disorders. Yet, the cure often contradicts its values meaning; the healthiest prescriptions are often of collective and communal value orientation, a direct contradiction of the European value structure. For the Africans, however, when they adopt and amalgamate his company with the other, he begins to directly feel the imbalance and cultural conflict with his innate artistic personality. The more the African tries to fit into this western narrative he begins to recognize the false persona or masking of his true self, i.e., Black Skin, White Mask. Even more alarming is that the field of psychology orients itself from a European value orientation imposed on non-European people; we see clear evidence of the continual decay of the African personality. To be explicit, I find it interesting that, after this disingenuous letter from APA, APA has worked harder to keep corrupting the minds of some of our Black folks with the creation of a sub-subdivision called African/Black psychology and launched the inaugural Psychology of Black Women conference in the year 2021-2022 (to be discussed later). As Barbara Sizemore said 25 years ago, "[some] Black folks just don't get it!"

Critical consciousness focuses on cognitive awareness of disparity and unequal social exchange between the oppressor and the oppressed. The development of critical consciousness serves to provide the oppressed with cognitive skills to generate change and the need to create social change strategies. Critical consciousness, in essence, is associated with empowerment theory, African/Black Psychology, and Liberation Psychology; however, little attempt has been made to connect factors in developing critical consciousness to learning, cognition, and knowledge acquisition to critical consciousness. This discourse will attempt to connect key elements of learning, cognitive processes, and knowledge acquisition to the development of critical consciousness and explore how to impact/influence behavior toward social action. Cognitive and informational processing will be examined to highlight the influences of social and environmental context and instructional methods. The advantage of this connection is that it would help to identify what types of cognitive styles exist, what mental processes are involved, and what innovative instructional methods should be used in developing critical consciousness. This chapter will discuss the essential beginning of consciousness to combat conceptual incarceration, scientific colonialism, transsubstantive errors and European hegemony.

When sociopolitical, community, and individual factors are examined, components of critical consciousness are discussed. For the sociopolitical environment to change, real change must occur within the cultural psyche of the oppressed group (i.e., the African community). Examples of critically conscious individuals will be revealed, and the need to withstand compromised mental integrity is a demonstration of activism. To set the record straight, literature has not openly tied the development of liberatory psychology to African/Black psychological literature. For this discourse, critical consciousness is African/Black psychology. Africans must begin incorporating critical analysis into their sociopolitical condition and authentic spiritual self by enhancing their cultural awareness. Nobles (2006) describes a brilliant concept based on the Songhay people of West Africa:

For the Sonay (sic) people of Mali, the word for Black is bibi. Bibi is actually a concept used to refer to the essential goodness of things . . . similarly, the Sonay (sic) people use the term, Ay moo hari bibi (Give me Black water) to signify water that is from the deepest part of the river and the most clear and clean. Bibi in this context represents the depth or essence, clarity, and purity of a thing. (p. 329)

African social scientists must pursue examining the deepest water to understand and determine what it will take to reconstruct the fragmented African self. In other words, when we seek the deepest parts of the Ay moo hari bibi (Give me Black water), African or Eastern psychology represents the river's source, providing the essence of what is needed for African people. The foundation of the sociopolitical atmosphere stems from the base of a group's culture. Culture informs consciousness. Consciousness is a type of power. It is believed that when critical consciousness is developed within groups' consciousness, they will need to change their social actions. This will assist in refining the critically conscious skills required to generate social change strategies. More importantly, if Africans were to enhance their critical consciousness, they could become more involved in social action for change.

We have to stop compromising our mental Integrity

The most serious mistake you can make is to utilize or try to use white definitions to define and understand black phenomena/black behavior. To use white definitions as an explanation for the world, they (whites) will rule over you. (Bobby Wright)

We must stop compromising our mental integrity. African social scientists have been trained to think within the confines of a Yurugu virus. Mama Ani discusses this yurugu virus as representing white male patriarchy which denies the natural order of the universe and acts to promote disharmony. The yurugu virus works to portend African human well-being and limit their intellectual ability. Limited intellectual ability compromises cognitive constructions, which seek to adjust and adapt to a colorblind mode of operation. It promotes itself as being open-minded in an ideological fundamentalist political structure. Consciousness is power. For a group to have authority over a people, they must reinvent that group's consciousness. For example, color blindness is a false consciousness, a false sense of objectivity. It is subject to three focal ill-disposed fundamental character critiques that hinder African social scientists' critical consciousness. When a group wants to use people, they intend to control their consciousness.

Baba Nobles provides three essential critical analysis tools when examining the limitation of advancing African/ Black psychology when taking on a color blindness perspective. First, by definition, color blindness cannot recognize, let alone correct, the *conceptual incarceration* that exists. Second, colorblindness's insistence on objective standards and universal procedures provides a smokescreen for *scientific colonialism* and thus entertains a self-justifying guard for conscious and unconscious racism. Colorblindness imposes white Western European political, social, and *cultural hegemony* by upholding institutional provisions which personify the residuum consequences of overt historical racism. Colorblindness imposes white Western European political, social, and *cultural hegemony* by upholding institutional provisions which personify the residuum consequences of overt historical racism. For example, Zora Neal-Hurston understood in her early writings that to be objective is to evaluate from the white man's eyes and realizes that to understand African life is to become a subjective participant to capture its richness and value. Zora Neal-Huston could not in all good consciousness operate from colorblind perspective when this colorblindness comprises a race-neutral universalism that inhibits race consciousness or race-based decision-making. Zora Neal-Hurston's commitment to accurately and validly capture the cultural essence of Africans in the Caribbean and United States represents her as an authentic cultural anthropologist and should be seen as a guide for Black social scientists to be authentic in capturing themselves, African life, and ways of knowing the world as they operate. However, in the current climate, the idea of colorblindness denies Black social scientists the opportunity to advance the interest and image of African people in research and theory development. It does not justify our contribution to the forward-flowing process of human civilization, or group identity consciousness, for that matter. For instance, in these post-racial times (if this truly exists), the current state of affairs disparages and depoliticizes acts of collective Black political consciousness and organizing. Amos Wilson reminds us that the history of white psychology and the teaching of its theories are, by nature, political. We must understand to elevate these individualized theoretical concepts to group-level analysis to grasp the heart of this politicization. As a result, African/Black social scientists tend to demonstrate an incarceration of the conceptual mind (conceptual incarceration).

Conceptual incarceration was provided to us by Baba Nobles in his work Black People in White Insanity: An Issue for Black Community Mental Health. He described how African social scientists are trained to think, theorize, and examine human conditions' problems from a White European cultural lens or frame of reference. In other words, the African social scientist is indoctrinated into believing and conceiving the Western conceptions of reality. For the past 17 years, every semester, I presented to my classes at two HBCUs, Kambon's rendition of worldview cosmological schemas– African versus European. This chart consists of characteristics of Ethos/ Basic Reality Orientation, Philosophical Values, and Customs, Psycho-Behavioral Modalities, and Mode of Production. Students are asked three fundamental questions: which cultural environment would allow them to (1) be successful in life, (2) accomplish their goals, and (3) contribute to humanity? African students who choose the white cultural structure justify their choice by asserting they must adopt the parameters defining mental and behavioral expectations of being race-neutral. This race neutrality constitutes a made-up consciousness forced upon African people from the indoctrination of an oppressive ontological and alien ethos orientation. This Baba

Nobles calls *conceptual incarceration* of the African mind, and *"the immediate task is to become conscious of our own consciousness."* Our consciousness has been created by someone else. The state of consciousness you are in determines what you are capable of doing. Not to use our consciousness is to be non-black or non-African. One of our most significant challenges is trying to achieve our fullest potential. Knowing how to control our consciousness liberates our mind from mental bondage. Bobby Wright tells us that the biggest challenge is the fight for the African/Black mind. We cannot develop and become aware of our intrinsic African self if we can not think for ourselves, describe ourselves, and define what it means to be a health-conscious African. Mama Ani represents this *challenge* as the effects of the Maafa, which means horrific tragedy, the fracturing, splintering, and shattering of the African consciousness. This disruption of consciousness has limited our exploration of African social life predicated by white male institutional scholarship in establishing scientific colonialism.

The second challenge brought forth by Baba Nobles in Extended-Self: Re-Thinking the So-Called Negro Self-Concept of our consciousness is that of Scientific colonialism, similar to Guthrie's scientific racism. Scientific colonialism occurs when the discipline of psychology and other social sciences are used as tools of oppression by placing White psychology, its conceptions, and formulations as the standard for which all other groups are to be measured. I can't help but consider the Black Lives Matter/ Say Her Name movement. First, because of the spectacle of seeing people take offense at the very notion of valuing a Black life, but also because I realized that the pre-eminent concern is that Black lives matter to Black people. This connects to Black critical consciousness. Too often I see Black people operating as though their personhood is dependent on societal norms (which essentially comes down to $$). Without defining the essence of a social fact or phenomenon, scientific investigation of African reality, be it personhood or social life, utilizes philosophical or theoretical assumptions already formed in the literature, which informs the final product. Western scholarship and African reality are philosophically different. Scientific racism as an instrument of oppression and domination, can have predeterminants beyond empirical given phenomena. The phenomena of cultural and historical consciousness are the primary tool used by European psychology in making the mental connection of the subservient African. The establishment of ideologies from European scientific racism is racially biased. For example, it was argued that the differences between the races were fundamental to a natural hierarchy, with the white race at the highest level and Africans underneath. This opinion developed and propagated these beliefs and is generally accepted in the Western psychological field. As a result, the existence of multiple selves instead promotes the idea of numerous consciousnesses. For instance, Nunn captures Western thought according to Harris:

> *[W]e are not born with a "self," but rather are composed of a welter of partial, sometimes contradictory, or even antithetical "selves." A unified identity, if such can ever exist, is a product of will, not a common destiny or natural birthright."*

Europeans have for centuries tried to deny the value and genius of Africans. Instead, they have indoctrinated that for African scholarship to be valued and respected, it must emanate from European thought without challenging Western consciousness. For example, one of the most widely studied identity development models is the Nigrescence model. Nigrescence uses the philosophical assumptions of "a priori" identity as its fundamental premise of Black identity. The same belief in white identity theory (*[W]e are not born with a "self"*).

The original philosophical assumption in Nigrescence is

that at the first level of consciousness, pre encounter phase, the Black individual does not recognize his blackness (non-being). His consciousness of being black only occurs with whites violating his humanity. Furthermore, the model reveals multiple levels of consciousnesses that lend little support for a collective conscious construct. The highest stage of identity consciousness rests on establishing meaningful relationships with whites. This consciousness phenomenon serves as a willingness to develop joint multiethnic forces. Black social scientists who master this level of consciousness drive themselves to be with the whites in every situation. These individuals will incorporate European ideology of scientific and philosophical investigative methods (scientific colonization) to explain African phenomena. We have yet to yield any advancements for the Black community out of a condition of oppression. This lack of consciousness allows us to continue using the Black community as a commodity. Only the Europeans themselves reap multiple benefits of this cultural exchange. The advantage of us Black social scientists come from white academia and institutions of publishing in the form of narrowly selected publications, recognition, mass media, partnership, alliance, and jobs that pose no threat to the status quo. It is only through the advancement of their careers that they do nothing to advance the understanding of African reality or existence. The Black social scientists who come to HBCUs but move on to PWIs see that experience as a stepping stone for their climb and security.

We see how Black social scientists pretend their *"quality of education." Scientific* inquiry is equal to European/Western objectives. Yet, when creating change or power, it collapses under the wheels of diversity, equity, and inclusion. Diversity, equity, and inclusion are falsifications for the creation of true advancement. Some nuevo affirmative action. When recognizing this falsification, notice exactly how the unconscious mind is created through content, instrumentality, and information processing. Consciousness is about power. What power do you have to incorporate the values of your people? When you decide to use your consciousness, do you see that you will get rid of the white man's power over you? We must begin to assess our capabilities objectively. What kind of interrogation do we engage in when analyzing how capable we are of achieving this goal? What type of knowledge must we have to accomplish this goal? However, if you are satisfied working for white establishments and institutions, what is needed to consider?

How different would that education be if we went to school to learn to create theories and conceptualize jobs by ourselves? How do we build the appropriate standards for defining what African people are made of? What are the goals of African people as a nation-state? What are the purposes of our community? True consciousness will help you decide what kind of education you need to achieve those goals. However, the type of education we're getting today has the goal of working for white people, adopting European ideology, and forever serving the white man in some form or another. This anti-black consciousness and or intellectual stance proclaims that Africans are inherently inferior more effectively than whites ever could. Black social scientists who can not think for themselves and create for themselves adhere to this scientific colonialism that contributes to the domination and oppression of people of color and yields gross transsubstantive errors.

Lastly, in Baba Nobles' Transsubstantive errors in Understanding Human Transformation; The Praxis of Science and Culture in Seeking the Sakhu: Foundational Writings for an African Psychology, he discusses when social scientists ignore the ideological integrity of one group and transform this into the substance of another cultural group. The task of science is to establish and enhance our knowledge concerning the group we are investigating. Scientific methodological standards and systematic exploration are to generate assumptions and rules and provide the basis for making predictions and testing and interpreting results based on the ideological integrity of the group studied. The challenge with committing transsubstantive errors occurs when you may have the logical skills but need more to let you value African people and culture. So, when you think and process phenomena from what you know using abstract thinking and logic, it will be processed under European ontological ethos. However, serious errors occur when the reality from an alien culture is used to analyze African phenomena' social life.

You are thinking for a reason, not just for living. Thinking is not just about displaying knowledge; it is how you engage in the information process to achieve a particular goal. So, therefore, our desires, needs, values, interests, aspirations, and ideals have a sense of purpose. Our consciousness's whole direction and purpose are to organize how we think. Our consciousness motivates us to know what instruments we are to use and what knowledge we should use to achieve specific goals. If the goal is African liberation, you have to value African people. You must be empowered, free, and self-sufficient. European hegemony does not allow for something like that to happen. What is the value of trying to achieve the capacity for great logical and analytical thinking if you are using and applying the thinking processes of false information? You are still going to come out to be incorrect. To control our consciousness, as defined, is to fill our minds with irrelevant or no knowledge. We will have knowledge based on false beliefs and wishes of all kinds of fantasies.

The cultural substance of African people is predicated on their cultural factors (ontology, cosmology, and axiology) and cultural aspects (ideology, worldview, and ethos), informing perceptions and behavioral manifestations. For instance, our consciousness determines the survival thrust of our group's behavior expectations. For Africans, the survival-of-the-group mentality values interdependence, group-oriented activities, and interpersonal style of relating. However, when we examine notions of a healthy sense of self from the European structure, we see tenets of individualism, autonomy, and ego-centeredness. As a result, misinterpretations and de-legitimization occur when using contradicted cultural substance and knowledge. For the individual in African life, healthy consciousness is predicated on self, community, and spirit. As previously established, conceptual incarceration uses cultural ideology that does not fit with the doctrine of the examined cultural group. The problem occurs when Black social scientists do not understand African cultural substance (cultural misorientation), operating from a culturally misoriented stance and thus interpreting African behavior according to European cultural expectations. This contradiction will undoubtedly create transsubstantive errors when researching the reality of Africans. Due to such errors, the responsibility of a critically conscious Black social scientist is to eliminate the dehumanization of Africans by (1) not fully accepting an alien science that is in contradiction to the African cultural episteme being investigated; and (2) beginning to initiate and develop authentic science methodology for accurate representation and expression of the reality of African people if true liberation is the goal.

Critical consciousness is essential to eliminating transsubstantive errors that do not support advancing our understanding of unity and wholeness of the African human experience. African science reflects the African consciousness, and the style of thought generated by that consciousness comes from this cultural substance and its ideology. This is done by us creating new mechanisms for examining the African human phenomena based on implicit assumptions and behavioral costs helping form new theories. When we utilize indigenous and innate ways of knowing (episteme), we begin to authenticate what it means to be African through our interpretations and social organization that will help us create solutions to the African problem. Right now, the African problem is for us to gain sovereignty and agency over our lives for the future development of our community and the restoration of our minds. Cultural integrity and interrogation will demonstrate our ability to contribute to understanding our humanity. Still, we must first combat and repair the damage that has been done due to the maafa. All three of these treatises are the result of European hegemony.

European Hegemony is the control and dominance of one group or state over others: European/Western ideology and values are a set of attitudes towards others based on an inferiority/superiority complex. When has there ever been a time in history where whites have not exhibited xenophobia? This hegemonic culture encourages people to identify with the habit, sensibilities, and worldview supportive of the status quo of the dominant group. According to Western hegemonic culture, its primary function is to persuade people to 'consent' and acquiesce to their oppression and exploitation. Western narrative, philosophy, and logic in its arrogance is presented as the way to understand all things in the world. This hegemonic culture's success is persuading others to depend on its constructs and meaning of functioning. Their view of the natural order of things receives little resistance.

Western/European psychology has positioned itself as the purveyor of world culture in which all norms and cultural practices are considered superior to other world cultures. For example, when we examine the origins of Western psychology, it presents itself as the cultural status for all other cultural groups to follow. It is not by accident that the field of psychology offers Greek culture as the foundation of psychology when, in fact, we know that the Greeks learned what they know from KMT. The original understanding of the human mind was seen as the study of Sakhu. As Akbar reminds us psyche is a derivative of Sakhu. Sakhu translates to the study of the soul whereas psyche is the study of the mind and soul. However, there is no theory or discussion on soul/spirit in Western psychological tenet. Psychological textbooks do not make any attempts to correct this fact, and the American Psychological Association (APA) has yet to attempt to state this accurate information since they provide guidelines for psychology curriculums in the U.S. and abroad.

The globalizing of Western/European culture continues to be the most effective strategy to spread their egocentric cultural values. The European hegemonic culture is "a set of values, beliefs, ideas, and cultural practices always willing to control, dominate, aggress, and exploit other cultures." This is racist and fuels racism. Since racism is a system of ideas that are made to keep inequity going, the inequity of blacks being inferior is built into the fundamental cultural values of the Europeans. Baba Nobles reminds us that "science is the formal reconstruction or representation of a people's shared set of systematic and cumulative ideas, beliefs, and knowledge stemming from culture." This meaning relates to how psychology continues to shape and control science based on a white supremacist perspective. Marimba Ani, Frances Cress-Welsing, and Amos Wilson articulated how Western culture has systematically developed a culture based on dominating and controlling other people's consciousness. European hegemonic culture automatically brings an individualized consciousness mind. For the sake of studying critical consciousness, the cultural Hegemony of white ideology, ethos, and worldview reflects the cultural substance of the European with no room for different cultural psychological perspectives. As discussed, four conditions exist in the psychological science field as we know it:

1. Transsubstantive errors will likely occur when the

dominant culture translates findings with a hegemonic cultural lens.

2. Scientific colonialism will use the discipline of psychology and other social sciences as tools of oppression when those other works (psychology of culture) do not fit the cultural consciousness of the Europeans.

3. Conceptual incarceration is when a cadre of intellectuals cannot explain and translate from the lens of hegemonic culture African social life. This is problematic because one continues to demonstrate the dominant culture's consciousness with relative ease for accessibility and explanation.

4. European Hegemony as a praxis continues to ignore other psychologies and use language that will require some degree of compliance with stereotypes.

Western values, consumption patterns, and way of life spread worldwide through several strong influence channels of globalization. This process is believed to bring impactful changes in the mindset and culture of social life resulting in the homogenization of the world, a flat, globalized world.

Adopting theories and research that fail to operate from the essence of who we are, contributes to committing "transsubstantive errors." For example, I remember reviewing a study examining African adolescent females' risk factors and psychological distress. The results demonstrated a significant correlation between interpersonal style of relating and depression. The author interpreted the findings as Black adolescent females who connect with their peers were at risk for developing depression. The lack of value for African socialization practices allowed for the interpretation to essentially place African youth at heightened risk for the adverse psychological effects of being African. This is a perfect example of "transsubstantive error," explaining African reality through the lens of European worldview when the African reality represents an African worldview phenomenon. Our interpersonal style of relating, the oneness of being, cooperation and commonality, and having a sense of shared fate with others is a proactive approach for increasing adaptive functioning within African youth. However, we see through scientific colonialism how European science reflects the European consciousness and how their philosophical/theoretical assumptions limit their understanding of African social life. The recovery of historical memory is to combat and restore our African way of being. European hegemony automatically brings an individualized consciousness of mind instead.

Black to the matter at hand. What clouds western trained Black social scientists' thinking is how they internalized non-native conception of knowledge. When we repeat their truth as our truth, we demonstrate what Nobles call the "Triangular Law of anti-African reality: (1) the law of (mis)knowing; (2) the law of (non) Being; and (3) the law of (un)doing." This can undoubtedly lead to conceptual incarceration, scientific colonialism and transsubstantive errors. This hindrance imparts the belief that the African mind is explained through a Western European lens. The African inherent knowledge recognizes and avoids unknowingly committing transsubstantive errors. The true African mind limits the quality and understanding of the expression of European utamawazo.

Since the inception of Western psychology, the grand narrative invoked is a science of universal truth. The grand Western narrative has an ahistorical presence, meaning that as a hegemonic cultural tool, there is no acknowledgment of previously constructed cultural systems or meanings. No other cultural opinions or facts are to be established. The claim that there is an impartial reality does not exist detached from philosophical and conjectural ideations. European hegemony has positioned Western psychology as a science of universal truth, ahistorical predicated on scientific colonialism. For example, History and System curricula promote that the fathers of philosophy are Aristotle, Socrates, and Plato. Yet, we do know that Plato traveled to KMT to learn in the African University system, which was known to reveal, "we are children to these (African) people." How can someone become the father of something when the father taught them? With that being the case, isn't it proper to presume that they learned philosophy and its underpinnings for thought and inquiry about the world from African scholars? And if that is true, how could they become the fathers of philosophy when they went into KMT to learn? This hegemony has not changed.

My internal awareness cannot allow for the gross undermining of the contributions of African/Black psychology. The re-establishment of African psychology is fundamental to African-centered consciousness. For the African mind, we must confront Eurocentric hegemony and combat scientific colonialism.

Bolekaja is a Yoruba term meaning, "Come on down, and let's fight."

In this section, I conclude that Black Critical Consciousness is necessary. This first work of Ubuntu Musing is designed for us to critically examine, reflect, introspect, and revere in the value and need for African/Black Psychology from a Black Critical consciousness. I do not believe that there is anything about African/Black Psychology that makes it suspect. What if our traditional worldview had no idea of mind, body, and soul and didn't conceive of emotion, thinking, and feeling? In particular, if we continue to tell our story through the lens of an alien paradigm and worldview, no matter its praxis, we are bound to continue to believe that our way of thinking and knowing is always in reaction to or sublimated by European ideas and thought. What does the African have to do with his current condition for freedom and justice while operating under white supremacy? Finally, what does that do to our understanding of possessing Black critical consciousness? As an unasked challenge, this "muse" is necessary as a bridge to and necessity for "the recovery of historical memory to combat and restore the function of the African mind." I discuss three branches of psychology for developing Black critical consciousness. In Branch I, I examine Liberation psychology as a *"muse"* for Black critical consciousness. In Branch II, I critique Community Psychology as *a need* for Black critical consciousness and point out how it is theoretically consistent with African Psychology. Finally, in branch III, I specifically discuss how African/Black Psychology is a necessary base for Black critical consciousness. All play a role in their potential formulation and underpinnings for creating authentic Black critical conscious development. In addition, these psychologies will be examined utilizing building blocks for Black critical consciousness:

1. Does it advance the interest and image of African people?
2. How can/does it contribute to the forward-flowing process of civilization?
3. Does it lend to the liberation of the African Mind?
4. Does it engage in the empowerment of the African Character?
5. How will it enliven and illuminate the African Spirit?

I will reveal, within their praxis, the need to combat psychosocial injustice by actively increasing critical conscious resistance to the deceptive and treacherous systemization of white supremacy and racial oppression in the minds of Black social scientists, even at times when we recognize the thievery of our ideas. Hence Black Critical Consciousness is necessary.

Liberation Psychology

The musing of Liberation psychology requires thought or pondering of its true introjection of freeing a people from the conditions of oppression. How has liberation psychology demonstrated its usefulness to the life experiences of African people? First, this discussion will contemplate as a psychology how liberation psychology advanced the interest and image of African people. Next deliberations will be conducted to see how liberation psychology contributes to the forward flowing process of civilization from an African centered perspective. Then, reflections of how liberation psychology actually liberates the African Mind. To follow introspection of liberation psychology process for the empowerment of the African Character will take place. Finally, reverie will take place to show liberation psychology can enliven and illuminate the African Spirit.

Contemplate as a psychology how LP advances the interest and image of African people

Liberation psychology implies the appeal of psychology in a participatory approach to pursue change and promote community-based equity. Liberation psychology concerns the experience and knowledge of the excluded and marginalized. How has Liberation psychology aimed to hear, amplify, and incorporate in theory and practice the voices and wisdom of African people who have experienced some of the most heinous acts of oppression? In her scientific colonialist mindset, Heitz makes conflicting assertions in the development of liberation psychology. For example, "Martín-Baró's understanding of psychology as an "instrument of change"... was influenced by... Black psychology in the United States." She says, "Aligned with White's critiques of Western psychology, liberation psychology... prioritizes the voices of marginalized groups, resists oppression, facilitates awareness of social inequities, highlights strengths, and empowers marginalized populations." Heitz would have you believe that a theory could be influenced by yet influence the approach that influenced it. She exhibits this when she says, "Martín-Baró's writings, as well as other...(Black scholars Frantz Fanon, W.E.B. Du Bois) influenced the development of Black Liberation Psychology," in the same breath, "liberation psychology has been widely incorporated into Black psychology." How can we go from Black psychology spawning liberation psychology yet only to have liberation psychology influence the development of Black psychology? From White's assertions in the early 70s, liberation psychology had not hit the scene. Even to the present, the academic discipline of psychology has traditionally been complicit in scientific colonialism by dominating the narrative, intentionally or not, by misguidance. This makes me think about how anti-blackness is so deeply established in the "Western" mindset that the act of giving African people credit for anything causes a kind of dissonance that leads to this kind of doublespeak. This is someone who feels an unction toward the truth but struggles with their own anti-Black conditioning. Our cultural and intrapsychic alertness should allow us to stop accepting such erroneous explanations. Western psychology has a history of outright denying the advances of the interest and image of African people even when the science of African/psychology spawned liberation psychology. These tactics were designed to keep African people confused and "conceptually incarcerated." The unspoken lie is that beyond Western systems and structures, there is nothing at best and at worst a wilderness that is not survivable. The truth is that if it is just wilderness beyond Western thought, then that wilderness is a place of life and possibility beyond racialized capitalism.

How liberation psychology contributes to the forward flowing process of civilization for African people

While there have been discussions about how theories can influence the development of critical consciousness, if not from an African-centered analysis and perspective, we will continue to unknowingly demonstrate conceptual incarceration, scientific colonialism, and transsubstantive errors. Liberation Psychology focuses on the battle between freedom and the sociopolitical status of oppressed groups. It has been suggested that Liberation Psychology demands that a change in power dynamics requires efficacious functioning and full participation in controlling one's life. Frantz Fanon first introduced concepts consistent with liberation psychology into the literature. Fanon's classic works Wretched of the Earth and Black Skin White Mask (1963, 1967) offered a critical analysis juxtaposing oppression's impact on the mental health of the colonized Africans. Fanon eloquently examines the role of white supremacy as a pathology that challenges Africans to live free and fulfilled lives. For example, in "Wretched of the Earth", Fannon states, "Inside the political parties, and most often in offshoots from these partics, cultured individuals of the colonized race make their appearance. For these individuals, the demand for a national culture and the affirmation of the existence of such a culture represents a special battlefield." In this case, confronting the intellectual wisdom of the African who decides to respond aggressively to the scientific colonialism theories of savagery, imperialism will react only slightly and still less because specialists in the dominant field widely obfuscate the ideas developed by the up-and-coming cognoscenti. Even in the field of liberation psychology, there has been no advancement of the forward-flowing process of civilization for African people. It is, in fact, commonplace to state that for several decades large numbers of researchers have rehabilitated the African mind. The passion with which these young intellectuals defend the existence of European cultural thought is a source of astonishment. Still, those who condemn this passion are strangely apt to forget that their psyche and selves are conveniently sheltered behind European hegemonic culture. Fannon goes on to say, "[we are] ready to concede that on the plane of factual being the past existence of an [African] civilization does not change anything very much in the diet of the [African] of today. I admit that all the proof of a wonderful Songhai civilization will not change the fact that today the Songhais are undeterred and illiterate, thrown between sky and water with empty heads and empty eyes." Black social scientists, when will we carry the passion about searching for a national culture that existed before colonization and find its legitimate reason to be shared with our young intellectuals to shrink away from that Western thought and culture? As Fannon claims,

> *"to claim a national culture in the past does not only rehabilitate that nation and serve as a justification for the hope of a future national culture. In the sphere of cycle effective equilibrium, it is responsible for an important change in the native. Perhaps we have not sufficiently demonstrated that colonialism is not simply content to impose its rule upon the present and the future of a dominated country. Colonialism is not satisfied merely with holding a people in its grip and emptying the native's brain of all form and content. By a kind of perverted logic, it turns to the past of the oppressed people, and distorts, and disfigures and destroys it. This work of devaluing precolonial history takes a dialectical significance today."*

The principal characteristics of liberation psychology should incorporate awakening, affirming, and grounding as sequential and complementary.

We have to challenge our own reliance on European

academic institutions, lest we find ourselves existing as a colonized bourgeoisie. We can establish the research criteria that are necessary for understanding our existence. How can we be liberated by thinking and structures that have historically relied on our degradation?

Reflections of how liberation psychology liberates the African Mind

Liberation psychology invites excellent dialogue, reflecting and constrained by our cultural disposition, group history, and spiritual commitment. For example, during the civil rights and Black power movements in the 60s, the Association of Black Psychology was derived from the maelstrom of social, cultural, and political unrest. Within Liberation psychology, this locates the psychological work within a paradigm of activism and change. The Black Panther Party carefully addressed the significant social problems from the cultural context that wittingly or unwittingly catalyzed the Black community toward positive change and impact on the status of African people. Arrangements of power were challenged. Racial injustice was confronted, and institutional racism was targeted head-on. It was the Black Power movement that gave direction to Liberation Psychology. It allowed for cultural identity to grow and be respected, Black spaces to be accepted, and encouraged our intrapsychic epistemology, the knowing of Black history and Black contributions to the world. As a result, San Francisco State University established the first Black Student Union and Black studies program, Northwestern University in Evanston, Illinois, launched its "For Members Only" Black student organization. Black Studies programs began to pop up around the country. One of the most significant accomplishments was the formation of the Association of Black Psychologists in 1968 and later the formation of Black StudentsPsychological Association

(BSPA), a group of young Black psychology students who took matters into their own hands and demanded change. They held a symposium called "Challenge of Change in 1969: Black Perspective in Psychology." This fervor and these political actions all culminate and activate almost in unison, reflecting an intrapsychic episteme. This intrapsychic episteme was needed to create a deep dive into interrogation, distribution, and re-scripted implications and values being African, Black, and free-minded, free-willed people. Liberation psychology emanated from these actions of African people fighting for justice. The values, inspirations, and energies that emerged from this era allowed for the expression of imaginative, artistic, religious, and spiritual displays that redeveloped methodologies and practices of meaning oriented from the liberated minds and lives of Black folk. Fanon states, "This rush of negritude against the white man's contempt showed itself in certain spheres to be the one idea capable of lifting the interdiction and anathemas." Because the African intellectuals in America found the strength to rise above the ostracism and delivered collectively against the contempt of white supremacy, their reaction was to sing compliments in admiration of each other. This is how African liberated minds reflect the initial tenets of liberation psychology.

I'm thinking about how the African aesthetic is also liberated. What happens when we reconnect with how our ancestors defined beauty? Is it not fascinating that the European mind first fears and then endeavors to emulate African aesthetics in all creative expressions? There is also a lie being told about Black progress. A colonized mind will assert that we can only make progress when our lives meet the criteria for white success. The truth is that those measures of white success aren't working for white folks either, which is why they elected a fool who would say anything to maintain their illusion of superiority.

Empowerment of the African Character in Liberation Psychology- Ayiti (Haiti) revolution

Paulo Freire's *Pedagogy of the Oppressed*, conscientization recognizes the importance of helping oppressed people enhance their internal power and critical consciousness of their status to liberate themselves from oppressive forces. A liberatory mindset must be tied to the oppressed group's collective liberation instead of an individualized notion of being. Critical consciousness as it relates to the collective instead of the individual illuminates the systemic nature of oppression and liberates one from the perception that one's condition is due to personal flaw. By the same token this collective liberation deepens a person's ability to love their people and in relation themselves. It's really Freire who understood the role of love in liberation. There is no possibility of sustaining love and hope from an individualized position. This is significantly evident in the Haitian revolutions sparked by the practice of Vodou from 1750 to 1804.

African Vodun/Vodou/ Vaudou (African/Haitian variations and spellings). Vodou derived from African-Haitian collectives during the Atlantic slave trade of the 16th century. The Africans brought to Haiti came from various areas of West and Central Africa and traversed from the Congo to Senegal. Most were taken from West Africa; the second largest contingency came from Central Africa. These tribal nations comprised Benin (Ewe and Yoruba), Kongo kingdom (Kongo), and Togo land. The Spanish imported Senegal and Guinea in the sixteenth century, and later the French. In the 18th century, Cameroon, Nigeria, Ghana, Togo, Sierra Leone, Windward Coast, Angola,and Southeast Africa (known as the Bara tribe of

Madagascar), arrived in Haiti during this period. Haitian culture and Vodou mainly originated in the West Africa Vodun of Benin, particularly pre-colonial Benin, known as the kingdom of Dahomey, where the word *Vôdoun* signified a spirit or deity. The French-based Haitian Creole language has influences from several African languages, including the Fon language. Yoruba and Fon tribes were predominant during the 18th-century era.

In Haiti, *Vodou* came to refer to a small subset of rituals, usually a specific style of dance and drumming. Vodou has been described as a monotheistic religion teaching the existence of a single supreme God. This entity, believed to have created the universe, is known as the *Grand Mèt, Bondyé,* or *Bonié.* The latter names derive from the French *Bon Dieu* ("Good God"). For Vodouists, Bondyé is seen as the ultimate power source and is responsible for maintaining universal order. Bondyé is also regarded as remote and transcendent, not involving itself in human affairs. The lwa are regarded as the intermediaries of Bondyé and as having valuable wisdom for humans. Where does the power of lwa (loa) come from?

Houngan, also known as a voodoo priest, papa, or papa-loa, in the vodun religion, is a man who summons vodoun gods to divine the future or heals. *Houn'gan* or *mam'bo* (priests/ priestesses) of the *Oum'phor* rely on their knowledge of voodoo rites and their ability to alter the mindset from being oppressed to courage and sacrifice for freedom if they can explain or predict various events. *Houn'gan* (priests) or *manbos, mam'bo* (priestesses) involved in powerful mystics are known as a "bakor" or "boko." Power, energy, or empowerment is called "Bo." It is believed that the "Bo" can safeguard and dictate human events. The "Bo" constituted the capacity to energize and evolve symbolically as God. "Bo" composes the sacredness of living, clock, and space. Mentally, the "Bo" indicates that humans are to understand and employ the belief of the unseen onto the seen. The "Bo" depicts the possibility of human will and reveals what is hidden as a potential strength. The word "Bokomon" or "Bakor" means master of the "bo" knowledge. "Bakor" is a synonym for "Houngan."

One of the first acts of liberation psychology occurred due to the Ayiti (Haiti) revolution, where the practice of Vodun (Voodoo) played a vital role in the fight for freedom. This revolution, reflective of liberatory psychology, was sparked by the ancient Spirit (inspirations and energies) of the vodun. Vodouists usually meet to venerate the lwa in *Oum'phor (ounfòs)* temples run by *oungans (Houn'gan* or *mam'bo)*. Through ceremony (community performances and voices that encourage dialogue), vodun enabled the people to come together (cultural spaces), form political and cultural ideals (practices of the meaning), and serve as the staging arena (redevelop mythologies) for proindependence (methods of empowerment) to get their message across. Not only was voodoo an essential part of family life (paradigm of reciprocity), but it has also played a significant role in politics (attempt to recompense status inequalities) at the village and state levels. Vodou would be closely linked with the Haitian Revolution.

Many Vodouists were involved in the Haitian Revolution of 1750 to 1804, which overthrew the French colonial government, abolished slavery, and established an independent Haiti. In reflecting on vodun, we must tour the two important figures, Mackaland and Dutty Boukman. Two of the revolution's early leaders, Dutty Boukman and Francois Mackandal, were reputed to be powerful *Houn'gans*. Francois Makandal was a *nganga nkisi* or "a creator of objects" possessing spirits. Makandal comes from Mayombe, a region of West Africa, and the name is associated with abilities to identify sources of illness, cure illness, or cause it. Makandal was a Bokor or Houngan or educated by a Bokor. As a Bokor knowledgeable about the Bo, Mackandal understood the invisible power in plant nature, similar to hidden power (bo). His connection to the

"Bo" (power) Spirit is evidenced by his knowledge of the secrets found in plants to heal our kill (the chemical compounds found in the plants). Mackandal used both to protect and direct human events, and the role of African spirituality played in his successes, including the fight for freedom. Mackandal was recognized as a leader for his ability to escape bondage and encourage many Africans, including the Moors, to revolt and take revenge on the whites. As a voodooist, Mackandal served as a living example of the idea of being a free African. His behavior is consistent with characterized behavior of resistance, revenge, and revolt.

Boukman sprang the revolution that would eternally modify the face of St. Domingue. Dutty Boukman, a Jamaican-born Houngan who had been enslaved by the British, was sold to the French in Saint Domingue. The French could not recognize Boukman's identity as a master of the knowledge of Bo or the African Spirit of a Boukman. His stature as a Bokor is knowledgeable of the Bo (the sacred). According to legend, on 14 August 1791, a Vodou ritual occurred in Bois-Caïman, where the participants swore to overthrow the enslavers. The Bokor was seen as a mouthpiece of the invisible spirits or deities (Iwa). Once the lwa possesses an individual, the congregation greets it with a burst of song and dance. It was midnight, Thunder! Lightning! The whole area is trembling. Presiding over the assembly were Houn'gan Boukman (priest) and Mam'bo Cecile Fatiman (priestess). Boukman and Fatiman forever lost their chains with music, dance, and spirituality. Boukman declared when the revolution would start as the attendees chanted, "Eh! Eh! Bomba! Heu heu! Canga, bafio te! Canga, moune de le!" whose fiery words exalted the conspirators. In the Dogon language, *Nommo* means "to make one drink," the power of words to create harmony and balance in the face of disharmony.

Similarly, *Ofo Ase* is a Yoruba term meaning the generative ability of the spoken word to evoke or call into existence the ancestral spirits that it represents -- the force that gives life to everything. The earth seems to shake, and that's when they get together in this voodoo ceremony, and everyone together says it's over, slavery's over. At a signal from the priestess, they all flung themselves to the ground. They pledged indiscriminately to follow the instructions of Boukom, who had been proclaimed the supreme chief of the rebellion. Boukman's and Fatiman's ceremony inspired the masses to fight for freedom on 14 August 1791, and they conducted a freedom ceremony at the Bois Caiman. They made the sacrifice of an animal, a black pig, and everyone touched the blood. The ceremony ended with Boukman and Fatiman leading the gathering in a blood oath to take revenge against their French oppressors and told the group, "*You want to win? Cast aside your white god. Embrace your African Spirit. You are free,*" as C.L.R. James recounts. Consequently, the status of a *houn'gan and mam'bo* can change and appease or manipulate the public through their gift for predicting the future. We can see how African science is inspired by the details of commands from both "Bo komon" and "B mena," that male and female complementarity.

The words and instructions from Boukom sparked the Haitian revolution via the energy or Spirit vibrating between worlds of the unseen and the seen, leasing the "Irritated Genie" that symbiotically infected African minds and dictated syntonically behavior consistent with resistance, revenge, and revolt. Dutty Boukam is reported to have given the following prayer:

"The God who created the earth; who created the sun that gives us light. The God who holds up the ocean; who makes the thunder roar. Our God who has ears to hear. You who are hidden in the clouds, who watch us from where you are. You see all that the white has made us suffer. The white man's God asks him to commit crimes. But the God within us wants to do good. Our God, who is so good, so just, He orders us to revenge our wrongs. It's He who will direct our

arms and bring us the victory. It's He who will assist us. We all should throw away the image of the white men's God who is so pitiless. Listen to the voice for liberty that speaks in all our hearts."

Boukman sprang the revolution that would eternally modify the face of St. Domingue.

Here is a personal account of contemporary participation in Vodou ceremonies by Nancy Johnson: "I attended several Vodun ceremonies in New York. One that sticks out in my memory is when the Lwa/Loa Ogou descended. It was a similar feeling that I have experienced in certain churches and bembe (Santeria) when even the air in the room gets heavier. These experiences of spiritual forces being called down require the will of the collective. It's not an individualized experience. Anyway, that night Ogou was all up in everybody's business revealing secrets and every – thang. The other consistency is that one does not leave ceremony or the bembe or service without being fed. A mambo explained to me that to go out into the world unfed while still spiritually open would make a person vulnerable.

This spiritual force is frightening to many non-Africans. But the other thing that is frightening is that Vodou (and other traditional/indigenous Religion) can't be forced into a Europeanized hierarchy. The Houngan or Mambo leads and serves but anybody can embody (be ridden by) the Lwa and anyone can connect with their ancestral knowledge and strength. The spiritual force is called by, and called to the community."

The most well-known anecdotes regarding oppression involve the Ayiti Boukman, which sparked the wheel of ceremonial sacrifice with a ritual that has since gained mythic proportions in Ayiti culture and consciousness. In the square house (see pic below), *Oum'phor*, the Boukman, judged Ayitian critical consciousness. Ayitian critical consciousness had complete faith in the powers of the *Houn'gan*. Boukman could achieve a significant following and impact on the political spectrum with the population's trust. Black social scientists must embody the strength, power, and courage of Houngan Boukam and Mackaland to spark a revolution of the mind for freedom. This liberation psychology evolved the perspective or consciousness with community performances (rituals, drumming, and dance) and voices that combine dialogue, creative thinking, and fantasy for future potentiality and possibilities. Rituals were performed, dances took place, and initiation rites and lamb sacrifice were completed. The European world calls this "spirit possession," or "black magic," whereas Africans' understanding is seen as the expression of the Khaba (African spirit science). Today it is just a modest village. Nothing at Bois-Caïman commemorates the momentous events more than 200 years ago, not even a plaque. This sacred oath of liberty was most important. The question conceived a revolution that would result in the creation of the first free black Republic on earth, and it all began with a voodoo religious ceremony held on this very spot. Vodun represented the cement.

Hazard, Samuel. *Santo Domingo, Past and Present; With a Glance at Hayti.* New York: Harper & Brothers, Publishers, 1873. Page 284.

> God who answers,
> Would you who makes water burst forth from rock, remind us that you are a God who responds to our exhaustion and defeat? Just as you had Moses cling to an artifact of memory to meet the present moment, would you grant us physical artifacts which call us back to visceral emotions of our own stories, recalling how you have brought freedom and care to us before. Let us grasp the staffs of our past believing in their power even now— that we would be a people who meets desperation and sorrow with a remembrance that protects us from despair. Let our elders go with us to the rock, knowing they hold memory for us, increasing our belief and resolve. And as we approach the hopeless stone of our lives, let us meet the face of God, seeing that we aren't standing in the traumatic memories of the past alone, but with the breaker of chains and maker of water in the wilderness. We have not been forgotten.
>
> @blackliturgies

Enlivenment and illumination of the African Spirit in Liberation Psychology

Liberation psychology invites excellent dialogue and reflection that can only be constrained by our own level of cultural consciousness and spiritual commitment. For Liberation psychology to be a vehicle for Black critical consciousness, embedded within its methodological and theoretical approaches should be the nurturing of cravings of the African spirit (Spiritual, Intuitive, Reparative, Flexible, Balance, Optimal, Restorative, Harmony, respect for elders, obligatory non-reciprocal sharing, complementary role performance, sense of oneness, Collectivity, family group centeredness, shared responsibility) an not alien spirit as that of the Yurugu. Liberation psychology, therefore, should enliven and illuminate the African Spirit for African people. What is this muse for enlivening and illuminating our spirit?

First, we have already imagined what it should be like for fair and serene communities to exist. We ponder these ideas all the time. This pondering can be called our spiritual thoughts, dreams of a utopia, or prayers for a better communal way of living. But where do these thoughts and ideas come from? I would say the spirits of our ancestors as well as gifts from God (Adroa, Amun, Ausar, Auset, Inkosazana, Kibuka, MA'AT, Modjadji, Nana Buluku, Obatala, Olarun, Oludumare, Olu Kulu, Sango, Nun, and Nunet, Muhammed, and Jehovah to name a few). It is the spirits that inform us of what it should mean to be free beings operating from our ontological episteme. Therefore Liberation psychology should cultivate, as demonstrated by our internal awareness, an intentional awakening and affirming strategies designed to eliminate internalized and externalized oppression. Within the teachings, preachings, and practices of being one with God and acting in God's nature, we free our souls, develop our character, and walk in the light. These foundational acts are designed to enrich gratitude for one's culture, spirit, and consciousness. This is African liberation psychology that operates out of the justice of MA'AT. Liberation psychology focuses on the battle between freedom and the sociopolitical status of oppressed groups. However, that critical element of spirit is missing in Liberation Psychology, much like psychology in general. My spiritual, social, racial, political, and academic journey is what makes me whole.

Undoubtedly, the liberation of a people was evident within religious circles for thousands of years. The Black church served this function for hundreds of years. More recently, James Cone's work on Black liberation theology espouses that the experiences of African American people be acknowledged and tied to spiritual teachings. Cone states, "Black people physically and politically and economically did not control their spirit. That's why the black churches are very powerful forces in the African American community... Because religion has been that one place where you have an imagination that no one can control. So as long as you know that you are a human being nobody can take that away from you." The vitalization of spirit requires us to examine what does it mean to be human. As human beings, are we not knowing and knowable spirits? What possible ways of knowing and being in our spiritual communities might we offer? It has been well thought out that Pan-African psychology is founded on the notion of *Sakhu or Spirit*. Baba Nobles informs us that being in spirit is to operate in our "Spiritness." Spiritness for African people is based on their experience. Like Black liberation theology, it is through experience that Africans and African Americans know that they are alive and feel the forces of phenomena or energies in the living world. This is what is knowable in the lives of African people. Liberation psychology must muse through this understanding to illuminate the essence of African people toward true freedom of mind and critical consciousness. Liberation psychology acknowledges the prominence of giving precedence to African people's power to define for themselves practices of empowerment and attempt to repay inequalities of status in the psyche and the world.

Community Psychology

Critical consciousness is essential to the needs of Community Psychologists. Community psychology as a discipline has yet to challenge the continued system of inhabited scholarship in its hegemonic values. Community psychology has fallen short of a critical examination of knowledge production to erroneous assumptions and conclusions discussing oppressed groups. Simple approaches for explanation also restrict the field, like community psychology, to methodological limitations and experimental methods that contradict its aim of empowerment and liberation only to reproduce the identified dominant group's ideas, attitudes, and beliefs. African community psychologists must engage seriously with epistemic reflections as an orientation. New methodological approaches, internal discourse, pedagogical and political practices, and creating institutional spaces demand critical conscious review. For emancipation and liberation, power must shift to the Africanization of knowing, being, and doing. Like liberation psychology, community psychology looks to empower its constituency, operates from an emancipatory praxis, values the community's strengths and social justice, and sparks the spirit of disregarded groups. However, how has community psychology effectively confronted the dominant worldview of white supremacy/racism? Essential to the need for critical consciousness, a common thread in Africanization of community psychology praxes will serve as the role to critique the effect, embodiment, and spirituality in social change efforts to combat the system of white supremacy. At the heart of white supremacy, even within community psychology, is the dehumanization of people who do not fit the norm of the white, male, hetero-patriarchal individual. In this section, I will attempt to establish the essential need for African-centered critical consciousness (i.e., Black critical consciousness) to combat contradictions embedded in community psychology. As previously attempted, I will examine this need as essential for African community psychology within the parameters of critical conscious analysis of:

1. Advancing the interest and image of African people.
2. Contributing to the forward-flowing process of civilization.
3. Liberation of the African Mind.
4. Empowerment of the African Character.
5. Enlivenment and the illumination of the African Spirit.

Advancing the interest and image of African people within community psychology

True Community psychology should be about increasing power, identity, and knowledge production constructed from native cultural ways of knowing, being, and doing. Critical to community psychology is the necessary know-how to identify ideological support for communities burdened by experiences of collective trauma and oppression that mainly produced or amply funded the impairment or injury of the community psyche. For community psychology to assist in healing and focus on building well-being, there must be an ontological orientation of understanding rooted in the community to liberate individuals who feel shackled. As for the Black social scientists, self-determination is needed to develop a psychology that adequately addresses the community from which we arose to accomplish and deal with this unique disequilibrium. In this case, how do we advance the interest and image of African people locally and globally? Key to this ideological conceptualization centers on identifying that African community psychology exists. Integral to African community psychology are ontological, cosmological, and epistemological features that feed communal participation, social empowerment, and political action. African community psychology should articulate an examination of epistemologies (asili), ideologies, and worldviews (utamawazo) which in turn allows for reflection of cultural manifestations of collective behaviors and real feelings (utamaroho) as factors of empowerment and liberation.

The examination and utilization of African community psychological science require the investigation of communal values concerning the conditions of injustice and oppression. In its stated goal, community psychology, by intent, recognizes the psychic consequences of power disenfranchisement. For African community psychology, the effects of the maafa (horrific psychic disaster) need to be examined, along with identifying ancient traditions that may help create solutions from the community level. However, we use western science as a model of community psychology. In that case, we must be prepared to recognize how little, if any, strides have been made in developing or empowering the Black community. Perhaps the power structure that created the disenfranchisement and disequilibrium operates from the same psychic network or consciousness.

For Black social scientists, no enduring good can arise from subservience. We must conduct ourselves with utmost attention to work consistently and with keen assessment as this is inviolable. As black social scientists, we cannot become leaders in our community by subjecting our people to the same brainwashing tactics that afflicted us in the first place. Affecting the mind of African people requires us to reject accepting lowered expectations of others and applying those low expectations to our community, particularly those who did not choose to take their role in creating the condition we are in. We must continue to speak up and speak out for standards that reflect our innate genius and for justice on behalf of our community using psychology as a weapon. If community psychology is about supporting the efforts of collective community liberation, empowerment, and justice, then who should seek the best for our community? We must not be held hostage to pitch to ourselves how others choose to see us or treat us but instead continue to chart our path, demonstrating the understanding, commitment, and integrity that defines us. This is tantamount to the work of African/Black social scientists; this work is hard, but to achieve at the highest level, we must be strong in our convictions and insist on treating our community with fairness from a political justice stance. Our community needs us, deserves us, and will always seek justice from us with immense gratitude for our support in improving the lives of those in the African community. Therefore, African/Black critical consciousness must examine scholarship and artifacts that reflect the people's psyche from an African-centered perspective.

Community Psychology and forward-flowing process

How might we begin this process of contributing to

African life and show how African life contributes to the world? Like liberation psychology, community psychologists can help co-create spaces where group and community members can listen to their dreams and aspirations (episteme), work through conflicts, and deeply inquire about the type of change (transformational) needed to solve our problems. One example is social action research as one paradigm in Africanization community psychology. Epistemic mutuality can occur if we prioritize historiography and geographic currents rather than individualized intellectualism. The lack of centering African ideals in community psychology requires African-centered community psychologists to point to an orientation—a global direction that is always from, by, with, and for Africa. This eco-cultural psychology helps facilitate understanding to reestablish the ideals of true community to end ongoing breaches due to cultural mistrust, power imbalance, and political miscalculation as a vehicle for creating confusion. Where are community psychology's actions for social change supporting reparations? If Community psychology is true to its intended purpose, it should act as a conduit to repair and rehabilitate African communities' physical, psychological, integrity, and dignity. The liberatory African-centered community psychologists must assume a political stance and resist precise definitions as they may sabotage effective engagement in emancipatory traditions within African ontology and epistemic exigencies. African-centered community psychologists (Black critical consciousness social scientists) should serve to guide how we enact psychologies of the community from a native perspective.

For example, ABPSi's rejection of APA's apology reveals that the politics of their monopolistic position continues to concentrate wealth, power, and influence in the organization responsible for maintaining the disenfranchised status of Black people and other people of color. They continue to abuse this power by not following the tenets of community psychology and not advocating for the empowerment of marginalized and oppressed groups. We can't be fooled by the presence of figureheads who can't wheel this type of power, yet they try to speak on behalf of the Black community without empowering the district they represent. Whom are they fooling? For us to move in a forward-flowing process, we must reject European epistemes that seek to justify notions of inferiority, indignity, and essential differences between Africans and Africans in the world by harnessing authentic knowledge systems and histories for the purposes (re)asserting the dignity and humanity of Africa. For instance, APA claims to be the leading organization in applying psychology to improve society; community psychology, as a discipline to remain viable, only needs to engage in dialogue with marginalized groups and place them in vulnerable positions so they can continue to maintain the privilege of Euro-American psychology. Case in point, where is APA and community psychology fighting against states that want to wipe clean from memory the vestiges of slavery and restore the invisibility of the Africans in America? When has the white community psychological field demonstrated real empowerment engagement and liberated praxis with the African community? Black social scientists, particularly community psychologists, should not be fooled by the political actions of the so-called purveyors of psychology. Instead, as constructed, the field places them as provocateurs and not as true facilitators working with people of color. Nurturing critical psychological consciousness requires connecting with Africans by enmeshing their lives with the social life of the Africans for healing.

Through correct ethos, paradigm, and praxis, the field of community psychology should take on the mantle and fight for reparations. We need critical community psychologists to support the fight for reparation through advocacy, social action, change, and transformation. Africans who are descendants of slavery are owed reparation. Africans whose family members were taken from them are owed reparation. Reparation denotes the progression and product of alleviating the impairment or injury caused by the maafa and subsequent inhumane acts of violence against a group and community. Just like we take a thorough history of the client in individual therapy, there is a history of the groups who have terrorized, tortured, maimed, vilified, and hung from trees, all for the sake of killing the spirit and psyche of a people. APA is complicit in these acts of violence as they participated and promulgated narratives to keep the Africans in a state of subservience. APA owes reparations to the Black community for subjugating the people in those communities to this harm and ills. There is a need to deconstruct the history of slavery and its momentous and continued affliction resulting in the lack of advancement of social, economic, and political life for the ascendents of enslaved Africans and for Africa. Community psychology's obligation has not made reparation a priority or an element to confront hegemonic, ancillary hidden, and repressed narratives that have contextualized current psychic horrors and community life. It must be recognized within community psychology that reparation must "comprehensively " restore any damage, including any material or moral damage caused by Europeans, Western psychology, and APA for their role in the aforementioned wrongful acts. The goal here is to utilize Black critical consciousness as a source to fight for reparation and healing from the damage done by past colonialism, inequality, and political and economic exploitation. Black social scientists in the field of community psychology should be obligated to make the case of reparation a reality.

Liberation of the African Mind in Community Psychology (CP)

Decolonization never takes place unnoticed, for it influences individuals and modifies them fundamentally. Frantz Fanon P.36

Liberation of the African Mind requires Community psychology, in its thrust, to extend the analysis of disproportionality caused by systematic racism and white supremacy (xenophobia). Examining the yurugu (exploitation, domination, and destruction) effect of the maafa (horrific terror), manufactured environmental and psychic disruption, and capitalism is paramount. From an African-centered perspective, community psychology is the field of study that addresses challenges European/western psychology still needs to accomplish as a discipline. Community psychological praxis requires critical reflection and action to transform and ameliorate structures of inequalities and policies that engender unfair outcomes while simultaneously coming up with solutions for a new vision of change. Critical to community psychologists' work is the need to work with communities to authenticate common knowledge (cultural manifestations of collective consciousness, behaviors, and fundamental feelings), use culturally relevant paradigms, and foresee deep-seated transformative praxis that engenders novel and innovative solutions due to African critical conscious development. Therefore, community psychology theory, research, and practice should be rooted in values and commitment to liberating psychosocial change. Instead, hegemonic knowledge and current science production reinforce and reproduce marginalized statuses. When Black social scientists, unbeknownst to them, ignore their epistemic agency, they subject the Black community to inadequate research methodology interventions that do not capture their essence.

Epistemic agency, concerning psychosocial change, is necessitated to transform from the subjective and objective interpretation of experiences. To understand these experiences more clearly, a methodological approach for examination and interrogation requires the carving out of black spaces for black thought to manifest in questions and answer format that would allow for excavating through contradictions. In addition, since an element of community psychology relies on collaborative approaches with community members, potentiating African psychological community work means ferreting out the look, feel, and utility of epistemic agency. For example, we managed to create what is known as "the ritual circle," an empowering collective presentation-feedback response process. In assisting every member of the collaborative group, each one is evaluated, whether student or professional, and the presenter must listen to everyone's feedback. All who attended the presenter's presentation performance are required to give feedback. The goal is to assist in influencing the presenter, be it an expert or novice student, for the emancipatory formation of their work, refining methodology, gaining more knowledge, or perfecting their skill as a presenter. The community should help the presenter/researcher refine his tactics, information, and processes within their delivery. The presenter must listen intently, think through the community's responses, and incorporate this in their work. This African-centered community research refinement process aims to recognize the stimulus of collective thoughts, feelings, memories, stories, and questions to solve problems.

The starting point of this reflection and dialogue process is for Black social scientists who claim to be committed to liberating the minds of African people and establishing psychological, social, political, and economic justice research. This epistemic shift requires a methodological intervention that calls upon committed Black critical conscious psychologists to dismantle anti-white thoughts, contest the status quo, and challenge unwarranted truths. The supremacies that enlighten western research with an obligatory researcher-participant dichotomy in participatory action research have no benefit to the African community.

Thought-provoking and agitating dualistic association of authority dynamic is part of the process of undoing. Fanon's description of experiences *"from below," from within,* and *through* the bodies, lives, and social disorder we can see new methods for data collection and impetus for social change. This proposes a novel direction in the research paradigm. Three critical figures for laying the foundational work in community psychology reveal the importance of the object of research serving as the purveyor of what needs to be known. Frantz Fanon's "Black Skin, White Masks" encourages innovative practices of inquiry centered on the person's political, historical, and cultural dimensions as part of critical consciousness reflection. Paulo Freire made relevant the essential practice of meditation and action called conscientization, the praxis *of* and *for* liberation. Finally, Martín-Baró created a method of research concept of de-ideologization as the process of fetching the awareness of foundations, practices, and interconnected systems of oppression.

Another methodological approach that could benefit community psychology research is the interpretivist and constructivist methods. This approach examines the global human experiences and rejects the power dynamic of one reality over another as universal truth. Often community psychology research captures the existence of multiple subjective realities that occur in different contexts and through different lenses and interactions. Other times it is socially constructed. An interpretivist and constructivist paradigm are not just events but meaning-making phenomena, giving rise due to historical events shaping the psyche community. Individuals' behavioral, interpersonal, and emotional responses within the community context allow the individual and community participants to be seen as co-researchers to counter any perceived power differences in the researcher-participant or "research subjects/objects" dyad. Identifying as co-researchers also ensures that individuals' experiences were privileged as they took the expert role and assisted in data collection and analysis via the qualitative interview. Knowledge, methods, and critiques that counter-hegemonic tradition lends power to liberate the mind of people of color, who are often targeted objects.

CP and Empowerment of African Character

Empowerment of the African Character is transformative psychopolitical validation. Transformative psychopolitical validity prioritizes liberatory practices as the potential of collective actions for ensuring individual, communal, and holistic wellness in *all* actions and interventions. The challenge, of course, is for the field of community psychology to promote conscious change and a positive impact on the psychological health of the African/Black community. The goal is to fend against scientific colonialism at its primary intent and to avoid transsubstantive errors when interpreting the cultural reality of the Blacks and their communal way of living. By helping the black community to identify and hold their values through vision, Black social scientists should be bold scholar-activists with the aspiration to make reparation a reality. Full empowerment of the African Character for people of African ascent rests on kujichagulia (self-determination) and ujima (collective work and responsibility) for healing as needed components to develop, define, and articulate the needs of the African community. This is the purpose (nia) of African/Black critical conscious psychologists (all Black social scientists).

Questions of identity and belonging are often the result of interconnecting dimensions of race, class, gender, nationality, and other significant factors in forming a community. Multiple meanings of the *community* consist of place, relational time, and assemblage forming community identity -- psychological-emotional connection, action, space, motivational, cultural, social identity, to sense of community. Membership or sense of belonging, mutual influence, and fulfillment of needs are representations of shared emotional connection. Within the community, concepts are the notion of a sense of connectedness -- through topography, collective history, culture, a sense of fitting, inspiration, success, and effective communication channels. In addition, the community is collaborative and transformative, a "unity potential solution" with collective forces (asili) of a people proactively addressing their problems. While communities have several layers and dimensions, the value of communality speaks of ontological and epistemological correctness within the African community. The shift from *community* to *communality* as ontological nature and epistemological understanding within African-centered community psychology operates from the ethos of kujichagulia (self-determination), ujima (collective work and responsibility), and justice (MA'AT) in resisting the status quo. The true essence of communality is balance and harmony, being culturally syntonic. In our communal wanting, imagining, visioning, intending, and acting together, we find peace, harmony, and balance of power. It means that we honor and absorb the wisdom of our cosmologies (ancestors) that prioritize the interconnectedness and interdependence of our humanity and be embedded in relationships, relationality, and collectivity as positioned. This epistemic stance roots in liberation theology but has utility in community social action research.

Communality establishes creative coalitions involving mutual learning without harming others. This Africanization of communality consists of constructing counternarratives, counter-knowledge, and counter-practices that seek to eradicate patterns of oppressive relationships and thoughts and move toward condemning exploitation, neoliberalism, patriarchy, and racism. The fundamental transformation begins with Black social scientists imagining terms of being concerning production, defining, and being in their light. Kessi, Suffia, and Seedat eloquently state, "Denying an individual's or a collective's right to their beliefs and values undermines their agency and self-determination." There is a need to reduce relations of structural dominance of people down to personhood when these are reciprocally related. There is no personhood without people, and there are no people without personhood. The essence of people and personhood enlivens and illuminates all spirits.

Does Community Psychology Enliven and Illuminate the African Spirit

"It is the undeniable desire of one's spirit to connect, merge, expand, and extend into a greater oneness with another (spirit)" in community." Baba Nobles

Critical consciousness encourages research to explicitly focus on the psychology of activism, challenging power, inequality, and political change through psychopolitical activity. How do we use the intellectual work of engagement and knowledge production as essential for psychopolitical gain? Psychopolitical validity is the intersection of meaningful terminology that encompasses political status and psychological factors when analyzing power, wellness, and oppression. For instance, linguistic analysis of terms' advantage', 'significant, and 'majority' demonstrates positive implications of assets and resources linked with the word, perversely, signifying a position of power and authority for Whites over those who have been identified with contradictory terms as 'disadvantage,' 'marginalized,' and 'minority' statuses. Analysis of these terms demonstrates undesirable connotations of deficit and lack of association with those they describe. The Black critical conscious community psychologist must ward against the use of psychopolitical latent concepts and definitions as we are bound to repeat the truth of the oppressor. We must decolonize our minds and establish authentic cooperative and collaborative terminology when working with the villagers. Mutual construction of new possibilities can create a unique design for living and a pattern for interpreting reality, grinding in the appliance to continue reevaluation to promote positive and restorative social change and community well-being. There is always a power differential, for example, in collaborative writing and thinking. One prominent example is the student-Jegna relationship, where the latter's voice is often weighted heavily over the student simply because of status. If the goal is empowerment, there must be an equal exchange between two joint forces to create a sense of collective voice within context and content. This can be done in illumination.

Illumination sessions activate our imaginations and visions to empower the constituency and operate from an emancipatory praxis. Illumination sessions value the community's strengths and social justice and spark the spirit of slighted groups in confronting the dominant alien worldview of white supremacy/racism. The session must incorporate asking questions to generate group discussion, pondering, contesting, and reformulating the active juices of our spirit. Questions asked would initiate liberatory African-centered psychological processes in the context of "look and feel like," "*from below, from within,* and *through," and of* and *for* activating spirit in psychosocial exchange. African Community psychology requires groups to operate with critical consciousness of everyday situations. Other elements of this exchange method are location and collective occupying of space—being in the same room. Second, stories become vital because we hear what illustrates possible epistemological, political, economic, theoretical, and social solutions to respond. Therefore, listening as a skill set is essential. When we listen with intent, we aim to recognize the stimulus of our thoughts, feelings, memories, stories, and questions. The challenge is to work through psychologically demanding faculties of anxiety and guardedness. This collaborative method can allow one to be with others in a new and uncommon way for actual psychosocial change in the Africanization of community psychology. African community psychology is premised on centering the knowledge and capabilities of those who reside in African spaces and different locales whose values and beliefs are African, valued, recognized, and represented in theory and praxis.

Communal spirit is the engagement, convergence, expansion, and extension into a greater oneness with others. Therefore, African/Black critical consciousness must examine scholarship and artifacts that reflect the people's psyche from an African-centered perspective. Through storytelling, artistic expression, social theater, and academia, to name a few. These expressions of culture will shed light on the functionality of both injury and wellness from, by, and within our group, relying on the ontological orientation, cosmological understanding, and epistemological knowing for an emancipatory vision of justice, resistance, and revitalization prioritizing our humanity and community of connectedness.

African/Black Psychology as the basis of critical consciousness

> *"We, who call ourselves psychologists, must refigure psychology to reflect the realities of Africa and her children worldwide."... "...Black African psychologists [need] to use African epistemological reflections and subsequent skill sets to meet the challenges of our time in every context and to*

engage in policy and program development wherever African people exist." (Baba Wade Nobles, 2015 p.401)

The field of African/Black psychology is rooted in critical consciousness. Operating from the ontological Spirit, cosmological orientation, and epistemological knowing of being African-centered, African/Black psychology in paradigm and praxis is the basis of critical consciousness. By mining deep-seated African ideas from African cultural integrity, with collective awareness, and spiritual embodiment, the return of what it means to be African is Black critical consciousness. It all started in 1968 when some sistas and brothas at the APA convention realized Western psychology did not have the Black community at heart regarding theory, research, and practice. As a result, Baba Robert Guthrie produced his seminal work detailing the history of White psychology. In his book, "Even the Rat was White," he revealed the legacy of white psychology's history of racism, describing American psychology's role and using psychological science to reinforce and perpetuate the myth of white supremacy. Guthrie noted that this science was always suspect and coined scientific racism. Joseph L. White's foundational article "Toward a Black Psychology" called for creating a psychology grounded in the cultural and ethnic authenticity of Black people. The works of White and Guthrie demonstrated that at the base of critical thought is the need to understand African/Black people, their culture, and how we have contributed to the world.

Critical consciousness requires the agency to reflect on theory and practice and to examine their utility and application to Black folk. Suppose the result does not promote a greater understanding of our contributions to the world and advance the interest and image of Black or African people. In that case, you are beginning to engage in critical thinking processes. However, you have to go much deeper than just criticizing white psychology. Black social scientists who continue to think from a white cultural lens end up just painting white theories black, using the exact psychological science to reinforce and perpetuate the myth of white supremacy. A case in point is the Nigrescence model. Baba Wade Nobles provides us with an understanding of African/Black Psychology as "African peoples' psychology [being] fundamentally derived from the nature of the African spirit and determined by the African spirit's manifestation as a unique historical and cultural experience," Skh Djr (illumination of the Spirit). This requires us to create a psychological science to reinforce and perpetuate an African power of potentiality in our conscious psyche. Therefore the idea of Black social scientists is to recognize her African essence and to operate from that ontological Spirit. Our Spirit is our consciousness. We have to use the Spirit of consciousness to create liberating psychology. Black critical consciousness is the state of mind that places African thought, worldview, and episteme as the foundation for analysis. As Baba Nobles articulates,

> *"African Black Psychology [is] an African-centered interdisciplinary and multidimensional investigation of African philosophy, literature, languages, history, politics, aesthetics, spirituality, and science. As a global discipline, Pan African Black Psychology would allow us to approach questions of human essence, experience, and expressions (i.e., values, customs, beliefs, conduct, etc.) important to all cultures—the nature of the beautiful, the meaning of human existence, the search for the divine, the nature of historical epochs—through an African-centered interdisciplinary and multidimensional studies." (p. 404)*

Baba Wade Nobles instructs African scientists to "think deeply" about what it means to be African. He (Dr. Baba Nobles) taught me two essential inquiry questions when examining, critiquing, and analyzing information and material: How does whatever information you receive advance the image and interest of African people? And how psychology's science contributes to the forward-flowing process of civilization for Blacks. Furthermore, three key elements can be added to establishing the bases of critical consciousness inquiry as extolled within the mission of ABPSi, are we liberating the African Mind, are we empowering the African Character, and have we enlivened and illuminated the African Spirit? How do our knowing and knowledge production, restorative practices, community revitalization, and dissemination of science (CABP, 2021) help advance Africans' contribution to the field of African Psychology?

In my most profound thought and understanding, which I instilled from my early life experiences with Babas Hilliard, Nobles, Goddard, and Kambon, I attempted to articulate that African cultural psychology emanates out of the deep culture of African people. I discuss the highlights and illuminate that psychological processes and resources for a positive human being reflect their cultural, psychological, and social authenticity in the world. These critique elements make our decisions deliberate and in the interest of African people viable and venerable. When we examine intensely what funds human beings and how that significantly shapes our responses and reactions to living, we will learn the value of being African. We must utilize our *Ngolo* (self-healing power) and *Nkali* (power of storytelling) to define reality on our terms and respond to our definition of correct and proper conduct. The utmost essential reality to demarcate is the sense of our health and wellness! African people's commitment to comprehending their undeniable association with their Africanness, which brought the Africans into existence, formulates critical consciousness. In other words, it is imperative that constructing African-centered theories authenticating correct and normal functioning must incorporate mutually verifying constructs within the culture about the African nature of human functioning. John Egbeazien Oshodi presents to us the notion of the power of potentiality. He discusses the nuances associated with psychological power in terms of desirable characteristics of acceptance, identification, controllability, and jurisdiction. The psychological process of power should serve as a guide for empowerment, restoration, and repair of our being. When examining these terms of intentions, evaluations, sacrifices, gains, and contributions identified by African-centered theorists and scholars alike, we can determine how our way can serve as a guide for establishing critical consciousness within the bipolarity of worldviews.

African world view	European worldview
Spiritual	Material
Transcended Self	Self-actualization
Heritage	Capital
Black	White
Whole	Part
Development	Industrial
Land	Sea
Flexible	Complex
Poly	Mono
Even	Odd
Intuitive	Investigate
Peace	War
Universal	Unilateral
Collective	Discrimination
Communal	Racial
Inherent	Imperialism
Balance	Hegemony
Optimal	Ultimate
Circular	Linear

Reality	Romantic
Restorative	Destructive
Diaspora	Transatlantic
Experiential	Experiment
Reparative	Provisional
Vital	Physical
Qualitative	Quantitative
Maternalistic	Paternalistic

While recognizing the power of potentiality and nuances associated with these psychological powers from contradictory worldviews, we must also give license to ancient African critical terms as the power of potentiality. The use of African words is required to keep our rhythmic Spirit alive. Uniquely African in harmony is our pattern of conveyance. Traditional African terms in our ancestors' languages are essential because they are found in ancient teachings illuminating our African beingness and psyche. We must become familiar with these desirable characteristics of knowing mechanisms and terminology which should be adopted in our daily practice. Some critical language to recognize and understand is revealed:

Ago – Amę
(ah-gooo) (ah-MAY) - - "Ago!" means "Listen!" or "come to attention, get ready. "Ame" means "I am [we are] listening. We are ready". This call and response traditionally represented a call to arms and the people's readiness to take action (AkanTwi - Ghana).

Alafia (Ah-lah-fee-ah) - - The state of perfect and total peace. (Yoruba)

Alasal Tarey (ah lah sah Tah reh) - - The process through which one comes to know and understand one's origin, essence, and unfolding as a human being to serve humanity (Songhoy-senni).

Ashe (àṣẹ) (ah shay) - - So Be It. Ashe is the power to bring things into existence, to make things happen. It is the authority, power, and life force within all creatures. When you say Ashe, you are your knowing and knowable Spirit (energy) to affirm and make it happen.

Buka mu kati, ya buka ku mbazi (boo-kah moo- kah- tee yah- boo- kah koom-bah-zee) - - The Divine in me, heals the inside; The rest of us heal the outside. (Kikongo)

Kingongo (Keen gohn goh) - - A state wherein the inner Divine presence is in harmony (blends) with the self-healing power (NGOLO) as expressed in all forms of being. (Kikongo).

Kugusa Mtima (Koo-goo-sah em-tee-mah) - - Means "touching the heart." It deals with the capacity of the collective human will via the "power" to transcend and transform human consciousness. (Kikongo).

Kundalini (koon-dah-lee-nee) - - Is the evolutionary phenomenon that is a biogenetic, conscious, and transforming force. It animates the spiritual trajectory of our species and has been with us, consciously, for at least six thousand years.

Ngolo (en-goh-loh) - - Strength/power/energy. (KiKongo).

Ubuntu (oo-Bun too) - - Spirit in which Being and beings coalesce. It is the cosmic universal force. (KiKongo).

Zola (Love) (zoh-lah) - - Zola means love. Zola (love) activates 'Ngolo,' the energy of self-healing power (potential). It is the undeniable desire of one's Spirit to connect, merge, expand, and extend into a greater oneness with another (Spirit). Zola requires one value and to treasure another with caring and affection to sustain, promote, nurture, and inspire their 'perfectibility.' Zola (Love) is self and collective cherishment. It is the actual act of personal and collective preservation and actualization. (Kikongo).

For African/Black liberation Kambon's definition of African/Black Psychology reveals,

> *"as a system of knowledge (philosophy, definitions, concepts, models, procedures, and practices) regarding the environment of the collective cosmos after the evaluation of African Cosmology [meaning that] ...African/Black Psychology is nothing more or less than uncovering, articulation, operationalization, and application of the principles of the African reality structure relative to psychological phenomena (243)."*

We can identify the subjective-objective intentions of European terms and psychological characteristics embedded within their culture. Due to scientific colonialism and scientific racism and the history of the Europeans exerting their power to have others believe they created all that is, we must be willing to retake back what we knew as Africa for centuries. As established by African philosophers and historians, high culture grew out of the soil of Africa before any other civilization existed. A shift in consciousness began due to Africans, the Moors, imprinted on Greek culture during the Dark Ages back to Africa. Greece's originality was a copy of Egyptian thought. The first-ever available power shift from Ancient Black Egypt to the Hellenic phase, after Roman rule, then to the British government, is now being recycled into U.S. and African history. Baba Wade Nobles gifted us with deep thought of understanding the definition of power *as the ability to define reality and have others accept it as if it were their own.* Europeans have exerted a sense of power that Black social scientists need them when in fact, they need us. We can see from above how "Europe's psychological domination of Africa's mind can be understood as a clash of culture and consciousness" (Baba Nobles, 2013).

We must accept the understanding that the only way for Blacks to advance themselves is for African people to reunite with African history and culture for us to develop solutions to our problems. Black social scientists need to understand that only when we, as scientists of the mind and culture, begin to dip deep into the well of African history and knowledge as the vital source of our being will we be victorious and re-define for ourselves an authentic way of self. But we cannot win the psychological war by sleeping with the enemy as their subjective-objective terms of intentions have never served us well. As we know, APA and Western psychology have proven that they are the enemy, but for some reason, we have some black social scientists who believe that working with the enemy will help bring us to salvation. I will forever harp on how the abused *container carves a note of explanation for the* abuser and feel healed. That is like telling the wife who is abused, tortured, and constantly injured by her husband *to pen a message of regret for the* abuser and say everything is alright now. This is absurd and makes no sense in the healing realm. There is no power to escape the abuser. The abuser's power has now transformed into the abusee taking up for the abuser. There's no reconciliation here, no restorative process here, and no revitalizing or illumi-nating the African Spirit toward wholeness. Piper-Mandy and Rowe state, "If such effort is absent, it is fair to presume that [those] scholars' work does not seek to be located within the African-centered archetype." In the words of Barbara Sizemore, *"[some] Black people still don't get it."*

With this understanding, I have been inspired to help (re) establish and re-ascend our health and wellness knowledge. Three essential themes stood out from my thirty-plus years of interrogating and exploring the epistemological understanding of health and wellness within African/Black Psychology lit-erature: Connectedness, competency, and consciousness (three C's). In developing this meta-theory system approach for cen-tering our mental health, Baba Nobles offered to rethink the term mental health and interrogate the notion of restorative healing as an African process for capacity and restoration.

Restorative capacity is the ability to demonstrate healing as determined by our Spirit, emotion (sense of Connectedness), social life (competency), and sakhu (consciousness). I have tried establishing the Ubuntu restoration and wellness model: Connectedness, Competency, and Consciousness (to be discussed in Vol. II). The attempt is to reclaim cultural patterns, styles, and ways of understanding wellness for African people.

I espouse three pillars for restorative health in my Ubuntu restoration and wellness model. First, **Connectedness** is feeling a sense of belonging and bonding with others. Multiple terms reflect the power and potentiality of Connectedness: communal, interdependence, interconnectedness, consubstantiation, harmony, collectivism, cooperation, connectivity, longing, belonging, bonding, community, and social support. The next theme, **competency**, reflects skills and abilities to successfully function and maneuver through demands -- possessing skills and abilities allows for transferring energy to phenomena, connecting psychological, cognitive mechanisms, and neural substrates. Words have transformative psychological power legitimizing the material manifestation of phenomena. Known as *Nommo*, the generative power of the spoken word on Dogon, *Ngolo* (self-healing power), and *Nkali* (power of storytelling). The final theme, **consciousness**, is the collective consciousness of self, others, and the Spirit. The amaZulu of South Africa believe in the '*Uqobo*,' the truth or origin of living consciousness -- consciousness is the aspect of God in our Spirit (*Skh Djr*). This spirit consciousness examines all of our actions -- consciousness of self-analysis demonstrating internal and external awareness. The Akan of West Africa believes in the principle of two: *okra* (soul) and *sunsum* (Spirit), immaterial/spiritual and *human* (body), material/physical worlds.

In this model, the philosophical tenet of Ubuntu, the meaning of one's human existence, is directly related to the human existence of others. Part of the Zulu lexicon, the term

Ubuntu means *"the essence of being human…We are people because of other people."* The well-being of man depends upon his fellow man - "obi yiye firi obi." It is a Spirit of Being with other beings—a universal cosmic force. When the human Spirit is well, whole, and healthy, the *soul* **Being** is in the reality of Ubuntu, characterized by our interdependence on human wellness concerning each other's human wellness. I am claiming to be an African-centered scholar who accepts the responsibility to address and spark other African-centered scholars to work on developing sound practices from the African-centered space of knowing and social life. Baba Nobles reminds us that "accordingly, the experiences of being, belonging, and becoming and the principles of location and agency for reviewing and understanding African phenomena are epistemologically paramount."

One could argue that Bobby Wright's Psychopathic Racial Personality, Fred Phillips's Ntu Psychology, Kambon's African self-consciousness, Stevenson's Racial socialization, Shawn Ginwright's Healing Centered Engagement, Chioneso's et al. Community Healing and Resistance Through Storytelling in African Communities and Wilson's Ubuntu Model of Restorative Capacity and Wellness, exhibit Black critical consciousness at its highest level. From an African-centered perspective, healing is a community endeavor that involves maintaining a harmonious balance between the spiritual realm and the physical world. For example, (Re)establishing spiritual harmony with one's ancestors is a healing prerequisite that allows access to extraordinary cures. Like Wilson's Ubuntu Restorative model, community healing consists of three vital psychological dimensions: *Connectedness*, collective memory (*competency*), and critical *consciousness*. Integrating these key dimensions into community healing is an ongoing multilevel process whereby oppressed groups strengthen their Connectedness and collective memory through culturally syntonic strategies that promote critical consciousness to achieve optimal wellness. When an African discourse guides the theories of African thinkers, then new and more appropriate ideas, concepts, notions, etc., will become part of the scientific enterprise. Within the discourse of African scientific enterprise, African social scientists must commit themselves to comprehend their undeniable association with their Africanness (eliminating mental incarceration) to bring the African into existence *Spirit* and formulate Black critical consciousness psychology.

The need is for Black social scientists to liberate ancient African deep thought and re-establishment the operation of our natural essence. I concur that there will be the adoption of *Skh Djr* [development of a Pan African Black Psychology] as the process for understanding, examining, and explaining the meaning, nature, and functioning of being human. For African social scientists conducting a deep, profound, and penetrating search, study, and mastery, we must contend that African ideations must be a conscious awareness of our identity as a collective. We must realize that "illuminating" the human Spirit or essence is to denounce human degradation against African and struggle for an individual and collective effort to dignify our human experience. The task for all Black social scientists is to reject the essences and denial of alien ideological conceptions and constructs and to meditate intensely and vigorously about African meanings and understandings of what it means to be human. Moreover, consistent with Diop's (1974) directive, we are to replicate and exert influence on and use the history and tradition of contemporary African people. *Skh Djr* would require that African language and logic be redeemed to gain insight into the functioning of us as African peoples.

Liberation Psychology was mused as an articulation of freeing the African mind for critical consciousness. Critical consciousness is understood as indispensable to the needs of Community Psychology, which aims to challenge existing paradigms and praxis for holistic healing, calling for an African-centered and strengths-based framework. Ultimately, African/Black Psychology forms the base of critical consciousness in reformulating meaning, extrapolating spirit science in functioning and authenticating African life and wellness. In sum, Liberation Psychology, Community Psychology, and African/Black Psychology form the foundation for empowerment through black critical consciousness psychological framework.

Critical Consciousness

A key component of critical consciousness is the liberation of the African mind. Liberation Psychology articulates that a change in power dynamics is required for productive functioning and participation in restoring one's own life. Critical consciousness has been defined as "an individual's capacity to critically reflect and act upon his sociopolitical [situation]" p. 445). Therefore, through mature reflection and action as guided by an African discourse, the African social scientist will engage in the liberation of all African people. It is essential to understand that it has always been the complexity of the *Skh Djr* (illumination of the Spirit) that provokes the Africans' need to be free. Community Psychology seeks understanding, connections, and restoration of collective cultural strengths among key community agents. This critical conscious revelation allows African community social scientists to challenge and transform structures of inequalities with a *"service through science"* mentality. This memetic thought is the "motto" and inspired work of Institute for the Advanced Study of Black Family Life and Culture, Inc. Finally, African/Black Psychology cultivates the cultural integrity, authenticity, and spiritual embodiment of what it means to be human concerning one's social, political, economic, and psychological freedom. African/Black Psychology was spawned out of the critical conscious minds and established the foundation for the psychological framework of Black critical consciousness. African/Black Psychology allows us to set theories of African thought and practice as guided by African discourse. Identifying traditional and innovative ideas, concepts, notions, etc., will become part of a creative scientific enterprise. It is believed that African/Black social scientists need to define restorative capacity through the foundational expression of *Skh Djr* (illumination of the Spirit). All are designed to bring Spirit back into its rightful place as the factor for restorative healing. Baba Nobles provide us with a comprehensive understanding of African/Black Psychology adopted by the Association of Black Psychologists (ABPsi), defined as the following:

> *"African Centered psychology (Africentric psychology) is a dynamic manifestation of unifying African principles, values, and traditions. It is the self-conscious "centering" of psychological analyses and applications in African reality, culture, and epistemology. African centered psychology examines the process that allows for the illumination and liberation of the Spirit. Relying on the principles of harmony within the universe as a natural order of existence, African centered psychology recognizes: the Spirit that permeates everything that is; the notion that everything in the universe is interconnected; the value that the collective is the most salient element of existence; and the idea that communal self knowledge is the key to mental health. African psychology is ultimately concerned with understanding the systems of meaning of human beingness, the features of human functioning, and the restoration of normal/natural order to human development. As such, it is used to resolve personal and social problems and to promote optimal functioning."*

There are many ways in which African social scientists can challenge the status quo and work toward deconstructing oppressive systems. First, psychologists can facilitate structural change within academia. For example, academia needs to challenge its own bias against Black survival and wellness and establish methods of inquiry highlighted from the African-centered paradigm. Second, change can be fostered through initiatives and programs within professional organizations. For example, there is a need to establish an African/Black Psychology licensing program in the field. The Black social scientist *nkali* will authorize scholarship, creative scientific methods, and ownership of transformation for the African community. Lastly, African science and intellectual interrogation encompass the systematic study, understanding, knowing, and illumination (Skh Djr) of Be(ing) and all phenomena. Hence, without apology or permission, we declare and affirm that the ABPsi recognizes, reclaims, and respects our way of knowing and being and, therein, take the authority to certify the proficiency and mastery of the body of knowledge that defines the unique parameters and content of our Being as a science. These fields, when centered on people of African ascent, promote African cultural phenomena in (re)cognition. Therefore, incorporating these constructs provides a foundation to expand and develop a psychological framework of Black critical consciousness.

II

Developing Black Critical
Consciousness

Pedagogy of the Oppressed, conscientization, has received significant attention for helping oppressed people develop an awareness to fight against oppression by enhancing their level of consciousness. The field of African/Black psychology can no longer afford to claim African-centered approaches that do not meet the same standards of critical consciousness when trying to authentically affirm the normal and natural collective and ancient voice of African life. Contemporary critical consciousness is centered around changing the current socio-political state of affairs. However, one must first conscientize to understand the need for sociopolitical change. Critical consciousness can be defined as an individual's capacity to think critically, reflect personally, and examine the sociopolitical system concerning oppression and colonization. The essential constituents of mainstream critical consciousness consist of (a) critical reflection, (b) political advocacy, and (c) action. However, Black critical consciousness requires authentic African values in this analysis. *Critical reflection* involves thinking deeply in one's analysis (from an African mindset) of social conditions, considering historical and structural factors, and ethically discarding subjugation and inequality. Critical reflection is necessary if one is to attain an awareness of *political advocacy* with conviction in one's capacity to assist specific or collective sociopolitical modification.

Critical action involves moving from commitment to action, undertaken alone or with others, to reduce the level of oppressive thinking (use of white constructs when defining and describing African life) and a sense of empowerment (use of pro-African understanding for defining and describing African life). In critical conscious development, individuals need to examine their actions and be authentic in their truth. The Black Lives Matter movement took a stand for social justice by recognizing how white supremacy was the cause for the brutality of Black lives at the hands of law enforcement, demanding the rights of Black people to be treated as humans (to exist as a people). This critical consciousness psyche/sakhu required individuals within the social system to stand up to the sociopolitical forces and be familiar with the historical context and conditions they live under oppression and barriers to bring about change. Centering critical consciousness allows for an intentional, proactive consideration of the relationship between justice and cognitive thought processes.

Regarding critical conscious psychology, one must begin to be proactive rather than reactive to racism. This core value of critical conscious psychology is consistent with the role of social justice change agents. Missing from the equation is how *culture* shapes and informs critical reflection, political voice, and action.

Under the auspices of the White/European paradigm, the fields of psychology, sociology, social work, and psychiatry require a change in their socio-political sphere. Liberation Psychology's challenge is that it operates within an individualized western context, culture, and worldview. While others suggest several avenues that critically minded professionals could take to adjust the scales of justice, we must also begin to impart ways to develop a critically conscious community to our communities. Critical conscious psychology requires an in-depth understanding of the world, allowing for the perception and exposure of social and political inequities and practices that dismantle the social and psychological factors that uphold oppression—including institutional and internalized oppression. A non-critically conscious individual demonstrates a cultural misorientation persona. Cultural misorientation is the acceptance and utilization of a Eurocentric framework, psyche, or consciousness in people of African ascent who align with the social-political practices of the prevailing European-American culture. Oppression is the persistent denial of resources needed to generate self-sufficient growth and development. Africans in America present themselves much like that culturally misoriented and oppressed group. Amuleru-Marshall points out that African Americans in this country suffer from violent assaults of socioeconomic inequality and political disenfranchisement. Look at the prevailing gerrymandering assaults on Blacks having the ability to vote and for their vote to matter in the communities in which they live. Gerrymandering or redistricting of voting precincts has been the practice of choice and the most remarkable political weapon for discounting the power of the black vote demonstrating how whites and other political groups (latest Hispanic attack on black voters in Los Angeles) disenfranchise the Black vote. This disenfranchisement or oppressive condition affects every aspect of the African's life.

Africans have continued to struggle with the enigmatic synergism of race and class just to compete within a Eurocentric society. When individuals become dissatisfied with their circumstances, it can lead to an awakening of critical consciousness. Simply stated, when awakened to the plight of being African/Black, the oppressed must liberate themselves. For Africans in America, there are two existential and political choices: collaboration or resistance. Ethnopolitical psychology would lend more towards collaboration when utilizing the Nigresence model of identity development. This insightfulness conveys that, as a group, the oppressed can think critically about their world and engage in reconciliation with those who oppressed them. Resistance requires a different avenue to take.

Black Lives Matter began out of resistance to the killing of unarmed Africans in America. As critical consciousness was evoked, the movement started conceptualizing and igniting change within the oppression of Blacks in the United States, supporting empowerment and resistance to social injustice. To participate actively in changing the social conditions of the African community, an increase in this community's psycho-cultural cognition became paramount. To understand the psycho-cultural awareness of the contemporary Black youth, we must look at the historical development. This introspective approach allows young adults to identify and understand how values change over time and which values Africans in America are to embrace, both negative and positive (see appendix #1). This critically conscious understanding represents the forum in which critical action takes place.

Here we should give respect and deference to the many brave and tenacious young Black folks who decided that enough was enough and took to the streets to protest in the spirit of empowerment and resistance to social injustice. Their opposition to the deaths of Blacks at the hands of law enforcement required these African warrior spirits to rise up. These young courageous women and men sought the empowerment of their African character to fight and make known what was unjust. As it is within the heart of the African community, we keep the Spirit and voices of those we have lost to racial violence: Tyre Nichols, Breonna Taylor, George Floyd, Nina Pop, D'Andre Campbell, Tony McDade, Regis Korchinski-Paquet, Ahmaud Arbery, Jordan Baker, Victor White III, Keith Lamont Scott, Dontre Hamilton, Larry Jackson Jr., Jonathan Ferrell, Sean Reed, Steven Demarco Taylor, Ariane McCree, Terrance Franklin, Miles Hall, William Green, Alton Sterling, Eric Garner, Philando Castile, Sandra Bland, Trayvon Martin, Samuel David Mallard, Tamir Rice, Botham Shem Jean, E.J. Bradford, Antwon Rose Jr., Stephon Clark, Natosha "Tony" McDade, Freddie Gray, Brendon Glenn, John Crawford III, Yassin Mohamed, Wendell Allen, Finan H. Berhe, Darius Tarver, Kwame "KK" Jones, De'Von Bailey, Christopher Whitfield, Anthony Hill, Ezell Ford, Dante Parker, Eric Logan, Kendrec McDade, Jamarion Robinson, Gregory Hill Jr., JaQuavion Slaton, Ryan Twyman, Brandon Webber, Kajieme Powell, Michael Brown Jr., Laquan McDonald, Mario Woods, Jimmy Atchison, Willie McCoy, Trettrick Griffin, Jemel Roberson, DeAndre Ballard, Botham Shem Jean, Robert Lawrence White, Akai Gurley, Rumain Brisbon, Charly Keunang, Anthony Lamar Smith, Oscar Grant and, sadly, many more before and after - - we keep them enlivened and illuminated in our hearts.

Personal liberation is part of the process of collective liberation. Collective liberation begins with institution building, support of African life activities and practices, and cultural alignment with African culture. This requires us to assess our African educational experiences and religious traditions, acquire an African economic system, control our voices in the media, participate in African political activities, and objectify and promote African social life. When oppressed people begin the process of liberation, it becomes possible for all to experience emancipation and healing. African/Black psychology allows us to respond to our reality on our terms and define a new reality for Africans. This psycho-cultural cognition of critical consciousness occurs when individuals make connections between their own experiences and the larger society. This psycho-cultural critical consciousness is integrated with reality, cultural enlightenment, and critical understanding leading toward action or change. One can know only to the extent that one problematizes the dominant culture and historical fact in which s/he is immersed. The foundation of sociopolitical change lies within the culture and history of its people.

Black Critical Consciousness

In Ancient KMT, the basic principle is "man know thyself." Rooted in this principle are psychological evolution, maturation, and the foundation of consciousness. Consciousness has been understood in Ancient KMT for centuries. What guided this consciousness was the moral demand functioning of MA'AT. The concept of MA'AT represents ethical concerns of personal conduct, monitoring one's thoughts and emotions, and the quest for truth, justice, balance, harmony, and order. In ancient KMT, the goal was the transcendent self versus self-actualization. Africans have been demonstrating critical consciousness for eons. The Black conscious mind concerning critical consciousness was not developed from Prilleltensky's model theory of liberation psychology. In essence, emanated simultaneously with the 'Black' psychological explosion of the time, the Black Power movement. Black is Beautiful and Black Love were the ethos of the time creating Black solidarity, Black nation-building, and achievement. This Black consciousness allowed for Black people strived for psychological well-being internally and externally. On the political level, MA'AT works against injustice. The inception and formulation of the Association of Black Psychologists (ABPSi) in 1968 began from the Spirit of Black psychologists, recognizing that the oppressive praxis, pedagogy, and paradigm within the field of White psychology was not nurturing the Spirit of African people. If it were not for the consciousness of liberation of these Black-minded psychologists, the field as we know it would remain for the white mind. One would argue that these sistas and brothas demonstrated ancient wisdom of Blackness and Africanity and, like the proverb - - *"The freedom that comes from ignorance enslaves the one who entertains it,"* chose not to be enslaved anymore. This is Black consciousness at its best!

Black psychology promotes liberating the African mind. Individuals of African ascent who are self-determined to know thyself begin to make decisions that are in the best interest of African people. Black consciousness must act and address their condition's oppressive needs. This state of mind and under-standing allow individuals to work in MA'AT for truth and justice. Dr. Joseph L. White's seminal article "Toward a Black Psychology" (1970) advanced and challenged our intellectual Spirit by informing us how Western/Eurocentric psychology had no application to Black/African lives and called for the creation of a (new/old) psychology, Skr Djr (Nobles), to au-thenticate African people. In 1980 Dr. Bobby Wright informed us not to apply White social theories to the problems of Black folks in America and challenged Black social scientists to create their social theories. Furthermore, Baba Wade Nobles provides us with an early articulation of his latest mission toward establishing the Skr Djr, "...Black African psychologists [need] to use African epistemological reflections and subsequent skill sets to meet the challenges of our time in every context and to engage in policy and program development wherever African people exist" (p.401). This articulation, as guided by African/Black psychology, includes in its analysis the African meaning of identity, culture, and Spirit as critical components to mental liberation and wellness. At no time did these brilliant minds and souls suggest that our salvation would come holding the hands of the oppressor. As such, the mission of ABPSi and its destiny is "the liberation of the African Mind, empowerment of the African Character, and enlivenment and illumination of the African Spirit. It is African to see psychological dynamics as inseparable from culture and personhood. That liberation for the Africans is tied to the collective spiritual freedom of the group, community, and society (i.e., the development of Black critical consciousness).

I have been told that I am a radical in the field. This prompted me to identify what radicalism we speak of. The radical school of thought is bearing the critical methodology of constructing a conceptual framework within African/Black psychology. This constructionist methodological approach focuses on creating new psychological paradigms for understanding the African/Black experience through theory construction. This approach views that the work must promote African people's welfare and advance the growth of critical knowledge. Baba Kambon taught us that we need to create a theory that speaks to the nature of our African selves. I am not sure why this is radical since we know that in Ancient KMT, it is through consciousness that we live with intention in the world. Who were the Kamites radicals from? The radical school of thought is based on "an African-centered conceptual framework for Black psychology by emphasizing African culture and philosophy. A defining characteristic of the radical school is that it focuses more on transforming Blacks' attitudes about themselves. Examples of African/Black psychologists who embody both radical schools of thought and constructionist methodology include Linda James Myers, Cheryl Grills, Asa Hilliard, Wade Nobles, Na'im Akbar, Kobi Kambon, and Richard King, to name a few. This is Black critical consciousness at its best!

Black Critical consciousness is a prerequisite for the liberation of the African mind. Black Critical consciousness is a crucial component of our framework for mental liberation. When we, as Black social scientists, look to the African *asili*, we recognize the productive forces for independence. It is within the African asili that should ignite our consciousness of knowing. Through our experiences, education, and training, we should be challenged to begin defining what our nature is, thinking critically, and providing meaning to liberatory forces from our expressions. Black Critical Consciousness is the contemplation of sociopolitical realities by way of an African worldview, culture, philosophy, and Spirit, and to a great extent questioning and perspicaciously liberating the African mind and structuring knowledge to advance Africans' attitudes toward themselves through the African experience. Black critical consciousness in operation is a state of mind that allows individuals to make decisions that are in the interest of African people. We have examples of this Black critical conscious experience from the likes of Franz Fanon.

Fanon demonstrated his genius mind through his psychoanalytical-sociodynamics and existential model for which the African functioned. He identified how European cultural conditions promote cultural oppression/indoctrination. To get a sense of these times, it seems appropriate to try to understand the societal context in which the oppressed currently operate. Frantz Fanon, in 1963 noted that for the African to survive in an oppressive context, he must alienate himself from his humanity; he must come to some existential discovery for a new identity of the meaning of being Black. In this, we begin to see how theories can represent the cultural, ideological orientation, and sociopolitical condition of the oppressive progenitors. Amos Wilson reminds us that White psychology is a sociopolitical instrument designed to control those different from the White power structure. We see this in Fanon's writings, informing us that to survive at the hands of White rule, we must develop a different way of being. In keeping in line with Amos Wilson, we have to learn how not to be African. Case in point, the concept of learning in psychology centers around the experience of consequences around behavior. Our behavior is shaped and maintained by its consequences. While white psychology will have you thinking about personal conduct at the individual level in its collective praxis, at the group level, it is about controlling the group's behavior. When we think about the rat in the box, placed in an unnatural habitat and forced to respond or behave in a certain way to receive a reward or escape a negative consequence, we can begin to see the shaping of his behavior. So what does the rat learn? He learns that there is an entity far more remarkable than himself and that he is not allowed to function as himself if he wants to eat and stay alive. Ladies and gentlemen, Africans in any community dominated by White rule are the rats in the maze, and we have been forced to behave in ways that have become detrimental to our existence. Even money can't buy our freedom from the maze. Look at the latest example at the time of this writing. A Black man in America with wealth is not allowed to state that he is a Black Jew. He may have facts to prove this, but if he endorses who he is, then he is vilified as being anti-other which serves as a threat to them, and he must apologize to white Jews for his action while at the same time they strip him of portion of his wealth. This brother was publicly castrated in the minds of many. Hence the rat in the maze.

For the African person who disregards the psycho-cultural-spiritual self and accepts the social-political status given (to him/her), we begin to see imposed on the African mechanisms toward European actualization. Any African social scientist who accepts and adopts white psycho-cultural models as explanations for Black social life is actively perpetrating the fraud and perpetuating this cultural imposition of European thought and values on African people. This is a form of menticide and cultural misorientation. For the Africans and their sociopolitical context, we see how our reality lacks the availability of resources for securing our basic needs and our ability to feel safe in this European society. What is challenged is our identity and Spirit of just being by a system of *injustice*. Our desire for belonging within this society is derailed by our not feeling connected to other humans in our community. Fanon would explain this Black phenomenon using Maslow's hierarchical model as the Black recognizing her/his sociopolitical power, causing her/him to question their reality, personhood, and humanity.

I have heard too many times my students say they have no one to talk to when faced with challenges to their mental health and psychological well-being. This sociopolitical context does not lend Africans the affordability to acquire basic needs nor to feel safe in America–no matter what position one may hold. In terms of today's sociopolitical climate, schools provide content designed to meet the needs of politically empowered Whites and not to meet the needs of disenfranchised Africans. A more accurate use of Maslow's hierarchical model is to turn it upside down. For the African to operate from critical conscious psychology, he must first learn to self-actualize and see his value as an African, for this would lead to self-love, increase self-esteem/confidence, enhance his ability to care for others and belong, and finally, safety to secure basic needs. For these individuals, the demand for a natural, cultural affirmation of their existence is representative of a regenerative productive force that transcends self.

White psychology is predicated on restructuring the Black personality to contain their behavior. We cannot simply apply European theories to African people. To accept APA's apology is to deny the inconsistencies in their theories and practices as adequate explanations for the functioning of African people. The ethos in white psychology is that behavior is shaped and maintained by its consequences. To counteract such circumstances, African social scientists must begin infusing liberatory and emancipatory pedagogies through alternative programs. The Small Interest Group (SIG) of ABPSi retorts to APA's apology. By this warning, "we know that the white man will try to satisfy us with symbolic victories rather than economic equity and real justice, underscoring that while the apology and resolutions may appear genuine, it is far too late for it to mean anything to Black America and sorely lacks several opportunities for real and meaningful change." Black liberation psychology emphasizes the necessity of utilizing a system of critical thought emerging from our indigenous thought patterns.

Critical consciousness requires groups to express their beliefs, values, perspectives, and worldview -- ways of being (culture), understanding (cognition), and behaving (sociopolitical) -- to interpret and place demands on that group's existence. The African community is ultimately responsible for their liberatory education. Ancient KMT understood the importance of how our environment should *educe* the potentiality of the person; this mastery of thinking intelligibly about complex issues and answering a wide range of problems stemming from the essence of their culture. The APA's monopoly on Psychology as a field reifies the ABPSi's need to not accept APA's apology for their racist, oppressive conduct and calls to question the various areas they should work to enact effective change immediately. Social justice is a critical element of liberation psychology. Yet, those inside and outside the field have acknowledged that social justice has not been consistently integrated into the dissemination of science, knowing and knowledge production, community revitalization, and restorative practice (CABP-Wilson, Adeeba, Bethea, Ronke, Moukam, Robertson, and Baba Nobles, 2021).

Consequently, ABPSi's liberation psychology set the means for addressing this challenge. For example, elements of liberation psychology were utilized in developing interventions for Africans in America through rites of passage groups and guidelines for culturally informed educational institutions. Hilliard (1995) captures Amilcar Cabral's eloquent analysis of the role of culture in national liberation struggles, "these struggles are always preceded by an increase in the overt expression of culture by the dominated population; it is a means of negating the oppressor culture." As mentioned, the task for all Black social scientists is "to think deeply and profoundly about African meanings and understandings about being human. Consistent with Diop's (1974) directive to examine the domains of history, language, and psyche, *Skh Djr* would require that one interrogate the language and logic of traditional African people to gain insight into the functioning of contemporary African peoples" (Baba Nobles, 2015, p.409). We must understand that we cannot create knowledge just for knowledge's sake. The practice within the European intellectual domain. Africans invent things based on need, and Europeans invent something based on greed. The intellectual science and academia must reconcile the African way of understanding with the use of knowledge and wisdom. These insights may offer a framework for developing critical consciousness and establishing the need for cultural connection.

III

What is Culture?

When one gets to know himself, he gets to know other people. We must recreate ourselves in terms of one's own criteria and one's own values. (Amos Wilson).

To develop Black critical consciousness, one has to determine how immersed s/he is in her/his indigenous culture and compare this to how enmeshed s/he is in a dominant non-native culture. Culture makes up both a people's conscious and unconscious thoughts and values. People who daily receive a negative picture of Africa and African people can only retain a sense of dignity by drawing on the deep roots of their African values. Goddard et al. admit that culture sets the foundation for "the tone, character, and quality of life of a people, its moral and aesthetic style and mode and the conception of the course and purpose of events in the world as well as guidelines for the creation of the ideas and concepts about human life and living. This spirit, seen as a force or ethos, is the active agent that causes the creation of cultural thought and behavior" (p. 8). Culture is viewed as a medium that gives people a general design for living and patterns for interpreting their reality. The model of culture provided in this discourse combines Marimba Ani's and Baba Nobles' understanding of culture consisting of three levels: deep cultural, structural levels of (1) cultural aspects - Asili, (2) cultural factors - Utamawazo, and (3) surface level, cultural manifestations - Utamaroho (See Table 1). I want to make clear that in designing the Ani-Nobles cultural structure there were some liberties taken in aligning the two ideas of cultural construction. For instance, Ani makes it clear that she equates the Utamaroho with Nobles' ethos; however, it does not represent guiding principles as this would be closer to the Asili.

Cultural Core- Asili

The Asili determines the cultural essence at the deep structural level and explains man's existence. The Asili is the inertia of the developmental character or "germ/ seed," that puts into motion the character or essence of its origin. The aspects of the deep structure consist of 1) Ontology – the nature of existence/being, 2) Cosmology - the origin and structure of the Universe, 3) Axiology - which is primary universal relations to ethics, aesthetics, or religion, and 4) Epistemology - the theory of knowledge or ways of knowing or investigating the origin, nature, methods, and limits of human knowledge. Culture relies on the essential elements or the inertia of a particular group's conscious and unconscious composition. The conscious composition of reality (cosmology), root assumptions and beliefs (episteme), value systems (axiology), and conjectures about life, the universe, and the constitution of reality (ontology) is the first deep-level structure, the basic understanding of culture.

Cultural Template-Utamawazo

The Utamawazo is the self-conscious expressions and explains culturally structured thought and framework patterned by members of a particular group (Ani, 1994). This deep-level structure contains or consists of the cultural factors of philosophical, cultural construction, and thought processes that embody our Ethos, Worldview, and Ideologies. Ethos is the set of guiding principles shaping a culture's fundamental character or spirit. It consists of a collective emotional tone, the underlying sentiment of a group or society. The assumptions from people or periods help inform the beliefs, customs, or practices. Ideology serves as the body of doctrine or standard for revealing the truth. The conceptual basis of conduct reveals through myths that guide an individual, social movement, institution, class, or large group. The most powerful element of the cultural thought process is that worldview. Worldview gives us the most comprehensive ideas about an order. Worldview is the overall perspective from which one sees and interprets the world, a collection of beliefs about life and the Universe, and shared cultural experiences held by an individual or a group. Worldview embodies the principal definitional categories illuminating the reality of racial/cultural groups. These philosophical systems are interdependent within a given culture. They frame the primary source of the meaning of reality.

Cultural Orientation – Utamaroho

The Utamaroho is the unconscious level of feeling that dictates the vital or conscious energy (ngolo zasikama) force set in motion by the collective behaviors and fundamental feelings of members in a particular group. The behaviors and feelings revealed are the cultural manifestations of ideas that influence values, beliefs, rituals, customs, and practices at the surface level. At the surface level we demonstrate the self-worth and survival temperament within the culture. Culture structures behaviors, attitudes, language, symbols, inventions, mores, traditions, rituals, and ceremonies peculiar to a particular people, giving them a general design for living and patterns for interpreting their reality.

Authentic African cultural structure

African cultural aspects of the Asili represent a reflection of our essence for being -- *consubstantiation* (Ontology), *interdependence* (Cosmology), *harmonious relationships* (Axiology), and affective/symbolic meaning (epistemology). Ontology and Epistemology are related to the divine revelation of divine speech, and the basis of Cosmology is metaphysics. The indigenous culture of traditional African conjectures about life, the Universe, and the constitution of reality reflects the "Ontological Principle of Consubstantiation." It conveys that we are of the same spirit or essence. This principle translates to the "Oneness of being/Unity of all things." It means that all things in the Universe, whether animate or inanimate, have the same essence, i.e., spirit. In Bantu's cultural construction, *NTU* is the universal force in which beings and beings intermingle culture's conscious/unconscious dimension. African cosmology refers to how the Universe organizes cosmic, earthly, and human truths. The link between heavens and earth, Asa Hilliard reminds us how the Milky Way is seen as a "river in the sky"; likewise, the Nile is a river on earth - - so as defined above, so is below. This deep-level structure is the basic understanding of culture. It relies on the essential elements or the inertia of a particular group's conscious (*utamawazo*) and unconscious (*utamaroho*) composition of reality. In Ancient KMT, the Akhu was the center of intelligence and psychological perception; it is where we comprehend the entire mystery of the human mind. In Bantu, the *muntu* reflects the force graced with intelligence determining the philosophical orientation of God, spirits, the deceased, human beings, etc.

The *kintu* in Bantu is the endowed force that acts according to *the muntu's* directive. The axiological principle of harmonious relations exists between the heavens above–our ancestors–and the man below. We on earth speak of the nature of man being in rhythm with nature. For the Bantu, this embodies its root assumptions and beliefs (epistime-*hantu*) and its value systems (axiology-*kuntu)*. The African Utamawazo, the culturally structured thought pattern, demonstrates **transformation** (ideology), *cooperation* (worldview), and *communality* (Ethos). African social life reveals attitudes, values, self-worth, the practice of extended family, reciprocity with nature and divine law, and karmic and psychic spiritual reality. The Bantu's *hantu* provides how we see time and space. From the culturally structured thought pattern, we begin to set in motion the cultural manifestations at the surface level of the African Utamaroho that dictates the vital force or conscious energy (ngolo zasikama) force set in motion by collective behaviors and real feelings. In Bantu culture, the *kuntu* reflects behaviors and feelings revealed for beauty, laughter, etc., the cultural manifestations of ideas that influence our values, beliefs, behaviors, rituals, customs, and practices. These manifestations are characterized by the spirit of mutual aid and trust as people rely on each other in everyday life. **Ubuntu!** Ubuntu is characterized by the interdependence of our humanity concerning each other's humanity. Amos Wilson speaks on the need for knowing self: "When one gets to know himself, he gets to know other people. We must recreate ourselves in terms of one's criteria and one's values."

The kinds of questions asked and the answers received are culturally determined. What makes us human? Who am I? What is my relationship with other people, and what is my relationship to the natural environment? As humans, the African's goal is to find connections and respond to the energy surrounding him. The nature or essence of African beings is community, self, and spirit. The dimensions of humanity manifest through mutuality, complementarity, and interdependence, indicating that we are all connected to other people. At the core is the unity of being that we are one in spirit. You belong to family, community, ancestors, and the broader Universe. Reciprocity, mutuality, tradition, order, and stability of the group and collective identity are paramount to the African self-identity; (1) the survival of the group and (2) one with nature are guiding principles within an African worldview. Accordingly, the overall emphasis is on communalistic values.

Western scholarship and African reality are philosophically different. While African societies recognize individual needs, the African belief is that "social relationships are essential for every human. However, the notion of incompleteness occurs in insufficiency and independence; for no one is self-sufficient and therefore no one can, in isolation, function adequately in the social context." Nothing in the Universe, spiritual or experience, can be defined independently. African communalism is considered a natural state and a fundamental part of the African concept of society. The well-being of the overall community sets the basis for individual happiness and thriving. In contrast to the individualistic values of Western societies described below, such as freedom, independence, etc., African societies promote communal values such as "sharing, mutual aid, caring for others, interdependence, solidarity, reciprocal obligation, and social harmony. Africans believe in a fundamentally spiritual reality and that the material world we see and operate in, while not an illusion, is merely the surface manifestation of a more profound spiritual realm.

Whereas Europeans, in contrast, have no equivalent to the view of completeness of identity in their cultural system. The European cultural asili core reflects materialism (Ontology), independence (cosmology), conflict (axiology), and objectification/quantification (epistemology). This nonnative cultural structure, the principle of materialism, conveys a spirit of "individualism, objectification, and quantity." The European cultural utamawazo template is characterized by domination (ideology), competition (worldview), and individualism (ethos). It means that for all things in the Universe, whether animate or inanimate, man is to control and dominate; the spirit is not all-encompassing.

European social life reveals attitudes, values, inflated self-worth, xenophobia, and reduction of divine law. From the culturally structured thought pattern, we begin to see the unconscious and consciousness Utamaroho of European behavioral relations, the manifestations of conflict and separation, the high priority placed on man's mastery and domination over others, greed over his geographical and social space, and reality of the physical material. This surface-level orientation of the European Utamaroho dictates the vital force or energy force set in motion by collective behaviors and real feelings.

The Eurocentric view of the individual fundamentally differs from the world's majority ontological systems. European and European-derived culture and worldviews, be they blatant or abstract, are designed and grounded on materialism and display an epistemology, aesthetics, and ethos based on material values. The materialistic paradigm of Eurocentricity manufactures specific cultural determinants, which shape and direct all social productions within the culture. European guiding principles are (1) survival of the fittest and (2) control over nature. The advantages of freedom, independence, mutability, and division result in a greater emphasis on individuality and individual liberty. A dichotomous reasoning style, hierarchical ordering, analytic thought, and objectification increase levels of abstraction, dangerous rationalism, and a rejection of spiritual or sacred forces. At the core of European culture, we see racism, sexism, etc., flow from this worldview's conceptual system.

As we can see, there is a contradiction in meanings between African cultural structure of essentialism, substance, and essence and European cultural structure etc. which is ontologically oppressive, arrogant, and resistant to another perspective of meanings to reality. I remember while in graduate school when I engaged in discussions about reality, culture and behavior, I would insist that the lens used to observe African behavior placed them at risk for misguided interpretations. I was then asked, based on these discussions: "Do you think there should be a different psychology for different groups of people?" With an unwavering response, I said, "yes!" The professor responded that within the field of psychology this will never happen. The cautionary tale should awaken upcoming African social scientists. Psychology is seen only through the perspective of the European worldview medium (gaze) within the academy and that this alienating ideology corrupts the thinking toward European hegemonic explanation of African social reality.

Therefore, education, by way of an African paradigm, can provide a source of understanding for the development of the consciousness of Africans. The most important source of forming the infrastructure of intelligence are those social and educational interactions between the child's psychosocial and physical environments. The socialization process is one of the important aspects of a people's reality. It is a means of transmitting values from one generation to another. Values represent a synthesis between cultural orientation and concrete historical conditions of a particular group. African-centered consciousness is the identity of high cultural, personal, and moral aspirations. The ingredients, which are proportionally combined, can maximize critical conscious development. Culture has the potential to be a weapon for liberation. T'Shaka recognized the evidence of a culture within the Being of Africans:

> *"African American .....political thought contains an ancient and traditional African cultural, and philosophical*

continuum.....In spite of the Euro-centric war against Afri-can and African American culture, it is a testimony to the wisdom of everyday Black folk, and the persistence of African culture in the United States that Blacks have held onto their core truth of the cosmos." (T'Shaka, 1995: and 149)

Black social scientists must operate with the relevance of African people. This is done by examining the content of culture. Diop succinctly stated,

"I consider culture as a rampart which protects a people, a collectivity. Culture must, above all, play a protective role: it must ensure the cohesion of the group. Following this line of thinking, the vital function of a body of African human science is to develop this science of collective belonging through a reinforcement of culture. This can be done by developing the linguistic factors, by reestablishing the historical consciousness of African and Black people so as to arrive at a common feeling of belonging to the same culture and historical past. Once this is attained, it will become difficult to "divide and rule" and to oppose African communities one against the other."

Black social scientists' theories' ultimate goal should be the recreation of African culture. Bobby Wright reminds us that Black social theory determines the destiny of a people by establishing guidelines for life, defining the relationship of living things, values and rituals, methods of education, how enemies are to be dealt with etc. Wilson contends that culture is our personality and consciousness. Culture should help us solve problems. We must use African culture to establish our power as people to confront alien or Eurocentric cultural frameworks that work against us as Africans.

Culture's Influence on Critical Consciousness

Critical consciousness is raising awareness through a dialogue of the situation in which people find themselves. Group context in which consciousness-raising techniques are employed assists in developing critically minded individuals. Within liberation psychology, an individual holding a marginalized identity might experience anxiety in response to experiences of discrimination and oppression, emphasizing the role that larger structures and sociopolitical factors play in perpetuating the oppression at the individual and collective level. According to liberation psychology, marginalized individuals and groups experience prejudice and bias, internalize negative stereotypes, and are pathologized by Western psychology for identifying or responding to oppression–all of which make it difficult to experience healthy psychosocial well-being. Critical conscious psychology, I would argue, challenges the marginalized identity provoking anxiety in the power dynamics confronting discrimination and oppression with an awareness of the sociopolitical structure at the individualized level. Within liberation psychology, Martín-Baró suggests that the goal is to get the individual to rethink and re-enact a different kind of psychology that could take these social and contextual factors into account as it seeks to redress what ails one. The prescription for what ails a person is the usage of indigenous cultural assets and precepts. Cultural precepts are the ethos - - intrinsic principle, rule, or law that imposes a standard of action or conduct consistent with the culture. The following eight precepts serve as a guiding constitution for traditional African culture: (1) Consubstantiation, (2) Interdependence, (3) Unicity/Egalitarianism, (4) Collectivism, (5) Transformation, (6) Cooperation, (7) Humanness and (8) Synergism. Cultural assets are fundamental qualities of human beings and becoming. By infusing a sense of consciousness, confidence, competence, commitment, and character, the overall objective is to guide the development of a well-rounded human being with the ability, skills, and attitude to contribute to self, family, community, and society. In effect, one in his/her Being should reaffirm the inalienable right of African people to (1) exist as a people, (2) contribute to the forward-flowing process of human civilization (as contributors and not debtors), and (3) share as well as shape the world (reality) in response to one's conscious energy (ngolo zasikama) and spirit. The essential constituents of Black Critical consciousness with cultural precepts and cultural assets operate as an "instrument of change" rather than a program for adaptation or the maintenance of social dominance. Armah reminds me of the warrior spirit we need to have: "Where I come from, revolution is the only creation, and the revolutionary the only artist."

Whatever the conditions of a people's political and social factors under domination, "it is generally within the culture that we find the seed of opposition" (Hilliard, p. 57). Then by definition, culture has the potential to be a weapon for liberation, which leads to the structure and development of the liberation movement itself. Liberation for Africans must flow from within African/Black psychology, ancient Wisdom, and deep thought of African culture and psyche. Black Critical consciousness involves black social scientists being active in their engagement in the dialogue of the conditions faced in the context of the group. Next, the individual becomes aware of systems of oppression and mental and conceptual incarceration with the need for change. Black social scientists must then begin the process of mental liberation in how she/he thinks and how to think about the system. Lastly, Black social scientists must begin to understand the ability to actively shape their identity and their role in society by recognizing the role of culture; this part of the process includes a historical understanding of the self and community.

Other areas of psychology, such as cognitive psychology,

ignore evaluating the validity of information even though processes involved in perception, learning, memory, and inferences are discussed. The thought that learning is didactic -- from teacher to student or, more specifically, European values imposed upon non-Europeans -- suggests that information should be looked upon more carefully, particularly from the vantage point of the cultural group. The employment of non-African paradigms, ideas, and frameworks for viewing social reality generates in Africans a political, ideological, and psychological struggle for their heart and their mind. At a high cognitive level of processing, it is evident that one cannot apply European theories to explain the phenomena of African people. It has been observed that little is mentioned in relating cognitive processes as a true formula for accepting and believing information presented. Since the development of critical consciousness requires relational approaches to the subject matter, critically conscious individuals (groups) connect personal and social domains when studying problems. This is a form of learning.

If you do not understand racism which is White-Supremacy, what it is and how it works, everything else you think you understand will only confuse you. -Nelly Fuller Jr.

IV

Learning - What is it?

Critical consciousness exists as part of social life. Since social life is a motivator for liberation, then by definition, culture has the potential to be a weapon for liberation. Liberation, by definition, developed within a system of critical thought emerging from African pedagogy. What is the way of knowing that leads to the production of knowledge that reflects the basic elements of imparting and receiving wisdom? For centuries African indigenous societies have developed through experiences and explanations based on how they relate to the world. The African way of learning is based on authentic experiences and how people learn is culturally specific. Distinct cultures have distinct interpretations of the ways and experiences of social life for learning. From this, indigenous forms of wisdom, analysis of cognition, knowledge acquisition, and learning theory need exploration.

This chapter will explain how culture influences learning and critical consciousness when aspects of critical consciousness of worldview and cognitive styles present specific characteristics pronounced. For change to occur, the sociopolitical environment recognizes the type of change required for the African community to move forward toward community critical consciousness development. Autochthonous knowledge systems identify knowing as a key element to human functioning and are transformative with the acquisition of knowledge. The developmental challenge is the realization of how culture and community provide the skills and ability to build upon and marshal knowledge growth and capacity among its people. This knowing and knowledge production speaks to a liberating mindset (i.e., the right to exist as a people and the right to use indigenous structures for freedom). Learning from the ways of our culture and community, we must know, master, and create from our conditions–an important context for activities designed for liberation through critical conscious development.

We must fight against scientific colonialism as it has historically relegated African knowledge as local to the African continent and has refused to acknowledge African knowing in the province of being universal. For example, while Ubuntu has garnered global attention in the scholarly arena as the essence of Being, Europeans still cannot truly fathom the state of being concerning others. In a recent conversation with my daughter, she mentioned how the executive director, who is Black, would like for the concept of Ubuntu to be the philosophical tenet of their organization. However, predominantly White organizations have demonstrated difficulty accepting this concept for either fear of being accused of cultural appropriations or rejecting this African concept. This resistance reflects the hard wiring within European/western cultural asili and psyche. Thereby, the African social scientist's role is liberation, a systematic and cumulative approach to recognizing how African knowledge systems, due to historical power relations, can help change psychopolitical dynamics and influence what gets perceived as universal. In keeping in line with Baba Wade Nobles' moving us toward an Skr Djr, we as African social scientists need to confess *'our way'* of knowing and knowledge production that will enhance and sustain us as a people. We, as Black social scientists, must contribute to the global pool of knowledge in the search for sustainable solutions to global challenges (such as the recent success fending against the COVID pandemic, etcetera).

The Black social scientist must reject the mental pattern that Africa and Africans authenticate out of a *tabula rasa* as this reflects European concept. What other races of people are forced by such ideology and have adopted this line of thinking? It is shameful for us scientists of African ascent to accept and exclaim such an ideological reflection of Being. What, before colonization, was the African? African cultural systems knowledge should be the only means to validate the value of Africa's ideas, beliefs, and general way of life. Carruthers captures Diop's stance: "African philosophy would not develop but on the original terrain of the history of African thought. Otherwise, there is the risk that it would never be." (1991, 324) (p.25). We must retake our minds and rekindle how deep African thought illuminated the world. Based on this Afrocentric view, African indigenous ways of knowing and knowledge production should be considered scientific, cultured, and compatible with the restoration and recovery of the African mind. Learning can lead to a permanent change in our structured Being. Learning involves processing information into logical nuggets of knowledge used to form future learning, problem-solving, and decision-making. Lastly, the Western learning paradigm merely modifies a behavior or thought. This type of learning eradicates the crisis of imagination.

Learning Style

Learning style is a way of perceiving, conceptualizing, and problem-solving the essential characteristics of critical consciousness. Learning style comprises cognitive characteristics, affective correlates, and physiological and environmental factors. Essential learning creates the benefit of imagination, informing how we interact with the world. Dimensions found within learning style were: worldview, social cognition, stimulus variety, conceptual tempo, and field dependence/independence. Cognitive style, in general, comprises the way knowledge is acquired. Knowledge acquisition is defined as "rule sets" for selecting and organizing sensory stimulation and embodies both conceptual and personal-social attributes.

For critical consciousness development, elements of liberation, community, and African/Black psychologies are embodied in the way we learn. Integrating African indigenous knowledge provides the following opportunities: (i) To learn appropriate community attitudes and values for sustainable livelihood. The free African mind lives within his community in harmony with others. She/he utilizes innate resources and capacity to develop and promote sensitive and caring values and attitudes for the subject matter. (ii) Students learn through various cultural forms, for example, folk stories, songs, folk drama, legends, proverbs, myths, etcetera. The use of these cultural resources sparks African geniuses and ingenuity. It enables authentic conceptualized practices for problem-solving. Placing issues in both their immediate experiences and beyond (concept for those yet to be born). (iii) Involving community knowledge resources enables students to learn across generations hence making them cherish and admire the understanding of elders and other members of the community. Revitalizing African indigenous ways of knowing and knowledge production is the goal here: To bring to light knowledge acquisition that facilitates learning and critical consciousness. The internal or external cultural dialogue on ways of knowing, knowledge acquisition, and value systems enables African social scientists to better understand and reconstruct their critical consciousness. In the context of this discussion, learning is an agency for acquiring and transferring cultural rules that provide a common blueprint for living and marking for explicating real life from one generation to the next. Knowledge acquisition can be defined as awareness of facts or acquiring practical skills.

Knowledge Acquisition

"Knowledge, knowing, and knower are interconnected and must always be connected for optimal learning acquisition to occur." Nobles and Nobles, 2011, Postulate within Nsaka Sunsum

Acquisition of knowledge from the African perspective views complex interactions between various factors within and without the individual and the spatial and temporal arrangements in which these interact. The mind and the body are involved in knowledge acquisition within the ecology of the community. We, as beings, examine circumstances that are required for comprehension. So how is knowledge acquired, observed, and experienced in traditional African societies? Within the Ewe language, the thing observed is called *nunya*. What I find interesting about the word *nunya* is how similar it is in the black community vernacular. When someone asks you about what you are doing when not in their sight, some of us would say "none ya," short for 'none of your business.'

As you can see, this derivative of the word can be attributed to an African term revealed yet transposed. This interpretation of *nunya* reveals that 'we are as African as we are' in this experience, and the 'none ya' is inquiring about an experience you may not have been privy to. The *nunya* observed demonstrates the beginning of knowledge acquisition, which consists of two variant styles of experience -- analytical and relational (discussed later). Knowledge acquisition defines the rule for selecting and organizing our sensory experience and embodies both conceptual and personal-social attributes to be used. It is our cognition that represents processes in the act of knowing. Knowing includes processes of perception, memory, mental elaboration, and reasoning. The element of spirit and practical use are left out of the equation.

For Africans, the benefit of knowledge is in its practicality for the profit of use—akin to the vocational fields. As for social scientists, the performance of activities is rooted in the cultural psyche of us as a people. Starting with our wisdom, knowing, and knowable spirits lead to the creation of practices that maximize our *Being* and conscious development. In its finest form, all African life is marked as "Being, Becoming, and Belonging" (*Skr Djr*). Baba Nobles informs us that in Being *(NTU)*, life is indicated by elements of desire, thought, and action. These elements themselves are conditional on transformative processes to be "perfectible." Accordingly, *becoming* (desire), when "perfected" (transformed), demonstrates pure love. In belonging (*Thought)*, when transformed, transmutes to explicit comprehension, and *action*, when "perfected," becomes acts of self-immolation or act of kindness to benefit the whole. In becoming, one's basic beingness transformed into a more perfect knowable and knowing Being. For example, The "òyìnbó" in Yorùbá language refers to white people or non-Yorùbás. The etymological note of the word "òyìnbó" stresses the need for white people to become poly epistemic. In this discussion, however, the conscious reflection of white ideology within Black social scientists resembles the same significant note that the morpheme "bó" means "to undress." This analogy divulges the undertaking of Being by relinquishing white thought, the undressing of white identity, and false privileges associated with the nonnative episteme. The concept of Becoming here presumes an operation of 'disremembering' from the òyìnbó who would then latter the òyìnbòs in the sense that they should undress (bó) and discard (bọ) their reliance on an ingrained foreign ontological thought process for Belonging.

The African critique of science is in pursuing theoretical knowledge that bears no benefit to creating immediate practical results. This intellectual masturbation serves no purpose but to have people running around chasing their tails. As it is understood, the desire for knowledge in western science is to suit itself. African cultures' minimal desire for theoretical knowledge informs us that knowledge is revered with practical application for relevance. We tend to use knowledge to solve problems. Like when African clients see the traditional healer, seer, or therapist, they seek prescriptions. The performance of different activities also shapes knowledge acquisition. For example, regarding the use of maxims (proverbs), African maxims are generally the creation of the sages and intended to convey profound truths. Maxims give you the wisdom of your ancestors and show one's intelligence.

Swahili maxim: Experience is the mother of all knowledge.

The Akan maxim: All things depend upon experience. Maximal techniques rely on the tools of oral communication of pictures, symbols, physical objects, and group discourses.

Maxim for human knowledge: Knowledge is like a baobab tree; no one person can embrace it with both arms."

African knowing values, inspirations, and energies emerge from the ecology of community engendering imaginative, artistic, religious, and spiritual products. A knowing and knowable knowledge understood in all African societies involve rituals and extrasensory cognition. In Africa, it is clear that some individuals are born with the extrasensory ability to know. Different from experience and observation, another

episteme for knowledge acquisition is through spiritual energies and cosmological divination. This knowing is the ability
to communicate to the ancestors in the spirit world to help
acquire knowledge in the physical world. The most respected
persons in the village are your wise man, wise woman, shamans,
traditional healers, priests, and seers; they have the ability to
see your past, present, and future through divination and communication with the spirits. The spirits are our oldest form of
Wisdom that continue to be passed down, but the reclaiming
and maintaining value for such a knowledge medium requires
those not raised in African societies to free their minds about
the ideas and constraints of such practices. As discussed in
chapter 1, the Ayity's revolution was deemed successful in its
rightful fight for freedom because the people listened to the
Oum'phor, rituals were performed, dances took place, and initiation rites were completed. *Houn'gan*, or *mam'bo* (emperor/
empress) of the *Oum'phor*, revealed the spirits' strategy and
conveyed it to the people through the vodun rite. Through
divination and communication with the spirits the *houn'gan*
was able to affect the consciousness of the people to fight for
their freedom. As said, the performances of such activities are
granted to the acquisition of spiritual knowledge.

We also can use this form of medium for correct character development. When connecting our livelihood to current
activities and situations, the wisdom of our ancestors and their
insight can guide us to understand future outcomes as a form
of knowledge acquisition. In Yorùbá tradition, Orí guides us
on our path from the time we are born, and if we firmly
commit ourselves to this spiritual work, there is a knowing that
allows us to maneuver through our social world. Traditional
Wisdom is available for the potential African social scientist to
consciously illuminate how spirit guides and directs us toward
what it means to be human. To be human is to use our potential consciousness. Consciousness is spirit-driven, a spiritual

connection to God. Conscious spiritedness then allows us to obtain a liberated mind or psyche. Liberating our spirit frees our minds. This process of knowledge acquisition situates what should be the training module, paradigm, and pedagogy to the African graduate student and the requirement *to be about* the business of real healing and restoration. In their training, students should be required to visit traditional communities to nunya (observe the thing) ritual practices in the natural environment. However, as knowledge is already embodied in our spirits/souls, Black social scientists must be able to call upon this skill to frequently practice correct values and ethos. Community healing uses knowledge to solve African community problems and resist indoctrination with foreign antithetical orientations and paradigms (ontological oppression).

Within African knowledge acquisition, community psychology would suggest that individuals and communities are collaborative agents. Therefore, what is required is the continual renewal of culture, mythologies, and practices of meaning to orient our lives. While community psychology sounds good, there is a lack of true reciprocity and interdependence, which may be difficult when definitions and theories come from an arrogant axiological orientation. A founding principle for fostering positive acceptance of indigenous knowledge systems must be a partnership *among* stakeholders with equally shared interests. Due to European thought's arrogance and power structure, this may be difficult to accomplish, but this is our challenge. As African social scientists, it is our job to construct the precious African capital from the old days and give away or disband all that disenfranchisement and deskill. Remove all that is detrimental to the development of our consciousness that does not contribute to or advance our forward flowing progress of sustainability and contribution to civilization.

"Our way, the way, is not a random path. Our way

begins from coherent understanding. It is a way that aims at preserving knowledge of who we are, knowledge of the best way we have found to relate to each other, each to all, ourselves to other people, and all to our surroundings. If our individual lives have a worthwhile aim, that aim should be a purpose inseparable from the way". Ayi Kwei Armah's Two Thousand Seasons

Built on the spirit of Ubuntu, mutual respect and understanding, transparent and open dialogue, informed consent, and just returns for the indigenous knowledge holders and practitioners through the flow of rewards and benefits. African mythologies are valuable cultural factors (Utamawazo) reflecting community resources, serving as a reservoir of symbolism, inventions, mores, traditions, and practices for future expressions.

A people losing sight of origins are dead. A people deaf to purposes are lost. Under fertile rain, in scorching sunshine there is no difference: their bodies are mere corpses, awaiting final burial. Ayi Kwei Armah's Two Thousand Seasons

When people form lasting commitments towards the African episteme, they develop competencies, skills, and abilities to successfully maneuver the spirit within through life's demands. Enlightening our spirit and acquiring knowledge, skills, and abilities allows for transferring conscious energy (ngolo za-sikama) to phenomena, mental liberation, and connecting psychological and cognitive mechanisms and neural substrates. The Western worldview of "knowledge" indoctrinated in Africans lacked an understanding of the holistic nature and approach of pro-African ways of knowing and knowledge production. For example, when Baoulè is asked about a child in their custody: 'Is he your son?' Baoulè says yes, he is (spiritual connection).

For the European, this is not clear enough for him, so he presses the Baoulè: 'Is he your real son? From your own body?' (limited spiritual connection to direct bloodline only) and explains to him what this means. 'Real son' and 'adoptive son' are contradictory ideas, separated by a strict boundary of fact. Whereas to the Baoulè, they are overlapping (spiritual interdependence) and can be simultaneously true.

Cognitive Style

In Akan, *nyansa* means the ability to think, analyze, solve problems, pay attention to fundamental principles in human life, and ways to garner success in one's personal life. Cognitive styles define how individuals receive information, form concepts, and retain and process information. This processing of information stems from our perception, which is the basic process of cognition heavily dependent upon socialization and past experiences. Perceptions are formed and influenced by how information is received in the environment, as registered by the sensory channels. In psychic culture, nature continuously unfolds in communication through language, symbols, and images. Baba Nobles offer meaningful insight into how knowledge acquisition and cognition affect our ideas for being human through "memetic analysis." "Memes" are units of cultural gifts that are inherently designated by assets of their phenotypic outcome by a particular culture's survival thrust. The meme itself is, in part, evidence dwelling in our conscious minds. Baba Nobles argues that "memes" are "sensorial information structures" designs that mimic by symbiotically injecting into the human minds. The KaBa is responsible for sustaining sensory perception that is transmissible information. The Akhu is characterized by attributes of judgment, analysis, mental reflection and perception, and shifting behavior, causing them to promulgate to a higher Being. Functionally, memes are any contagious information patterns, in the form of symbols, sounds, or movement, that can be perceived by any of the senses and replicated by symbiotically entering the human being's "mind" and thus altering behavior in a way that propagates itself. Memes impact consciousness, and consciousness impacts behavior. Therefore, based on one's learning style, memes can assist in determining how one thinks and what to think. For instance, hieroglyphs represent memetic reflections. The psychostasis "The Papyrus of Ani" reflects the memetic messaging of ancient KMT. The weighing of the heart (Akhu) to the weighing of the feather (MA'AT) - - the Papyrus of Ani is the motif in which a person's life is assessed to determine their KA (soul) immediately before or after death to judge their fate to the heavens in picture form.

> *The Papyrus of the Ani demonstrates the beloved Scribe's reckoning divine offerings led by Thot, in which he brings his heart to be weighed against the feather of MA'AT (symbolizing Right and Truth). This homage to thee, Osiris by Anubis, Lord of eternity, King of the Gods, whose Ka is holy. I would strongly suggest you look at the depiction of "The Papyrus of the Ani," known as the Ancient Book of the Dead, which existed thousands of years before the Christian version comparing the act of one's soul weighed on a scale.*

Interestingly enough, other cult-like religions, like Christianity, have adopted similar storylines, like going to the Gates of Heaven, indicating the act of judgment and thinking. But what is most important is that Kemetic civilization *was* documented thousands of years before that of the Christianity, Judaism, and Islam religions as we know them. Other memes can be television shows, altars, tattoos, and human markings, which are also reflective sensorium information messages.

The cognitive style of Africans is challenged when we begin to think in a cognitive way based on other people's schema.

Na'im Akbar introduced to us the psychological chains of slavery, equating to Black social scientists' inability to examine African and African American reality outside European and American ideas. Conceptual schemas should reflect the cultural essence of a people's psyche. When our perception is distorted, we see a limited version of ourselves rather than seeing ourselves in terms of rich African thought or ethos that says we are equally divine. Instead, those who have mastered a subject matter from the other's paradigm cannot begin to think that what they know makes them less of who they are. Those who achieve such attributes and characteristics of the other's thought pattern will neglect the social and cultural cues of their divine self. Think about it: Africans' plight is beset with a very limited vision of what we can do with and for ourselves.

Let's think about the situation involving Deion Sanders. As a Black man, he sold the vision of how great he could make Jackson State University (JSU), but that entailed selling that vision to talented and gifted young black minds. He was on the path of greatness for Black America. Sanders is one of many who can help elevate JSU and all HBCUs. Imagine HBCUs regaining their rightful place and being the incubators for talented Black Athletes that could turn into cultivating and creating Black greatness in the classroom, community, and society. That was the larger picture–bringing the best talent back home for development in sports and the entire social structure. But what ended up happening is that Deion's vision of greatness involved taking our best talent to white institutions *in order* to have more Black coaches at PWIs. What he failed to understand by following the white dollars is that white America has never supported Black success if it did not enrich their pocketbooks first. Deion demonstrated that he had a fullness he needed to bring out, but he would be left with an emptiness that he would need to fulfill. So is his goal to bring more Black students to PWIs? Is his goal to create more Black Administrators at PWIs? Maybe his goal is to turn a PWI into a PBI (not spiritually the same as an HBCU) in the grand scheme. His vision for the greater good by not realizing an aspect of perception for cue selection; cue selection helps to inform us about choices to be made. I wish him Deion Sanders well but not at the expense of enriching white institutions and white folks over Black institutions and Black folks.

The second component of perception is analysis and organization. It is where one objectifies the experience and places it accordingly within a section to pull from for later use -- making the objective subjective. We organize our thoughts based on our mentality or types of consciousness as reflected in the different psychologies mentioned earlier: liberation psychology, community psychology, and African/Black psychology. We can recognize whether we are truly engaging in liberation and freedom. There is a difference in dealing with slave/colonial mentality, Black consciousness, Anglo/Saxon mentality, or neo-colonialist mentality by the way Africa is centered in their analysis. Even if a model uses *sensorial-information*, it is only available in non-linear processing mode that is not easily controlled using classical conditioning techniques. European processing structures *symbiotically* contaminate the mind's consciousness to reinforce the real as unreal and the unreal as real and the inability to not know the difference. Results eradicate the crisis for imagination.

Baba Nobles calls this "memetic ideation" by defining the nature of ideas as reflecting the substance of the behavior examined. As sensorial information structures, "memes" are carried out like messenger signals for the next generation to examine the core content, meaning, and capacity of the information they perceive. We are by-products of genetic memory. The conscious connection between you, your ancestors, and those yet to be born can be influenced by pathological memes when one is trying to process and organize information according to the ontological oppressor. Memes or sensorial informational structures come from ideas, symbols, images, feelings, words, customs, sounds, practices, or other knowable and perceptible stimuli. The most serious mistake Africans can make is to use white symbolism to direct their behavior. Symbols that do not correspond to African reality are not useful for inferring meaning to African life. When institutions such as education, politics, religion, economic, and military come into conflict, they will create a revolution. However, what upholds the revolution are the memes within institutions such as esthetics and arts, traditions, customs, and family structures where culture serves as the symbiotic display of relationships. Armah states: "Where I come from, revolution is the only creation and the revolutionary the only artist." Keeping consciousness alive, we have to use art as cultural analysis in memetic ideation. Then we must organize the integrated culture for critical conscious engagement. In all, the synthesis of analysis and organization begins with recognizing a group's inherent cultural virtues that empower the people and the belief in the power to improve their lived experiences.

What are these inherent cultural values?

The inherent cultural values are communalism, collective self-identity, and social relationships considered a natural state and a fundamental part of African social life. The African belief is that "social relationships are essential for every human person, for no one is self-sufficient and therefore no one can, by themselves, function adequately in the social context." Tradition, order, and stability of the group and collective African self-identity emphasize communal values. The well-being of the overall community sets the basis for individual happiness and thriving. Ideas such as freedom, independence, etc., African societies promote communal values such as "sharing, mutual aid, caring for others, interdependence, solidarity, reciprocal obligation, and social harmony. Africans believe fundamentally that spirit occupies our reality and that the material world we operate in allows for spirit and a physical manifestation simultaneously.

On a cognitive level, we must, from an analysis, respect the cultural integrity of African philosophical orientation - - (*utamwazo*) to the reality of African people. For the potential African social scientist, when one incorporates indigenous African cultural elements, like language, into their teaching practices, is regarded highly by students and clients as a collective awakening–the bursting of conscious waters (*hari bibi*) of thought-provoking essentialism. What then becomes *within* the learner is that such learning, when *experiential*, reveals the spiritual affective language giving meaning to other aspects of learning such as love, devotion, and sharing ("sharing, mutual aid, caring for others). This experience provides a feeling of autonomy by allowing learning from a particular cognitive style. For example, when Black social scientists are unable to reflect African thought and insight exhibit an *enit Orí ẹ Kòpé* (one who is unable to put his mind together). There has been some recognition that different cognitive styles exist. Therefore, a comparative analysis worldview is used to highlight differences in learning, cognition, and knowledge acquisition styles already discussed.

African Worldview vs. European Worldview Cognitive Styles

The core dimension of European intelligence is that

of rationality - - logical-analytical cognition. The individual can adapt and self-actualize. Western/European behavioral science considers rational beings more adapted to learning. The rational Being is stimulus-centered, field-independent, and reflective, a quality placed on disassociating oneself from the subject matter or experience which initiates learning. Manipulation without direct interaction is an essential function when problem-solving. This knowledge acquisition style construct opens the way for many futuristic possibilities that do not relate to an effective state of arousal.

Intelligence in Ancient KMT was considered to be located in the heart as rational thought - - spiritual and ethical. Ba (activating life) and Ka (physical form) operate as compliments to each other; as such, the KaBa produces emotion and motion. It is where we comprehend the entire mystery of the human mind. The Akhu is the center of intelligence and mental perception. KaBa is responsible for sustaining sensory perception. For those of African ascent, the essence of intelligence is affective (the intuit ability) and symbolic imagery (spirit and divine forces). Culture as a sensory component is supposed to help solve problems, suggesting that learning and problem-solving are holistic processes. The knowledge acquisition construct is "knowing," which is the epistemic character of "being." The Ptah is the intellectual soul associated with the mental maturity of the individual - - the synchronicity of the brain with the mind. The establishment of human identity–personal, social, spiritual, intuitive, and symbolic imagination – consists of synthesizing stimulus responses and intuitive epistemes making complementary the left and right brain functioning – di-unital logic. Di-unital, the logic of the right and left brain working simultaneously reflects African KaBa. The KaBa, a product of emotion and motion, physical form (Ka), and activating life (Ba), operate as compliments (in the same way) without contradiction to each other. The KaBa, in African logic, can be a thing and something else at the same time, providing meaning to understand one whole. For example, the maturity of the Ptah governs conduct and the person's ability to reproduce intellectually - - the ability to teach others. Vernon Dixon, in the essay, "African-Oriented and Euro-American-Oriented World Views: Research Methodologies and Economics," provides an outlook on connotation-construction and relationship to African logic that reveals the effervescent character of African culture and African symbolic language, which is supreme to grasping the undercurrents of African spirituality and thinking of the mind.

In summary, cognition consists of two components -- cognitive processes and cognitive contents. Cognitive processes concern how information is attended to, encoded, stored, and retrieved. Cognitive contents refer to the products of cognitive processes and include such variables as beliefs, self-statements, and expectations -- a force set in motion. Critical conscious psychology acknowledges the value of historical wisdom and existing curative paradigm. In contrast, Western psychology casts doubt and cannot find it in its own cultural schema healing component. The element of a healthy cognitive self is rooted in a more African cultural thought process. For instance, Ya Kimbwandènde Kia Bunseki Fu-Kiau left us with his divine wisdom for spoken medicine from the Congo: *Buka mukati, ya buka ku mbazi* (The Divine in me, heal the inside; The rest of us heal the outside). It is through chanting these words that each word carries a particular vibrational medicine as a healing therapeutic modality. The ability to attend to and make associations with deep thought requires skills in cognitive functioning. For critical consciousness, the process of decolonization requires a fundamental shift toward using African epistemic ways of knowing and being in the world.

Deep and Elaborative Processes

Two of the most powerful ways of attending to information for learning are deep and elaborative processing. Deep processing is the search for conceptual meaning, while elaborative processing is where the individual embellishes in thinking associations. Deep processing assesses the extent to which students critically evaluate, conceptually organize, and compare and contrast information they study. Elaborative processing assesses how students translate new information into their terminology, generate concrete examples from their experiences, apply new information to their lives, and use visual imagery to encode new ideas. *We must understand that d*eep processing requires finding the meaning or importance of knowing, which may be seen as knowledge promoting enlightenment and not just knowing for knowing sake. And elaborative processing may be thinking in-depth, as my Jegna would say, taking a deep dive into the subject matter, which may spark or bring change to one's sense of self. Self-knowledge with no purpose is empty knowledge.

This responsibility to define for ourselves the contexts and content of what Nobles calls core fundamental qualities of *Being*, *Becoming*, and *Belonging* will allow us to defend against his Triangular Law of anti-African reality: (1) the law of (mis)knowing; (2) the law of (non) Being; and (3) the law of (un)doing. Deep and elaborative processes reveal the imagination of possibilities.

The deep and elaborative process combines both states of material and invisible and of being and knowing. Synthesizing Baba Nobles' Triangular Law of **Knowing, Being, and Doing** with his core fundamental qualities of *"Being," "Belonging,"* and *"Becoming,"* we can see the type of deep dive needed when engaging in the "initiatory mastery" when processing our spiritual affinity. The deep process for inner development and critical consciousness requires discipline in thought and action, the ***Being*** within that says I have a mastery of self, and my commitment is the demonstration of such mastery through my thoughts and actions. In our **Knowing**, we see virtues extol the acceptance of truth when revealed. This faith, trusting the process, allows us to see beyond the (mis)knowing or that we have yet to see. *Becoming* is the essence of fulfilling one's destiny, an ongoing expression of **Being.** Only in our *Becoming* is there a conviction that truth will be divulged. It is during this process *of developing consciousness that we begin to recognize that our thoughts are not ours alone but rather reside in our interactions with others.* Based on how others project those interactions onto us, we run the risk of feeling resentful. Here we must free ourselves from feelings of persecution and accusations, a hard virtue to instill. Within the ontological spirit and cosmological connection, our consciousness demonstrates an ongoing expression of **Being** through our devotion to a higher purpose. *Belonging* is the spirit-conscious act of **Doing**. In our **Doing**, we are actively combating what is real versus what is not. It is our *Belonging* that allows us to manifest the spirit of Ubuntu. Marcus Garvey left with us the following:

> *"I trust that you will so live today as to realize that you are masters of your own destiny, masters of your fate; if there is anything you want in this world, it is for you to strike out with confidence and faith in self and reach for it."*

African science is real science but what is unreal is to continue to believe that we can coalesce in working with a foreign oppressive cultural group that operates from a psychopathic personality disposition. There is never a time, nor has there been a time when the slave and master can be on equal ground outside of African thinking. This active elaborative processing allows us, then, to defend against laws of *(mis)***knowing***, (non)***being***, and (un)***doing** in our psycho-behavioral disposition. Black social scientists must trust our ancient values and virtues in the process of *"Being," "Belonging,"* and *"Becoming,"* which defines for ourselves a normal and natural state of consciousness.

For the African, deep and elaborative processing is the conceiving of information that provokes meaning to one's life that began during ancient times. For example, the role of myth often used throughout Ancient times when taken as palpable and scrutinized symbolically raises the conscious expression for African thought and contemporary African conduct. Utilizing the virtues of the people is key to establishing critical consciousness. Hilliard reminds us of G.M. Jackson's corrective prescription within the educational process in ancient KMT times through the use of virtues:

Mastery/control of thought
Mastery/control of one's action
Devotion of higher purpose
Faith in the Master's ability to teach the truth
Faith in one's ability to know the truth
Faith in the ability to see the truth
Freedom from resentment when punished
Freedom from resentment when wronged
Ability to distinguish right from wrong
Ability to distinguish the real from the unreal

This is the process much like when the African Joel MBid of the NBA stated early in his NBA career "trust the process." He became this memetic reflection and is now known as "The Process" today. The virtues above allow one to access knowledge through deep and elaborative processing. In the ability to engage with the subject matter, the individual must see knowledge as the purpose of solving problems. What needs to happen for this to occur? We must infuse and incorporate new/ancient pedagogy from which we learn and teach.

Use of African Wisdom and Knowledge

Acquisition of knowledge is in fact the development of identity (p. 7)

The *Nsaka Sunsum*, which means "touching the Spirit," is an educational pedagogy and process that captures African Wisdom, consciousness, and information intermingling. In African tradition, knowledge is seen as a source of freedom, and Wisdom is seen as the ability to think and solve problems. The Ewe word for knowledge is *Nunya* thing observed. *Nyansa* is the Akan word meaning the ability to make success in one's life and pay reflective attention to human life experience. This deep-level processing occurs by way of elaborative processing. If Black social scientists were to operate from the *NSAKA SUNSUM,* then we must demonstrate the following:

1. Love for African Wisdom and knowledge.
2. Knowledge of the Culture of African people's social life.
3. Familiarity with the African Educational process.

This processing style has not been the focal point for intellectual activity or academic achievement.

Essential to critical consciousness is the ability to investigate or discuss truth as an active resistance to oppression and a vision of possibilities for freedom and wellness. For liberation to occur, knowledge and Wisdom must focus on systemic conditions, the need to solve practical problems, and gaining knowledge for liberation. In the current climate in America, we can see overt collective efforts to keep Africans from truly being free as evidenced by challenges to critical race theory and gerrymandering the black vote. But we also have clear demonstrations of *Being, Becoming, Belonging, Knowing, Being,* and *Doing* throughout our history. African communities have shown collective resistance to colonization and racism -- resistance that demanded radical change for freedom. In the late 1960s, the Black power movement helped redefine the image of the African. Imagine going into college as a "Negro" and coming out "Black." The Black Panther party showed leadership, protection, and force, by challenging the evil of institutionalized racism and concomitant inequities.

The transformation that took place required a deep dive into the meaning of the African and how we examine a new understanding of our relationship with the world. Before that, Marcus Garvey was clear: *"If you haven't self-confidence, you are twice defeated in the race of life. With confidence, you have won even before you have started."* Garvey laid the blueprint for warding against **(mis)Knowing**, *"If we as a people realized the greatness from which we came we would be less likely to disrespect ourselves."* Establishing the fundamental values of what it meant to be black by realigning against **(non) Being** *"we are entitled to our own opinions and not obligated to or bound by the opinions of others."* Knowing the history and contribution of Africa to the world, correcting the **(un)Doing**, *"Go to work! Go to work in the morn of a new creation... until you have reached the height of self-progress, and from that pinnacle, bestow upon the world civilization of your own."* After all, while all knowledge is experienced, not all knowledge lends itself to being purposeful.

It can be said that the war is not over. We continue to be in a race war, the war for the African mind. Critical consciousness in contemporary times requires a radical shift and radical response to current injustices -- one that moves beyond individual Eurocentric symptom reduction (reconciliation) and toward an African collective resistance to a new reality. Collective resistance to the dehumanization of African students aims to restore our intellectual dignity and warrior spirit in learning what we need to become. When examining the educational attainment of Black students, one can see how the dynamics of sociopolitical status interfere with academic performance and contribute to alienation and control. Research has demonstrated that teacher expectations greatly influence the performance of Black students. To the extent positive sentiments manifest themselves in rewards, a minority student will often be rewarded for failure and punished for success. (Read Dr. Jawanza Kunjufu's publications entitled *Countering the Conspiracy To Destroy Black Boys.*)

The differential expectations are the causal attributions and sentiments expressed by the teachers of the students. Imagine, if you will, when Black students whose characteristics do not live up to the teacher's low expectations, the students are not liked by the teacher. This response from an anonymous participant in training for teachers in a Pennsylvania school district revealed "the teachers are owning the expectations that they want students to form...If you do not respond in the manner that teachers approve, then you are not "right"--something's wrong with you...It reminds me of the whiteness of property again." As we can see, these issues remain. Teachers can influence students' learning through their attitude toward the student. Another participant revealed: "You have to think critically to do that, Dr. Derek, and we are not teaching critical thinking skills, or criticality ... because the learning is owned by the teachers...most teachers do the thinking, not the students...." How can students begin to engage in deep and elaborative processing when teachers do not expect them to gain the knowledge or experience the Wisdom they deserve?

Akoto reminds us of the power that teachers have: *"It is the confident, capable and the committed mwalimu (teachers) employing a broad repertoire of techniques within the interactive circle.....to recapture our people's minds, engender the liberated Afrikan personality, and reconstruct the Afrikan nation/world." (1994 pp. 335-336).* For the Mwalimu, this demonstration of Ptah reminds us of the power we have influencing conduct as they bring to higher being the ability to reproduce intellectually - - the ability to teach others. As evident in the breakdown of world-views and psychology, as it exists in the United States today, education needs to be equitably meeting the needs of all individuals and groups.

We can see how education and psychology continue to perpetuate inequities. Inequities extend beyond education and psychology, including, but not limited to, for example, the healthcare and criminal justice systems in the United States. There are ways psychologists can advocate for change, and it is our responsibility to do so. Thus the following maxims for knowledge and Wisdom are delineated:

> Experience is the mother of knowledge.
> All things depend upon experience.
> Knowledge is like a garden; if it is not cultivated,
> it cannot be harvested.
> Wisdom creates well-being.
> Wisdom is not in the head of one person.
> If a problem lasts for a long time, wisdom comes to it.

Black critical conscious psychology scholarship and practice should shift in focus on how we reinforce and define what it means to be human from the African episteme, explaining African cultural psychology. Once we grasp the profound agency in African culture of song, dance, and drum (personhood, familyhood, and social life), the political struggle occurs when Africans have to write in the language of their oppressors.

There are a number of African warriors who have begun to incorporate African cultural worldview approaches in the study of mental health and wellness. To this end, we must create and establish a nosological system of healthy functioning from our own cultural perspective and needs. What does this entail? For one, this requires we work even harder to uphold our mission and destiny to liberate the African Mind, empower the African Character, and enliven and illuminate the African Spirit. We must escape the indoctrination of western psychological science and be willing to define and determine who we are for ourselves. We have to locate the correct diagnosis of Africans in America through an African-centered lens when examining mental disorders. Akbar identified four basic categories of mental illness among Africans in America: The Alien-Self Disorder, The Anti-Self Disorder, The Self-Destructive Disorders, Organic Disorders. This spawned the development of a nosological system that would allow us to accurately diagnose and provide corrective healing practices to African people. We as Black Psychologists are responsible for creating our own definitions of what is "normal and natural" versus "abnormal and nonnative" and culturally relevant to African people. As a part of this theory of diagnosing personality functioning on an order-disorder continuum, a nosology system of diagnoses places at its center an African understanding of personality as a function of inheritance, social ecology and the interplay between the two. (Greater discussion will occur in Vol II.)

The foundation for transforming African/Black psychology into the "psychology" of Sakhu Djaer (Skh Djr) will be the work of the current and next generation of critical thinkers in the field. It is within this deep dive that further refinement and deeper extension of African cultural psychology are needed. We have exhausted the critique of European/Western psychology. Once we get beyond the need to think like white cultural expectations and operate from our own sense of meaning to the word, ancient African wisdom and contemporary African thought, then we can create and establish Black spaces, we can begin to unapologetically explore and define from an African episteme the working of the African mind. Demonstrating Black critical consciousness can lead us toward a path in creating the African structure of *Being* based on the constant, perpetual, perceivable, and continuous relationship between those who dwell in the reality of being human, the reality of spirits, and the Divine laws of nature. The goal of merely surviving within an oppressive society no longer meets the needs of African people. Black Critical consciousness occurs when Africans authentically begin to examine and master the multiple realms of African reality: *Being, Becoming,* and *Belonging* concerning our *Knowing, Being,* and *Doing* spirit, Skh Djr (Pan African Black Psychology). Furthermore, it is the Wisdom obtained that helps to create well-being.

The soul is the presence of being alive or the origin of living consciousness. **Consciousness** is the awareness of "I," self, and others. Consciousness is self-analysis demonstrating a level of internal and external awareness. The presence of "I" is Being. Being is behind all expressions. **Being in the** presence of life itself. We are conscious **Beings.** Our beingness is spirit consciousness. This spirit consciousness examines all of our actions. As spirit Beings driven, all expressions are God's consciousness. Consciousness is the aspect of God in our spirit (*Skh Djr).* God's consciousness reflects a man-God conscious state. To what degree can we appreciate ourselves as man-God conscious Beings as knowing and knowable spirits? As a knowing and knowable spirit, a conscious mind is liberated. A liberated mind is an empowered mind. An empowered mind is aware of the Universe as an unlimited resource. The unlimited resource of the universal spirit within is dedicated to liberating the African mind, illuminating and enlivenment of the African Spirit, and enlivening the African character. Those who operate without Black critical consciousness lack Skh Djr, the liberating force in our Being.

"You want to win? Cast aside your white god. Embrace your African Spirit. You are free. -Dutty Boukman,1791"

V

❦

Connecting Cognitive Characteristics to Critical Consciousness

...the future will bring increasingly valid models of how the mind works in the learning process. It may also bring pedagogical applications for these valid models' applications which improves teaching and learning. (Hilliard, p111)

How we perceive information and experiences varies from "direct experience" to "abstract conceptualization." We either perceive through our senses that which is direct experience or cognitively (cognitive is such a loaded term here) that which is abstract conceptualization. This maneuvering between the "perceiving" dimension relates to deep and elaborative processes discussed in the previous chapter. How Africans learn is how they perceive content. Autochthonous knowledge systems identify learning as transformative "sensorial information structure" patterns. In our transformation, we experience information or material through feeling and sensing receptors within the depth of processing (deep and elaborative). Africans' primary cognitive knowledge acquisition style is Sensing - primarily through six senses, what one sees, hears, touches, and spirit. Sensing people's experiences and facts to learn about things increases their knowledge. As discussed earlier, 'things' are experiences. The second sensory experience is Feeling - the emphasis is placed on the personal import of stimuli, which relies on different types of logic or wisdom being imparted. It must be noted that the sixth sense can inform the feeling, as this is true when we discussed *Being, Becoming, and Belonging*. In the African knowledge system, we know things for practical purposes or utility gain. Knowledge leads to wisdom, acting on our **Knowing, Being, and Doing** to help us solve problems and for well-being. For this discussion, the focus is only on how Africans relate to the world.

Researchers suggest that within the depth of processing, the primary task of critical evaluation is an intricate part of learning. Much like critical consciousness, situations are conceptualized within both context and content. This connection to critical consciousness helps to provide insight into how socially complex issues can be solved. Intellectual activity has been extensively dissected and experimented with within the field of cognitive psychology to capture which processing style is more effective in learning. Lewis conducted a study to show differences in the depth of processes among African students. Gender differences were identified as results revealed that African females engaged in more profound levels of processing than African males. Additional research demonstrated that African pre-high school males tend to use *feeling* rather than thinking as a preferred method for processing information than their eleventh-grade African female cohorts. African high school male students are likelier to incorporate sensing as a processing method than intuitive. Jensen reports that *sensing* (S) types learn best when they are moved from the concrete to the abstract in a step-by-step progression. They value practical knowledge. As for thinking (T), types learn best when the material is presented to them in a logical and sequential format. The *sensing* and thinking frequency, previously reported among college-age male Africans, is also verified among high-school African males. As we can see, this reflects the "sensorial information structure" patterns which emphasize the importance of symbiotic learning styles in the minds of Black male students. This demonstrates an African mind-processing technique, whether feeling, sensory, or relational.

Relational style learners tend to exhibit challenges when classroom environment expectations need to be more supportive. Expressiveness is exemplified by extraverted (acting on or **Doing)** elements and *Feeling* (F) type learning students. Students drop out before reaching high school when the school environment does not embrace these needs or meet the children's learning styles. For example, what should we expect when African high school male students prefer Perceiving (P) over Judging (J)? Black male students who operate from a perceiving style learning process prefer a more flexible approach to learning. Perceiving style learners tend to view learning as freewheeling and flexible. They care less about deadlines and the completion of tasks. They prefer open and spontaneous learning environments ("It's tactile, it's body-oriented, it's more personal") and feel "imprisoned" in a highly structured classroom. The Perceiving style learner discovers how to manage elastically and spontaneously while simultaneously solving problems. Those who put forth the theory of differences argue that black children require instructions that deal more with people than with symbols or abstractions. They say black pupils need more chances for expressive talking rather than writing. These educators say that black children also require more freedom to move around the classroom without being rebuked for misbehavior. Age may also show differences in the progression of the preferred depth of processing styles. Upper-level high school students engage in primarily thinking (T) style processing. The thinking type, characterized by logical processes, requires a more selective introversion perspective, as in science classes, than for the thinking dimension.

The critically conscious individual connects personal and social domains when studying problems or subject matters, much like the relational style construct for acquiring knowledge. The relational-symbolic-affective learner prefers high-stimulus social learning context, external stimulus, and diversity of experience for transformation. The dimension of affective symbolism (spiritual and personal-social), an element of relational style, is essential in developing critical consciousness. Research has found that relational styles learners prefer learning content on social issues. This relational style construct typifies visual attributes, self-centeredness, field dependence, and spontaneity. Self-centeredness is in those mental activities that use personal or social cues in learning for problem-solving. These individuals are people-oriented, field dependent. These individuals would do well with chakra training and divination. Body receptors allow for continued stimulus flow, searching rigorously for an underlying meaning without manipulation.

A paucity of black educators and psychologists believe that black children learn in distinctly different ways than white children. They have been urging schools to adapt their instructional methods to this difference. Those who put forth the theory of disagreements argue that black children require instructions that tap into the right brain and midbrain functioning. Africans typically rely on spiritual concepts like love, affection, and sharing within Ubuntu. Equal balances of rational and creative thought characterize the midbrain. Here we can see the ontological, cosmological, and axiological markers for how and why Africans think the way they do. Observing African children in social spaces, we recognize how they express their experiences with various field-dependent stimuli. When Black children operate in an open and accessible environment, their natural genius and inquisitive nature begin to unfold. Those who don't know how to handle or interact with our children will quickly label them behaviorally challenging. As noted earlier, knowledge acquisition requires experience and *nunya (observation)* with the environment, spirits, and analytical and relational essences. In our being, we know. In our becoming, we (re)know and confirm through our belonging. Yesterday belongs to me, tomorrow I know. Thus far, evidence shows how we can tap into critical consciousness connecting to polyepistemic ways of knowing.

Culture's Influence on Black Consciousness

"All mental functions are manifest through specific cultures, which include specific languages" (Hilliard, 1994 p.153).

We can add to the understanding that *Black critical conscious psychology* is being able to sit in the consciousness of being, in spirit, and in a divine dialectical dance of resisting the oppressive ontological psyche. We are reminded that during the earliest times, the undertaking of being and becoming a knowable spirit was to transform towards "perfectibility." The development of consciousness is a transformative process. As previously mentioned, since we are conscious beings and our consciousness is spirit-connection to God, we must operate in a man-God conscious state. It is this totality of consciousness of being, becoming, and belonging as knowing and knowable beings or spirits that we recognize the value of our Black consciousness. This Black conscious discussion needs to highlight and elucidate the psychological processes and resources of the Black man thinketh. In other words, it is imperative that constructing an African-centered authenticating correct and normal identity and behavior must 'incorporate mutually verifying constructs about the nature of the African beingness and African functioning.' We need to use the wisdom of Africa to recreate our identity and wellness. This critical conscious work centers on connecting varied spiritual and divine understandings for building on the African community. Black consciousness is the state of mind reflective of a positive self-concept, cultural pride, and centering of Blackness when making decisions that are in the best interest of African people. With this Black consciousness, you can walk in the world with confidence (self-esteem), a defender of Black people, and a feeling of self-assurance arising from one's appreciation of culture, Blackness, and spiritual connections of relationships.

The axiom that *"nothing happens outside of culture"* provides the understanding that culture is the medium for all human functioning. An examination of core African culture reveals that African social life places a high premium on group-centered cooperation and fosters cognitive, affective, and behavioral expressiveness of African beings. Technology and culture perform both a symbolic function and a moral demand function to humans. As a symbolic function, culture provides its set of signs, symbols, rituals, and rites that give meaning to human cognitive phenomena. Through these motifs, culture teaches the individual to recognize phenomena and the logical relations among phenomena. What does that mean for having a Black consciousness? The Black consciousness values the conception of African knowledge, recognizes African cultural phenomena, and enhances Black life. Now I am not speaking of the need for Black folk with self-esteem to want to coalesce with other cultural groups or nationalities. It is our Blackness first! Unapologetically, Blackness first. It is within our cultural schema that serves as an agent for this recognition. Schemas represent categorical knowledge according to a structure where values and attributes are placed. We know that knowledge is reserved in schemata where we organize knowledge and experiences. Hilliard reminds us that mental functioning, operations, and structuring are all culturally manifested and signify that knowledge acquisition reflects a particular worldview. Since schemata are influenced by worldview, the development of Black consciousness can only remember the consciousness of that specific group.

A multitude of meanings exist during the process of identity development and problem-solving; however, when one personalizes phenomena (affect) and establishes the use of metaphors, proverbs, and gestures (symbolic imagery), the synthesizing of these two constructs, affective-symbolic imagery, conveys a dimension of knowing as conscious dynamic, rational and creative. Embraced within critical consciousness is the first step of raising awareness through how we see ourselves and our identity. Do you belong here? Who are you connected to? To whom do you belong? Are you just another human being? What value orientation do you adhere to? What value do you place on your Blackness? How do you relate you are to the first ancestors who walked this life? Do you see yourself representing the power of greatness? In the end, can you answer all these questions without the thought of White people, Asian people, Indian people, etc.? The next step is to recognize the oppressive thought patterns that you have or the thought patterns of how others treat people who look like you. Do you push aside the slights that other socially constructed groups transgress against you? Do you accept the disrespect that other socially constructed groups express about people who look like you? Do you fight for and defend the right for Blacks to walk in the world based on their own accord, or does it require the need for all humans to get along? These are the beginning markers for Black consciousness and form your critical consciousness when in full operation mode. Can you envision a world of Blackness, illuminating possibilities leading to the following process of divine law and inspiration? Much like Lupe Fiasco's song *All Black Everything*:

Sometimes you just gotta... go!
You would never know
What you could ever be
If you never try
You would never see
Stayed in Africa
Where you never leave
So there were no slaves in our history
Were no slave ships
Were no misery
Call me crazy, or isn't he?
See I fell asleep and I had a dream
It was all black everything

Uh, and we ain't get exploited
White man ain't feared so he did not destroy it
We ain't work for free, see they had to employ it
Built it up together so we equally appointed
First 400 years, see we actually enjoyed it
Constitution written by the W.E.B. Du Bois
Were no reconstructions, Civil War got avoided
Little black Sambo grows up to be a lawyer
Extra extra on the news stands
Black woman voted head of Ku Klux Klan
Malcolm Little dies as a old man
Martin Luther King read the eulogy for him....

Uh, and it ain't no projects
Keepin it real is not an understood concept

Yea, complexion's not a contest
'Cause racism has no context
Hip hop ain't got a section called conscious
Everybody rappin' like crack never happened
Crips never occurred no Bloods to attack them
Matter of fact no hood to attack in
Somalia is a great place to relax in...

Uh, and I know it's just a fantasy
I cordially invite you to ask why can't it be?
Now we can do nothing 'bout the past
But we can do something about the future that we have
We can make fast or we can make it last
Every woman Queenin' and every man a Kingin'
When those color lines come, we can't see between
We just close our eyes 'til it's all black everything

....
All black everything
All black everything
All black everything

Do we continue by recognizing how we connect with and interface with the divine law in the face of oppression? We must recognize the strength, resistance, and cultural authentication of our ancestors. How did you get here? Through which channels and gates did_____ pass through? Think about the number of generations that had to pass 400 years ago, 1,200 years ago, and 3,000 years ago. What is your conception of your first ancestors who walked this earth? The critical consciousness of Skh Djr is our framework woven throughout the process of illuminating the divine within us and the recognition that our collective divine spirit will lead us to more authentic liberation. What are we fighting against? I will let you decide:

The white man has succeeded in subduing the world by forcing everybody to think his way....The white man's propaganda has made him the master of the world, and all those who have come in contact with it and accepted it have become his slaves. Marcus Mosiah Garvey

The question is to what extent our "cultural style" affects how we see ourselves? How has it produced strong arguments for the need to discern differences in the impact of social identity within context? What is the understanding or cognitive style of what it means to be African? We are informed by Baba Nobles' how our Knowing, Being, and Doing for Africans is challenged when living in an anti-African reality,

The first law of (mis)knowing -- "if you don't understand White supremacy, then everything else you think you know will simply confuse you".

The second law of (non)being -- occurs when "If you don't exist according to your cultural essence (nature/spirit) then everything that you think you are will only be a diminishment".

Lastly, the law of (un)doing -- "the experience of one generation becomes the history of the next generation and the history of several generations will become the tradition of the people - law of (un)doing.

This strategic critical conscious analysis can be seen in research on socialization's effects.

Elsie Moore studied the effects of how socialization affects learning in adoptive Black children by white parents. Moore asserts that the learning experience (socialization) accounts for differences between African American children and

White children and that this socialization of learning is culturally driven. Let's examine Black children being reared in white environments, whether they are adopted by white families or simply in an all-white community. The first law of *(mis)knowing* would suggest or instill in our children the need or desire to attain white value status. As discussed earlier, I open up with my class every semester by having students choose between African and European cultures. Which structure would allow them to accomplish their goals, be successful in life, be the best they can be, and contribute to humanity? Those African students who choose a white cultural structure justify this by thinking that you must operate like white folks to succeed. The thinking behind this is that one must accept and adhere to oppressive ontological ethos and reality orientation. This leads to the second law of *(non)being*; they are challenged regarding whose philosophical values and customs they participate in. When Black students claim to have good white friends but never think to invite them or make it an interest to join in a Kwanzaa celebration even though they believe they live in a diverse community of acceptance. Even within various communities, their existence is diminished every day, and they do not or have not been exposed to cultural celebrations that nurture their cultural essence (nature/spirit). Lastly, the law of *(un)doing* is the psycho-behavioral modalities in which Black students believe in the practices and values of European culture.

For example, belief in individualism and nuclear family structure, "do your own thing" mentality, and being emotionally distant from your group (see Table 3). Akbar would call these remnants of psychological chains of slavery. These experiences get passed down from one generation to the next and become the history of several generations, traditions, etc., that must be undone. Different child-rearing environments affect both learning and problem-solving processes. If you were to ask the average Black college student what it would take to solve the problems of the black community, they would not have an answer for you. We have work to do! Amos Wilson has begun to lay a plan and framework in his career, Blueprint for Black Power! Too many of us are scared to implement the plan for Black Power, which is why we need to develop Black Critical Consciousness.

Black Critical conscious engagement begins with recognizing inherent group virtues and culture that empower the people and the belief in the power to improve their lived experiences. While White supremacy contributes to oppression, black inferiority, and blaxploitation, Black critical consciousness needs to mesmerize us into our beautiful strength within undulating across the Black diaspora. We need to confront these hostile forces while fostering the virtues of people's individual and community strengths. Someone who proclaims to have Black Critical consciousness will navigate away from individualistic goals and trust and accept collectivistic survival thrust as a direct result of their connection to their community. This focus on "common collective struggle" is vital to Black critical conscious identity.

Collective wisdom and consciousness exist within the world's cultures. "knowledge is power" comes from collective wisdom, a display of critical thinking. Compelling arguments about how groups operate within a cultural context require an understanding of the way humans relate to the world,

> *The normal role of human beings in and with the world is not a passive one. Because they are not limited to the natural (biological) sphere but participate in the creative dimension as well, men can intervene in reality in order to change it. "Inheriting acquired experience, creating and re-creating, integrating themselves into their context, responding to its challenges, objectifying themselves, discerning, transcending,*

men enter into the domain which is theirs exclusively--that of history and of culture." (Feire p.4)

This demonstrates how critical consciousness is both an intellectual activity and a mental capacity, corroborating with the cultural substance of one's group.

Empowerment Theory - Political Falsehood for the African

Empowerment has been identified in critical, liberation, community psychology, multicultural counseling, and social work. Empowerment theory examines in context the social, political, and economic role of power and how relationships are carried out with those who identify with an oppressive group. This implies that empowerment theory examines person-environment perception from the individual, community, and systemic levels. There is an acknowledgment of mutual interaction and reciprocity between individuals, human-to-human interactions, and communities.

At the individual level, empowerment is primarily incorporated to assist persons with personal self-efficacy and coping skills as they maneuver through social environments. A key element within Empowerment practice is problem-solving. From here, we are to identify the strengths and problem-finding solutions, set goals, and perspective-taking. Community psychologists have also used the concept of empowerment theory. As conceptualized in community psychology as a process and an outcome, empowerment also applies to individuals, groups, and entire communities. Any advances in theory development of empowerment in community psychology have yet to make significant progress in problem-solving issues, particularly for marginalized groups. For example, from a systemic analysis, there has been limited discussion among community psychologists as a field expounding on the Black Lives Matter movement. This lack of articulation in the community psychology field speaks volumes to racial science oppression. It is safe to insinuate that there is a dual identity of Being; this is no different than Dubois' Double consciousness theory, played out between the oppressor and the oppressed. What are community psychologists here to do? There is a power relationship dynamic that identifies human characterizations at all levels within systems. For instance, there is a power relationship dynamic that recognizes the relationship between the slave and master. Those who identify as masters expect to be recognized by the enslaved person with little reciprocity expected in return, as the enslaved person is not to expect to be recognized by the master. These interactions profoundly affect people's views (dual identity of Being and Double consciousness theory). Does this mean Africans can think from an African thinking mind but are forced to see the world from a European worldview? We have proven in previous chapters the conflict between westernized thinking versus Africanized thinking. This dynamic power places empowerment theory and community psychology on heightened alert.

Empowerment theorists and community psychologists have been called social science activists. The primary focus has been on individual perceptions of personal control. We still see elements of learning theory where we recognize behavior according to consequences imposed by external sources passed down by the oppressor/master. Individuals without consciousness operate at this personal level and do not seek activist activities, and are likely to seek temporary relief and pleasure concerning external consequences handed down by the oppressor/master.

Some social scientists continue to operate from the enslaver/enslaved person dynamic in creating theories emanating from oppressive axiological thrust. For example, Racial identity development could be seen as part of the empowerment genre.

Racial identity theory posits that Black identity is created in response to the White identity social structure. Racial identity's primary goal is to reach internalization and commitment as the healthiest forms of identity functioning with claims that these levels guard and shield Blacks from psychological affront, supply a feeling of group membership and cultural grounding, and; provide an anchor or position of withdrawal for engaging in interactions with other cultural groups afar from their Blackness. The goal of this theory is to be an integrationist. Ultimately, the power structure here remains the same.

Studies have examined the relationship between racial identity and strategies for social change and how group consciousness contributes to political empowerment. Watts asserted that those with high Pre-Encounter attitudes were more likely to improve their status and engage in less intense social change strategies [(mis)knowing and (un)doing]. Those having Immersion and Internalization attitudes would favor more challenging strategies based on racial solidarity (Knowing, Being, and Doing). It was also discovered that those who held attitudes firm in Immersion and Internalization endorsed such strategies as picketing (Doing) while those high in Pre-Encounter [(mis)Knowing] perspectives had more promising approaches to racial integration [(mis)Knowing], socialization [(non)Being] and persuasion of White colleagues [(un)Doing]. A more critical look at the Pre-Encountered person posits that "such an individual is out of touch with his/her self and is in a pathological, misoriented or disordered state." This suggests that such an individual is spiritually isolated (Belonging), prefers to adopt an analytical style construct of thinking (Being), and is incapable of developing true critical consciousness (Becoming).

Empowerment and Critical Consciousness

Embedded in empowerment theory is the understanding and development of critical consciousness. To change one's thinking, we must acknowledge the markers of oppression and develop defiant actions against this recognized oppression. Counseling using empowerment theory is most often conceptualized as an individual psychological process. Empowerment in counseling involves working with clients to make changes they want to complete in their lives. To make such a change, an underlying aspect of empowerment theory discusses the development of critical consciousness with a shift in thinking. In societies scarred by inequity, disparity, injustice, racism, sexism, economic deprivation, and violence, counseling relationships may be vulnerable to even overtly reflecting these and other forms of oppression. Through training and education, counselors are in a position of relative privilege that, when unexamined, can contribute to maintaining the presence of oppressive social realities within the counseling relationship. Counselors ascribing to the dominant culture's values without examining the influence of their importance in counseling may define client problems and engage in inappropriate interventions for their clients. For example, counselors who fail to acknowledge the roles that racism and classism play in creating the environment of a low-income client of color may "blame the victim." Ginwright was forced to develop an African thought process when a young Black male exclaimed, "I am more than what happened to me, I'm not just my trauma!" This thought sparked a different way of engaging with and discussing challenges with our youth so that the community can help (us) heal. Ginwright's piercing model of shifting from a trauma-informed to a healing engagement paradigm represents, at a minimal level, liberation, community psychology, and empowerment theory from an African paradigm. This allows, at its core, the element of Ubuntu that humanness is found in our collective interdependence, which is an asset-driven and strength-based approach.

However, critical consciousness at the community level recognizes oppression at the group level on three psychological processes: group identity, group consciousness, and group efficacy. Theories of empowerment have tried to explain the development of critical consciousness at the community level for healing. Critical consciousness within a community seeks to enhance groups' civil participation to address concerns of disparities, inadequate funding, and community health statuses. Critical consciousness prepares community members for civic engagement and assessing community problems. Community healing involves collective responsibility and advances critical consciousness using culturally restorative practices. Self-determined cultural values define community resistance in empowerment theory. One element of necessary conscious development within a community is the use of griot narratives of the community. Griot storytelling advances community belonging and empowerment, interdependence, and endorsing the community's needs. Community advocacy is the resistance to disempowering values and systemic practices of inequities. Critical consciousness within organizational domains requires and highlights new community narratives and community action.

Healthy Black critical conscious individuals would demonstrate more of an African self-consciousness personality. The critical conscious mind would want to know how being an integrationist afforded your power in the context of white supremacy without denying living in a racist society. The Black critical conscious individual understands the need for collective conscious identity, African survival thrust, respect for all Africans, including support institutions, and an uncompromising position against anti-African forces. Toni Morrison wrote: "I spent my entire life, writing life, trying to make sure that the

White gaze is not the dominant gaze." This is an example of an embedded African self-conscious spirit personality.

In Seeking the Sakhu, Baba Nobles suggests that spirit or spiritedness is a complex entity within Being. This spirit is a manifestation of the material and immaterial, giving value to being human. Within the African process of being, we are to master or gain an understanding of divine laws that represent substance within, materializing, refinement, and kindness. The concept of 'spirit' or 'essence' as defined by African thought further suggests that African modes of inquiry for knowing should guide the examination of critical conscious psychology. The African understanding of Being, education, and history recognizes wisdom's power to promote wellness and problem solve. We cannot treat African people with non-African techniques of the oppressor and expect increased well-being; at the same time, we cannot expect to have a long-lasting effect of feeling empowered. Any conscious attempts to reach the goals of African people should be culturally driven. The use of cultural values influences both the need to solve problems and create well-being. As stated repeatedly throughout this discourse, examining what makes us human is paramount. The African conception of human Beingness in Bantu is NTU. NTU is Being itself, that force binding the Being and beings to unify as the universal cosmic force in all things manifests. This is Skh Djr, recognizing that our collective divine spirit leads us to more authentic empowerment and liberation of ourselves. We must begin developing ourselves and our consciousness to be free from White supremacist thought and practice. We are not allowing the white gaze to become part of our Sakhu / Skh Djr.

The African/Black psychological mindset will free us from the white dominant thinking mode for understanding the world. We need to Be African! Think African! This sparked the notion of what is right with us. Toni Morrison was asked why she writes stories that the white audience had difficulty comprehending; her reply was, "I'm not giving the "White gaze" the power and attention over how I see us." This is Black critical consciousness at its best–utilizing the virtues of African people's cultural values and critical consciousness in practice.

VI

The Need for Reprogramming

Beale Street is a loud street. It is left to the reader to discern a meaning in the beating of the drums. -James Baldwin

The inception and formulation of the Association of Black Psychologists (ABPSi) in 1968 began from the spirit of Black psychologists recognizing the marginalization, rejection, ignoring of African life, and oppressive praxis, pedagogy, and paradigm of the American Psychological Association (APA) and the field of White psychology. If it were not for the consciousness of liberation of these Black-minded psychologists, the field as we know it would remain for the white mind. One would argue that these sistas and brothas demonstrated ancient wisdom of Blackness and Africannity. These African psychologists chose not to adhere to Hegel's Master/Slave relationship anymore, as this was Black consciousness at its best!

APA comprises multiple divisions, which all can be seen as subdivisions. APA consists of over 50+ divisions. One of the divisions created was The Society for the Psychology of Women (APA Division 35). This division describes itself as "providing an organizational base for all feminists, of all genders and of all national origins, who are interested in teaching, research, or practice in the psychology of "womxn." To demonstrate our commitment to the inclusivity of feminists of diverse genders, the presidential trio has chosen to describe the division's purposes and activities using the term "womxn." The division recognizes a diversity of womxn's experiences which result from a variety of factors, including ethnicity, culture, language, socioeconomic status, age, and sexual orientation. The division promotes feminist research, theories, education, and practice toward understanding and improving the lives of girls and womxn in all their diversities; encourages scholarship on the social construction of gender relations across multicultural contexts; applies its scholarship to transforming the knowledge base of psychology; advocates action toward public policies that advance equality and social justice; and seeks to empower womxn in community, national and global leadership." This epitomizes inclusivity, pollyannaish, and intersectionality, and all rolled up into one. But what is the reason to start a subdivision within a subdivision? The one population who suffered some of the worst atrocities at the hand of its oppressors were our African women. But I have to ask the question: what would be the reason for an oppressed group to want to stay under its oppressor? What are we afraid of? Are we afraid of losing our investments with the white community? Are we afraid of bargaining and leveraging our Blackness? Is the social currency of being around and under whiteness, white organizations, and white connections more important than liberating the African mind? Like the proverb - - *"The freedom that comes from ignorance enslaves the one who entertains it."*

We are losing our way!

A people losing sight of origins are dead. A people deaf to purposes are lost...The remade are pointers to the way, the way of remembrance, the way knowing purpose - Ayi Kwei Armah (p. xiv, xv)

Unlike the 1968 group that saw itself as a separate entity, the Psychology of Black Women (PBW) became a subdivision with *sub-meaning* under a subdivision. With vision and perseverance, some extraordinary Black women who started as a committee on Black women's concerns gained a more prominent voice within Division 35. In 1984 Section I, The PBW began, now Division 54. As a Section, PBW has its bylaws and governance structure. It has scheduled time for invited presentations at the American Psychological Association's Annual Convention, and 2021 kicked off its inaugural PBW conference. They even went as far as to use African symbols in their advertisement. Operating from a Black critical conscious framework, what would be the reason to start a Black Psychology of Women and use African symbolism as a subgroup of an ontological oppressed organization that came out just months before admitting APA's long history of racism and discrimination against Blacks?

But why do we continue to create Black organizations under oppressive white social systems and white social spaces and say we are free? They cannot get away from functioning like Black Student Association still at a PWI. This is what they are used to. The leaders of PBW must understand that consciousness is a type of power, personality is a type of power, and culture is a type of power. If we let another group determine the complexion of our values, personality, and consciousness, they then achieve power over Black people. If personality, culture, values, and consciousness are gauges of power, they will use our consciousness, values, and culture as their power instruments. How does this work out in reality? Europeans will take our cultural products, our groups (PBW and BSPA), our music (theories), and our songs (stories) and use them as their instrument of power (APA's Letter of Apology) and benefit from them. So what does an African-centered consciousness look like operating under a white institutional organization with a history of oppression and racism? We begin to use African symbols under APA when there is nothing African about APA. When we compromise our values and consciousness to be regulated by other people, we become their instruments of power, and they will use us against ourselves. Some of our best and brightest Black intellect (who have access to up-and-coming emergent Black scholars and intellectuals in the field) would choose to be affiliated with an organization that admitted to a plethora of discriminatory and biased practices in its history that harmed the Black community. I am reminded of a powerful expose of a young up-and-coming emergent scholar when she was a student; the young sista Gadsen said,

> *"I found a language to communicate and articulate my barriers and challenges as a Black doctoral student. I was introduced to readings in Black feminist thought and Black psychology that helped me understand how I was viewed as a Black woman and an African person. I learned more about the meaning of working harder and still being treated as less competent than my White peers...Navigating through a PWI has been a taxing and, at times, hostile journey for me. Similar to my experience, many Black students at PWIs have reported experiences of chronic implicit and hostile racism, and isolation."*

Her words speak volumes about why we would create a subdivision of the Psychology of Black Women. Now, they may have begun establishing an African/Black Psychology sub-division within APA. This makes no sense. *"[some] Black people still don't get it."* You have failed to create an image of empowerment for our upcoming scholars. Chancellor Williams identifies this "View from the Bridge" as a grim expectation for Black empowerment and liberation when he stated back in 1987,

> *"For white people, still masters in the world do not have to yield...The Negroe drive to be with the whites in every situation is equaled by the white determination to prevent it. Yet the whites must truly feel a deep sense of pride in seeing this Negro leadership so clearly validating their own belief in white superiority. Their pretended "Quality of Education" objective actually collapse under the wheels of busses for "racial balance."...Here we have, **Within the race**, the intolerable situation of an anti-black group proclaiming the race's inherent inferiority more effectively than the whites ever could, precisely because this group is regarded as "black."*

As a budding young scientist, her involvement with ABPSi has led her to recognize how "Black feminist thought epistemology centers the sovereignty of Black women, voicing their history and struggles to empower, heal, and resist oppression...the miseducation of African people in psychology...the obtainment of this knowledge demands action in voicing and dismantling Black oppression." At least this young, dynamic scholar gets it where she admits, "Black women at PWIs have explicitly reported daily gendered racial microaggressions, such as experiencing projected stereotypes of the angry and strong Black women, being silenced and marginalized, being sexually objectified, and receiving assumptions of their beauty." Psychologically speaking, how do you ignore the collective consciousness of the oppressed and still believe that the oppressor is the best fit for you to operate as a sub-organization? Why are we quick to revert to European/Western thought and rule? Come home to ABPSi!

White supremacy is deep!

We still go to the oppressor to affirm our Blackness to prove who we are. Just having proximity to white people does not make you more valuable or solidify your beingness. What has this pseudo-association done for the Black mental health of the Black community? What we do know is that APA "...acknowled[ed] psychology's role in creating, perpetuating, and failing to challenge racism and the harms that have been inflicted on communities of color as a result...psychologists understand that racial inequities result from laws, systems, policies, practices, and cultural narratives that reflect racial bias and White supremacist ideology and that psychology has an important role and responsibility to disarm and dismantle racism in all its forms. Since its origins as a scientific discipline in the mid-19th century, psychology has, through acts of commission and omission, caused great harm to communities of color..." How do some of our best and brightest keep running to the master oppressor for freedom? The same questions apply. What are we afraid of? Are we afraid of losing our investments with white institutions? Are we afraid of bargaining and leveraging our Blackness for true liberation and empowerment for the entire African community? Is the social currency of being around and under whiteness, white organizations, and white connections more important than liberating the African mind and the African community? Like the proverb - - *"The freedom that comes from ignorance enslaves the one who entertains it."* In the words of Frances Cress-Welsing, "If you don't understand white supremacy, then everything you think you know will only confuse you." Our consciousness has been abducted, and *"[some] Black people still don't get it."* Come home to ABPSi!

When APA came out with their false apology to communities of color, admitting that they have neglected and weaponized psychology against the Black community, the question is: What has the APA done to make Black lives better? Has APA gone public by going to the mountaintop and telling the world how they will carve out reparations to the Black community for the damage they have done? How has the PBW under the APA made the Black community a healthier, safer, and empowered community? The inaugural PBW conference under APA is blatant hijacking and thievery of black consciousness. The mere fact of this group using African symbolism in their inaugural conference is a false sense of identity. Being under a white organizational structure in the name of Black women's empowerment can be construed as a false sense of security. Essentially, what was done and conveyed was to provide a space for black conversation so they would not have to listen to our brilliant Black women discuss our issues. Can you call yourself a conscious and empowered organization if you use the same structure and function as your oppressor? Questions remain: Who are you afraid of? You can't be scared of your people (ABPsi)! What has this *pseudo-association* done for the black community since the Black Lives Matter (BLM) movement? What has this *pseudo-association* done for the Black community since their 'false' apology to the Black community? Are you more willing to fight for creating a Black identity under white spaces and for psychology that does not reflect us, your group of affiliation, your Blackness being the majority for the intersectionality of your other *identities*? Are we afraid of losing our investments with the white community? Are we afraid of bargaining and leveraging our Blackness? Are the social currency of being around and under whiteness, white organizations, and white connections more important than liberating the African community? The epitome of an African woman scientist is

Zora Neal-Hurston, an anthropologist who stated, *"The life of [Africans] is far more entertaining than that of the letters in a typewriter. Go hard or go home."* As the African proverb states, *"The freedom that comes from ignorance enslaves the one who entertains it,"* and yet *"[Some] Black people still don't get it."* Come home to ABPSi!

ABPSi vs. APA (Pseudo Association) is analogous to Negro Leagues vs. Major Leagues. This pseudo-association takes some of our most talented people, upholds them, places them on pedestals to placate their consciousness of success, and gives them a false sense of power as a reward. Not all come with this level of ignorance. An emergent scholar I am proud of, a former student of mine, Oba Woodyard, eloquently revealed, "the quest toward the liberation of the African mind requires a critical exploration and immersion into the reservoir of deep African thought." This young man shows great understanding and insight as an emergent African scholar in psychology in his knowing that the "exploration and pursuit of the deepest water [thought], in order to understand and determine what it will take to reconstruct the fragmented African self...is the art of the regenerating power of *kinkete mu dikitisa ngolo* as extolled by Fu-Kiau...as this collective or communal process is intended to restore the [African's] [conscious energy (ngolo zasikama)] or life force and promotes a self-conscious transformation of the social reality through social and political struggle." The real power is making our communities and families whole, having them use their sense of agency and advocacy, and recognizing their funds of knowledge. My real passion is creating a system of thought based on African meaning to the world. We need our best and brightest to come home. ABPSi is the premier international organization for the concern and welfare of all African people worldwide, including all identities (intersectionality included). How is it that our best and brightest keep running to the master for freedom? *"Black people still don't get it."* Much like the Parable of the Master and Servant:

> *But who is there among you, having a servant plowing or keeping sheep, that will say, when he comes in from the field, "Come immediately and sit down at the table," and will not instead tell him, "Prepare my supper, clothe yourself properly, and serve me, while I eat and drink. Afterward, you shall eat and drink"? Does he thank that servant because he did the things that were commanded? I think not. Even so, you also, when you have done all the things that are commanded you, say, "We are unworthy servants. We have done our duty."*
> — Luke 17:7-10

Guthrie's work shines a bright light on the contributions of black psychology activists and scholars. Still, it also reminds us of how much work has yet to be done in psychology and the service of racial equality. Come home to ABPSi! ABPSi is our Black space, with Black freedom for black creativity. We did not begin ABPSi to keep returning to "Another Pseudo Association" (*APA*) for black people. The Psychology of Black Women is rightfully part of the African/Black Psychology field and not the other way around. Man, this White supremacy is deep. It is so deep that you feel you *belong under* APA than *within* ABPSi. This book is to provoke black critical consciousness and, as a result, liberate ourselves from white rule, create a greater community for us as African people, and to operate from a power of Africanness and Blackness through real empowerment. Maybe you can leverage your connections with APA since they apologized for their misdeeds to advance African psychology, write letters of support to all 50 states for the Black licensing program, and support increasing the infrastructure of psychology programs at HBCUs. ABPSi is not a sub-organization, and African/Black psychology is not a subfield. It is a field of study that began thousands of years before the conception or inception of white psychology. We need to affirm ourselves based on our own accord. I find it shameful that we keep running right back to the same organization that disrespected, displaced, and disregarded black life and called ourselves free, empowered, or self-affirming.

Barbara Sizemore's message over 25 years ago reminded us then, "When it gets to the point the way we live becomes destructive and leads to our extermination in thought, mind, and body we need to take a long, serious look at culture, particularly the culture we are adopting. Culture should influence and nurture the mental, spiritual, and physical health of a people to recreate/procreate." Culture serves as a means and will for survival. For example, in the debate of Rap/Hip-Hop lyrics being used to convict Black artists, I heard an artist say, "My art is not a reflection of my character." We need to see that the art he is creating is the other's culture, the meme. Since art is the aesthetic demonstration of culture at the surface level we need to understand its impact and import to creating a culture that black has adopted. We interpret art, art captures a point in time and representation of history, and art subliminally and overtly conveys the meaning and characteristics of a culture. What culture is the rap artist referring to? What is the character of this rap artist? The same questions apply to PBW. This happens when you adopt the oppressor's culture with no political guidance. How do we call ourselves conscious if we keep using our oppressor's language and rules of engagement? We continue to be prone to demonstrating the Triangular Law of anti-African reality:

1. The law of (mis)knowing.
2. The law of (non)being.
3. The law of (un)doing when we follow the guides of the destructive culture.

A colleague revealed to me her apotheosis of understanding our challenge to teaching Black students, "I learned from The Black Teacher Project that prior to integration, 50% of Black professionals were teachers. Now 80% of public educators are white women. Black. males are needed in educational spaces, but they have to be more than Black. They have to come with the critical consciousness to educate Black males in a way that helps them navigate hostile spaces while claiming and defining their own identity and humanity. I would think the same is true for what mental health provides. It's not enough to "show up Black." You have to be equipped to engage in transformation."

Our reanalysis of culture, nature of being, personhood, and familyhood can cover a more profound comprehension and reveal a rich, hidden landscape we had not recognized before. Nevertheless, what is common among various African nations or communities is the centrality of the African spirit that comes from our cosmology, knowledge that comes out of our ontology, and an understanding of the human relationship to the world that comes from our axiology. Together the deep structural components represent the African Asili of Being in our diversity. Still, more importantly, this is what makes us powerful people with similar philosophical and cultural ways of knowing the world. This commitment to the Multidimensionality of who we are within our African spaces, communality, and mutual respect as African people demonstrates our love and fight for our need to exist together. *Black people, we need to get it!* Now is the time for black folk to get it! Black folk, please get it! Come home to ABPSi!

Cultural authenticity and Self-knowledge

How do we use our authentic cultural self to develop critical consciousness? We must first study the cultural artifacts of Africa. This knowledge comes from us learning the African way of being. In our reanalysis of culture, nature of being, personhood, and familyhood, we can cover a deeper comprehension and reveal a rich, hidden landscape we had not recognized before. We must set our standards for knowing. This standard of knowledge must reflect how we socialize our community to establish the correct way of being. What I know is that this is familiar. African wisdom has been around for thousands of years. There is nothing new under the sun. We must study our history and learn our way of being, but we need more than looking. We must operate from and within our cultural interest and image that reflects our profound cultural heritage. We must become immersed in living and social life and not live by white validation. Asa Hilliard provides us with the charge,

> "We have all that we need to do what is necessary. We can come to know what we need to know. We, however, must choose to do what is necessary and make the sacrifices that we need to make. Today, we have more resources, books, computers, etc. Still, we waste far more resources than we need to take care of the socialization requirements. Now is the time to save us. The struggle continues." (p. 54)

How do you claim to be conscious when using the same thought pattern of the oppressor? This book intends to combat the desire of Africans thinking in the same way as those they wish to be accepted by on their cultural terms. We need to operate out of our reality. What is the reality of Africans? African socialization is not dead. The sources of traditional African ways of existing in texts of ancient and contemporary times, oral traditions of elders, participants' observations, and nurturing and affirming African culture. The cultural wealth of Africans lies in our indigenous traditions as many of us still experience the world at a deep structural level. We must continue to rescue, reclaim and reconstruct the most viable aspects of our African culture.

"Practice without thought is blind; thought without practice is empty." Kwame Nkrumah (p.78)

The goal of becoming a critical thinker is to use it as a baseline of one's cultural standard. Black Critical consciousness is the examination of any subject matter from an African perspective. With an African mind and culture as the driving source, we can examine a thing in itself whose parts influence each other. This holistic approach to examination takes into account the wisdom of African people and the purposive use of knowledge. When examining issues and problems we must go back to the purpose for what is knowledge and wisdom from an African standpoint. When information is related to experiences and examined within the socialization of culture, this allows for connections that will shape thinking. The result leads to making explicit any contradictions that may exist. When history in its various contexts, personal, social, and political contexts are examined by the cultural framework that allows for synthesizing of cognitive and affective products. This provides for the development of critical consciousness. The practical application of such practices can be seen within the experiences of the community.

Use Within Classroom Instruction

To a critically conscious person, society is a human creation, which we can know and transform, not a mysterious whirl of events beyond understanding and intervention (Shor, 1992)

The first example describes an "in-process" research

dialogue inviting students to speak about their concerns in consciousness-raising group discussions. Once a problem or concern is identified then research should be divided into three separate areas: 1) on news and public data information versus movie and television; 2) identifying whose interests are being served; and 3) focusing previous questions into an action-oriented project. One must look at the power relationship between Europeans and Africans and question if that fundamental power relationship has changed at all. The role of the teacher is to strive for mastery of what they teach. Many terms reflect the role of teachers; "Jeli" or "Jelimuso" in West Africa, "Sba" and "Sesh" in ancient Kemet, and the "Jegna" in Ethiopia. As a Jegna these individuals meet the threshold for educational expectation for African students of a *"sense of excellence"* and *"sense appropriateness."* Attributes of Jegna are that they have gone through trials in war and struggles, they manifest warrior disposition, they demonstrate conscientiousness, and resolution to our people, they pledge to safeguard people, culture, and space, and always speak the truth. They can be deeply spiritual people and are members of families and the community.

As a Jegna it is my job to understand the problem posed and to empower students to come up with solutions from an African cultural context. To do this, the fundamental power relationship must transform the learner to take action on the problem and reflect critically on that action taken. Therefore, it is Jegna's job to challenge the students and resist conventional and fundamental relations of power....and address the specific social problems they have identified. For example, I am reminded of my time as the Assistant Director of the African American Student Affairs a.k.a. 'Black House' in a well-known university in the Midwest. The following email correspondence was found and reminded me of the type of Jegnaship provided by interrogating demands imaginative and real potential possibilities for human action:

"...[name student] said something yesterday that hit me. Throughout all the time that you were with us, you never failed to encourage us to get up and take action if we were displeased about something. That's exactly what we're doing now. Remembering your own advice is what is driving us now and it's what's going to help our voice be heard. "Be independent and get up and take action." Those are the words that we are remembering. You remember one thing too, Derek, and that's no matter what happens, we have your back."

Another example of demonstrating critical consciousness is teaching students how they should not take what is written as a fixed statement of history but examine between the lines what is and is not being said. For example, let's examine how critical consciousness can be developed within a classroom assignment. Students were asked to analyze that part of history about Christopher Columbus "discovering" America. Students not only had to scrutinize the language concerning how this piece of history was written, but they had to compare several historical texts and pull-out differing portrayals and perceptions. They were shown examples of how the word *discovered* was falsely used in the accounts of Christopher Columbus. If one were to discover a purse that was in use by someone else, could s/he claim this purse as hers/his without being called a thief? How could someone discover a habitable land and claim it for her/himself without being called a pirate or thief?

Critical consciousness began to rise as students were introduced to critical accounts of history by differing cultural perspectives about Christopher Columbus. An example of a different cultural perspective can be found in accounts presented by Native American Indians that included such information as Columbus taking Indians as slaves and selling them; ordering for the cutting off the hands of any Indian person not bringing in a three-month quota of gold; and, also, finding out that one particular island called Hispaniola had all of its habitants wiped out in forty years due to the Spanish invasion. These students had to synthesize what they had been taught (content) and who in our society would have an interest in this inaccurate portrayal (context). Their task was to rewrite this part of history virtually from their language. This was determined by students doing research on the collective text of the group (Native Americans) and creating a narrative of group experiences (minorities in this country) to help the students see any common positions they hold in this society.

This problem-posing task reveals elements of elaborative processing, connecting the content to the context. Before, some students would have cared less about who Columbus was and may not have made any significant connection to how this affected their lives (elaborative process). However, once students received various lessons of history from a culturally specific or critical evaluative paradigm then words like *discover* and *Columbus* took on very different meanings (elaborative process) and significance (deep process). This example reveals students questioning the narrative of a story and allows for different choices and speeches to manifest critical conscious development, which ultimately for them changed the meaning of the history of Columbus. This example exercised the complex powers of thought and avoided the passive transfer of information.

Seizing the Power of Experience

"Seizing the power of experience" was the theme used at a 1995 summer institute on "Educational Excellence of African American Students". The focus of the institute was to show the successes of teachers and school-site administrators who in their practice of culturally consistent education incorporated

and honored the knowledge and life experiences of their students. The organizing questions of the institute were:

What are some principles and practices of successful teachers of African students?

Why do educators need to know about and be involved in the community where their students live?

*How do we help African students recognize and value the knowledge and experiences they bring to the
classroom?*

What curricula materials are effective for African students?

*Why do African students consistently achieve educational excellence in some teachers' classrooms and not in
others?*

What has culture to do with it?

How does this translate to practical application within schooling, in particular, the development of critical consciousness? It was first determined that African American social practices set the tone for a social context within learning. For example, the practices of communalism and mutual aid can be translated into collaborative learning experiences (Hollins and Baba Nobles, 1995). As a result, high regard is placed on verbal astuteness, and public performance is embodied as representing acquired knowledge. Secondly, external support systems should reflect that of the extended family. Thirdly, the educational process is relationship-driven and determines the meaning of scholastic outcomes. Finally, governing the educational expectation and performance is that of a *"sense of excellence"* and *"sense of appropriateness"* for African American students.

Several studies were examined to determine how culturally patterned interactional style played an integral role in the educational performance of African American students. However, one study warrants special mention here for the fact that its style and structure of instruction/teaching resembled aspects of developing critical consciousness. What made it even more intriguing was the subject matter -- teaching high school algebra to students in middle school. This project was known as the Algebra Project. First, the central aspect of the project took the position that every child can achieve math literacy. Teachers become learners; the project mandated parental and community involvement and established the need to create a new learning environment for math. All parties were to become mathematically and scientifically literate by learning algebra in the same fashion as they would seek political power. Akoto mentions that "problem-solving and inquiry skills in math and science can be developed using social, historical, or technical situations that involve Afrikan people (p. 334)." The infusion of political dimension was evident within this project.

Students were to move from the familiar to the symbolic representation of mathematics. Step one introduced students to a new concept by engaging them in a familiar physical event to which they asked questions they knew they had the answers to. The purpose of this was to provide the basis for which they could reconnect and assimilate concepts and unfold complex arguments when moving toward consciousness. This allowed them to actively link the physical world to the abstractions of mathematics.

The next steps in the process are designed to increase the students' consciousness and mastery of concepts. The second step of making pictures to integrate the humanities demonstrates the relationships between mathematics and other forms of knowledge. This next step moved students to express the problem in their own language, in a less than formal communication style. This complexity required the individual to integrate information and elaborate on key points within their own language of communication. The Algebra Project believed that the students' language is an important resource, particularly for Black students. The fourth step is designed to help students express the physical event with an emphasis on using mathematical language; and finally, the fifth step introduces to students' mathematical symbols. Throughout the process, students came to recognize that mathematical symbols were created just as they had done to represent physical events.

These types of challenges to students develop high-ordered knowledge and skills. Becoming aware of the cultural resources that students bring with them bridges the process toward critical consciousness. The goal of empowering education is to have students share responsibility and authority for their learning. There was a certain point as I began to teach that I realized that education itself is therapeutic. Another example of developing and demonstrating critical consciousness has been shown through mural projects. Mural projects can be interdisciplinary blended between art and history; the goal is to give students an opportunity to cooperate in the creation of change in their community. Students can make a community mural devoted to groups often left out of history or given minimal recognition in traditional course syllabi. Mural projects are often begun with a problem-posing dialogue; students are given sources of historical information to consult about forgotten groups, people, and events. After the project, there is a process of discussion that takes place for students to reflect on the project itself -- a collective summary after each cooperative learning exercise.

Thus far these outlines offer students self-development in a cooperative and critical process. To think critically in this framework means to examine deep meanings, personal implications, and social consequences of any knowledge, theme, technique, text, or material. Critical thought about any subject reveals its internal structure and its connections to self and society. This in-depth scrutiny is research.

CLOSING

Cultural action in a classroom is unlike political action in an organization or movement. A classroom in a school or college is rarely a self-selected group seeking social change (Shor, 1992). One must understand the workings of that culture to understand the basis or foundation of a sociopolitical environment or its need to change. Through the orientation and manifestations of culture, the sociopolitical structure is revealed. Likewise, the sociopolitical structure is geared to protect the culture from which it germinates. Society does not place education as the center of power, but education is infused with a critical paradigm that can affect power. The critical paradigm respects the knowledge, experience, and language of students. The grasp of clarity of power relationships within a society catalyzes creating social action and social change; this provides the making of critical consciousness.

This paper connects critical consciousness with culture, learning processes, and group consciousness. However, since critical consciousness embodies both cognitive functions and affective states, the conception of learning, cognitive, and knowledge acquisition style provided us with meaningful interpretations. Now, empirical science must foster the need to support this type of research. Research is needed to clarify ways to establish a framework for examining the development of critical consciousness. As Freire states, "[i]f men are unable to critically perceive the themes of their time, men cannot perceive contradictions within their society."

Finally, this would not be complete without a critique of the origin of critical consciousness itself. Although the effort of writing this paper seems gallant, in the research of critical consciousness, it became clear that all theories emanate from a cultural epistemological framework. All theories must and will undergo some scrutiny of their own.

One critic identified the fallacy of creating a universally accepted Eurocentric theory. With no disrespect to the father of critical consciousness, Freire maintains a Marxist position, and his analysis limits issues related to culture and race. Freire's profound wisdom and understanding of culture provide no room for ethnic or cultural features as a part of developing critical consciousness. The insight here could be that the issue of race as a nationality construct does not exist in Brazil and other countries as it does here in the States. This lack of insight does not allow for an accurate assessment of the sociopolitical structure. These factors shape society's social interactions, relations, and structure.

Freire posits the acquisition of knowledge based on the "man-object" relation, insisting that critical thought only occurs through reflection. Akoto states, "he fails to acknowledge or factor into his theory the rich, varied, and vigorous cultural elements of identity for Afrikan Brazilians, who represent more than 50% of the population (p. 324)." Linking power struggles of European-colonized culture to indigenous ethnic/racial cultures counters Freire's view that national culture determines national existence. We must fight against cultural imperialism, scientific colonialism, and cultural co-option in our struggle for cultural authenticity. Black social scientists have been co-opted to work with agencies that do not serve the interests of the black community. If African culture is not attended to or not part and parcel of a political struggle, then liberation and empowerment have no value or vitality. Cultures may be transformed from within by the dialectics of their elements. We must understand how indigenous African culture has been co-opted, interrupted, and arrested by European white suprema-cists' cultural and political means. The cultural struggle is part of the political struggle. Once we grasp the profound agency in African culture of song, dance, and drum, the political struggle occurs when Africans have to write in the language of their oppressors: Who are they writing for?

VII

Evaluation of a Black Manhood Training and Development Program - The Importance of a Culturally Consistent Curriculum

Abstract

This research examined the effectiveness of the HAWK Federation Manhood Training and Development program in instilling an African-centered sense of Black manhood responsibility and character in African-American adolescent males. The three primary objectives of the HAWK Federation program were to develop cultural competence, cultural confidence, and cultural consciousness in young African-American males. Specifically, this study evaluated to what degree the HAWK program enhances African-centered cultural "values and consciousness" within African-American adolescent males.

Cultural values and consciousness in this context refer to the person's awareness of his African-centered cultural identity concerning his racial and personal identity, his purpose in life, and his path to success as an African-American male. It was hypothesized that African-American adolescent males who participated in the HAWK manhood training program experience would increase their African-centered cultural values and African self-consciousness along with their school performance [GPA and citizenship (CIT)]. The subjects consisted of 61 African-American males, 11-14 years old, 30 in the HAWK group, and 31 in the control group. The research employed a pre-test post-test assessment design using the African-centered values scale (ACVS) and the African self-consciousness scale (ASCS) to measure the rate of change in African-centered cultural values and cultural consciousness within these subjects. School grade reports were collected to measure changes in GPA and CIT. A pre-test assessment consisting of the ASC and ACV scales were administered to both groups before the start of the HAWK program. Subjects in the HAWK program went through 14 weeks of Manhood training. After fourteen weeks, both groups received a post-test assessment to measure what changes had taken place regarding their cultural values and consciousness. Pre-post GPA and citizenship measurements were also taken to determine whether there was a relationship between the HAWK program, cultural values, consciousness, and school performance. Results indicated that the HAWK program manhood training and development did increase ACVS, ASCS, GPA, and CIT performance. Correlational analysis revealed significant positive relationships between the HAWK experience and change scores for ASCS ($r = .4096$, $p < .001$), GPA ($r = .4630$, $p < .000$), and CIT ($r = .3893$, $p < .004$). However, there were no correlations between the ACVS and ASCS with GPA and CIT, thus, the change in GPA and CIT cannot be explained or accounted for due to increases in ACVS and ASCS scores. T-test and analysis of variance revealed that the subjects in the HAWK program experienced significant increases in ASCS, GPA, and CIT change scores over control group subjects. When pre-test and post-test differences in ACVS scores between the HAWK group and control group subjects were taken into account by way of paired sample t-test analysis, significant change scores for HAWK subject's ACVS over control subjects were observed. Analysis of covariance revealed an interaction in that the older subjects who participated in the HAWK program experienced significant increases in ACVS scores than the older subjects in the control group ($p<.034$). It was concluded that manhood training and development appears to represent a viable option as an intervention strategy to address the needs of African-American adolescent males and should be more widely instituted. Future evaluation research should incorporate a non-cultural African-American mentoring program as a comparison (control) group and identify culturally specific behavioral outcome measures to further examine the effectiveness of the HAWK program. Linking the training to existing cultural measures would bring greater clarity to the efficacy of culturally centered programs for African-Americans. Furthermore, we must begin to develop, identify and utilize more appropriate culturally-centered assessments/behavioral outcomes measures when studying African-centered Rites of passage programs.

INTRODUCTION

A significant difficulty for African-American male adolescents is that they are confused about who they are and where they are going. On the one hand, they seem to have unconsciously accepted the notion that "racism is dead," yet they are confronted with the same "real" inequality which faced their parents and grandparents. The myth-makers are popularizing the notion that things have become, and are becoming, better for African-Americans; on the other hand, there is the stark reality of unemployment, poverty, and inequality. As a result of the actual material conditions and the unreal illusions of progress, African-Americans males are becoming confused about what values to transmit to the younger generations. Already there is a subtle shift in value orientations among African-Americans. The society's masculine archetype is also that which has done the most harm. Yet it is often presented as the one model Black males must emulate in order to be successful or be recognized as human.

When young Black males reject White supremacist patriarchy, they are showing the presence of critical consciousness. But what becomes their North Star? Who guides them on the path? It is the work of those who guide them, to t to develop an understanding of masculinity that centers them. When this happens, those young men begin to life sustaining choices. They want to do more than survive. They want their families and communities to thrive.

The contemporary plight of young Black males in America rests on their race and gender while growing up in America. Latimer, in Emerge Magazine (1995, October), captures a mother's expression of her fears for her two sons: "Because of their race, because of their gender, my little boys are at risk of being beaten senseless by cops who act first and ask for identification later; of being run down in traffic to flee a mob in a White suburb; of being shot point-blank, stripped of their belongings and left to die, victims of some impulsive adolescent act. These are the kinds of things that have happened - and are happening - to young African-American males today. If you're a mother of a Black boy, you know the fear" (p. 38).

As stated directly and succinctly in Emerge Magazine (Latimer, 1995), "Much of the violence threatening inner-city youth and those "sheltered" in the suburbs is the result of poverty, crack cocaine and big drug money, the easy availability of guns and seemingly nonstop violence in the media and some homes" (p.41). The conditions hindering young African-American people persist and fester even when policymakers have the means to address them. The social maladies have had a detrimental effect on the development of young African-American males.

A greater encumbrance in the development of positive young African-American males is their awry sense of manhood. Many inner-city youths feel that they can consummate they're a man by joining violent gangs, participating in criminal activities, or by making a girl pregnant (Robert Hill, 1988). This icon of manhood is perpetuated widely by shows on TV and in the movies that glamorize crime, drugs, and sex. Moreover, societal norms make it acceptable for men to be unfaithful to women, but not vice versa, thus making the models which establish masculine attitudes for most African-American males today very negative and anti-female. Consequently, women's attitudes have responded in an anti-male position. Similarly, African-American males' lack of self-worth is a cogent factor for lacking certain academic skills and job skills. Further affecting the future of the African-American community, family, and relations.

American society does not place value on African-American males. As a result, African-American men must show young African-American males how to become more confident, competent, and conscious to be successful. Implementing manhood training would convince young African-American males that they have a future and that their life has meaning. Furthermore, African-American men must teach African-American boys how to be men and bear the cross of being African-American men (Monroe, 1995). Monroe (1995) captures this essence in a simple phrase from an African-American male, "I am Black, and I love my culture." (p. 28)

REVIEW OF THE LITERATURE

Manhood training and development aim to provide a relevant intervention/prevention strategy to address the problems experienced by young African-American males while simultaneously reflecting the historical and cultural integrity of the African and African-American communities, according to Nobles (1989). But not all Black male training programs take such an approach. Some of the earliest interest displayed in this area was during the 1960s when George Henderson (1967) found that African-American males in lower socioeconomic areas required more positive role models to be motivated and inspired to seek middle-class goals. Issues of identification, pro-social behavior patterns, and educational/occupational aspirations seemed to impede and/or stifle the progress/development towards success for the lower socioeconomic class of African-American males he studied. However, Henderson did not see the importance of providing African-American male role models as the critical factor for identification and success.

Contemporary scholar Ronald Taylor (1989) identified that the research done by Bandura and Walters (1963; Bandura, 1969, 1971) revealed a significant relationship between identity, acceptance, and role models. Bandura (1969, 1971) mentioned that acceptance and identification with role models do not occur at random but serve purposely to assuage the child as he relates to his personal and social characteristics while serving to facilitate the functional utility, attributes, and resources of the model. This early insight into what is appropriate role modeling suggests that young African-American males would tend to look toward older African-American males for images to imitate and adopt. Henderson did not believe racial identity acceptance would impact male role modeling for young African-American males. However, his findings suggest otherwise.

Henderson (1967) pointed out that those males who attained "successful" status did so by continuing to function as members of their cultural group, experiencing fewer adjustment problems than those who strayed away. This suggests that young African-American males who had an older African-American male involved in guiding and directing them toward more lofty goals proved to be an essential factor in their success. Thus, the need for African-American male involvement is deemed essential by this author when advising and instructing young African-American males toward success.

In looking at "success" for African-American adolescents, it becomes imperative for them to understand that operating successfully within the dominant European-American culture or "other" social environments may depend, to some extent, on their strength and/or desire not to displace their cultural integrity (George Henderson, 1967). Staying in touch with one's indigenous cultural/racial identity has been shown to serve more excellent value towards success than replacing and adopting a foreign cultural identity and values. This further suggests that an in-tack cultural identity serves to buffer any cultural/racial identity conflicts that are bound to occur. Suppose success is tied to a connection of racial identity. In that case, some questions to be answered are how does race influence self-esteem and self-identity/self-concept, and what role does it play towards the development and maintenance of success? Does self-esteem exist outside of a racial identity reference point, and at what point are African-American males vulnerable?

It has been noted that the academic vulnerability of African-American males begins around the fourth grade (Kunjufu, 1985). Jawanza Kunjufu (1985) identifies this as the fourth-grade syndrome, where young African-American males' learning environment changes rapidly. African-American children who were once eager to learn in a collaborative environment are forced to adapt to an individualistic and competitive social learning environment. This has profoundly affected the self-esteem of young African-American males (Spencer, 1991). Thus, mentorship programs should serve as a preventive intervention strategy in addressing the issue of self-esteem in vulnerable African-American males.

Margaret Beale Spencer (1991) studied self-esteem among African-American youth between 7-9 years of age. She found that African-American males exhibited more sporadic changes within various dimensions of self-esteem (e.g., student and intellectual self) than African-American females. It was noted that while self-esteem in African-American males increased with age, these identical boys saw themselves as less competent as students compared to African-American girls (Spencer, 1991). She asserts that societal factors complicate the development of African-American youth by forcing them to integrate the reality of racism and its effect on their biological, behavioral, and personal identity.

In other words, Spencer concluded that as males in American society, African-American boys adopt conflicting messages of manhood by portraying themselves as aggressive by nature, competitive and domineering, and independent and autonomous. Thereby, the role of male mentoring programs should nurture young African-American males to effectively discern appropriate attitudes and beliefs about what it means to be an African-American male. Not those previously described, and to positively affect the youth's overall self-esteem.

Courtland Lee (1991) points out that young African-American males in contemporary American society face significant challenges to their development and well-being. Social, cultural, and academic forces have combined to keep African-American males from assuming traditional masculine roles. Empowerment interventions for young African- American males must therefore consider African and African-American culture and its crucial role in socialization.

Festus Obiakor (1990) noted that the success or failure

of African-American children in school had been attributed to positive or negative self-concepts. He argues, however, that the construct of self-concept has been misused and misrepresented by educators and researchers. The traditional self-concept definition is based on the perception of the dominant society. The Emerge magazine article cited earlier purports that this would hold to be true, "There is an image that African-American males are threatening, that they're dangerous, and that people don't want to come into contact with them." ((Monroe, 1995, p. 22). This popular consciousness or global conceptualization is dangerous for African-American males because misleading assessments and unjustified interpretations are developed around the African-American self-concept (Obiakor, 1990). Young African-American men must be introduced to an operational concept of self-concept via qualities, attributes, attitudes, and responsibilities of becoming a man (Obiakor, 1990).

In African tradition, for example, male roles included different rituals at certain stages toward achieving manhood status (Nzenga Warfield-Coppock, 1992). According to African scholars, all people have four basic life stages (Mbiti, 1970; Nobles and Goddard, 1990, p. 101; Warfield-Coppock, 1992). These stages are birth, puberty, marriage, and death. The initial stages of birth and childhood establish the importance of procreation and protection. The act of procreation was done within the confines of marriage. At the same time, protection provided both external and internal practices, as in observing certain customary restrictions, i.e., abstention from sex with a pregnant wife to providing adequate nourishment for the family (Mbiti, 1970; Nobles and Goddard, 1990). During the puberty and initiation stage, the male supervises boys' ceremonial practices. Their primary function is to provide educational rituals relating to manhood's social and spiritual responsibilities, i.e., initiation (Mbiti, 1970; Nobles and Goddard, 1990). In the marriage ritual, the male is to supervise and educate by approving the son's or daughter's choice, negotiating and facilitating the marriage contract, and educating the younger males on the responsibilities of marriage (Mbiti, 1970; Nobles and Goddard, 1990). Finally, in death and the hereafter stage, the male is to investigate the cause of illness for dying relatives, facilitate and prepare the grave-burial ritual and distribute belongings of the deceased (Mbiti, 1970; Nobles and Goddard, 1990; Warfield-Coppock, 1992).

When developing a social and organizational structure for the development of African-American male masculinity, it becomes vital that we become acquainted with an African cultural developmental praxis that, through its intentions, preserves and ensures the cultural integrity of those of African ascent. Within the African cosmological view, the whole is made up of interconnected parts. Jeff Morris (1994) utilizes Molefi Asante's (1989) model of African ideals, thoughts, and social conduct as a way for individuals to function within a concept of knowing (cosmology) that they are connected to a larger group. The group governs the social order establishing what is right or just conduct. This then teaches all those within that society what is just while incorporating values of interdependence and corporateness. African societies understood that, for a person to receive the right to participate in family or village decisions, the individual was to demonstrate that he could carry out the responsibilities of manhood (Oba T' Shaka, 1995). In the African tradition, values and beliefs needed to manifest through "just and right conduct."

Ayittey (1991) articulates that many studies of traditional African societies have shown kinship to be the articulating principle of social organization as a whole and the basis of social integration. The emphasis, on the whole, suggests that there is no separation between thought and conduct, individuals and others, and social institutions, i.e., family, school, and law. Social organization engulfs all institutions and/or units. This integration requires that individuals master within themselves rules, laws, and social order to facilitate one's development.

Kenyatta (1965) identified that within the tradition of the Gikuyu cultural system of East Africa, the development of character within individuals is formed within the family circle and then within the local group, and then within the whole tribal organization through a course of initiation ceremonies which gives them the process of character formation. He further states (1965) that "Growing boys learn that they have one thing to learn which sums up all others, and that is the manners and deportment proper to their station in the community." (p. 103).

Warfield- Coppock (1992) articulates that "initiation rites for African-Americans serve as a vehicle of instilling a strong, positive sense of self and achievement and returning a sense of empowerment to African-American families and communities." (p. 472). In addition, it was noted that initiation served to preserve values, customs, and behaviors to be passed down to the next generation. The function of rites of passage for the adolescent in traditional African society, then, served as a developmental and educational process instilling knowledge, responsibility, privilege, and duty to become a respected adult member within their society (Ayittey, 1991; Coppock, 1992; Hill, 1992; Kenyatta, 1965, and T' Shaka, 1995). It was further noted by Coppock (1992) that today's rites of passage programs began as an effort to provide African-American youth with cultural-based information to address needs that generally would not be addressed in public schools. However, a significant difference between the two is that rites programs focus on the whole person instead of one individual aspect (i.e., academic need) through a system that is based on traditional African cultural beliefs (Coppock, 1992). (This system includes rituals, ceremonies, celebrations, and skills training, all done secretly within these initiation rites.) The African philosophical belief system provides the direction and guidelines within the social organization for these African rites group.

Reclaiming and revitalizing rites of passage ensures that African-American adolescents' values, customs, and behaviors are appropriate for transition into adulthood. Coppock (1992) states, "Passage refers to the movement from one stage to another" (p. 472). Paul Hill (1991) speaks of these rites of passage as a proper way for boys to enter manhood. The ceremonial rite represents completion and mastery marked by agreed-upon standards, activities, tasks, and trials that each youth must complete to achieve the community-sanctioned status of "Manhood." Advancing this same argument, Courtland Lee (1992) discusses the importance of African-American manhood training to promote the adolescent transition from boyhood to manhood. A critical component of such training is obtaining respected elders in the community to serve as male role models for African-American youth.

In addition, Paul Hill (1992) identifies that the socialization process must consist of an orderly process of maturation that prepares youth for adulthood. Ancient culturing of an individual's character represents the ongoing transformation from the inferior, individualized, separate being to a more transcendent self. This transformation process, known in traditional African society as a rite of passage, preserves African social organization. Rites of passage, which resurrect the way of thinking and doing, must become part of the contemporary socialization transformative process. Within a transformation model of prevention/intervention for African-American males, manhood training and development should have measurable effects on increased educational achievement and social empowerment.

Nobles (1989) contends that the African-centered model of prevention is, by definition, a systematic process whereby one develops and/or stimulates the learner's knowledge, skills, ability, attitude, and character. This becomes necessary for the person to understand socially defined goal-oriented and culturally meaningful activities designed to

1. achieve mastery in all levels of human functioning,
2. make explicit one's personality in the objective world, and
3. validate one's self and kindness.

This can be seen as the general purpose of manhood training and development, but what is the primary purpose or function of manhood training and development?

The primary function of African-American manhood training and development is to provide young African-American males with an appropriately culturally centered education. This is done through the implementation of an African-centered curriculum. Frances Powell (1991) captures Asante's understanding of what an African-centered curriculum consists of in the following statement: "It is both a process that centers around the cultural heritage of African-Americans and the infusion of the content of African culture that is designed to stimulate and/or reinforce the growth and development of African mental and ethical traits." (p.1) This becomes critical because the existing American educational curriculum is overwhelmingly European-centered and insensitive to African-Americans, creating feelings of disconnectedness within African-American youth.

Jerome Harris (1992), another researcher in this area, argues that a culture of success for African-American students must be created for African-American students to succeed. He proposed the creation of a multicultural education infusing African-American history and culture throughout the curriculum. Harris (1992) states, "The majority of urban public schools demonstrates a historical culture of breeding negativism and racist assumptions that guarantees failure." (p.46). The current educational environment does not foster adequate development for African-American students. The goal of the implementation of an African-centered curriculum would be to develop positive and appropriate attitudes among African-American students. Harris (1992) states, "Immediate actions should take place since the problems of African-American students have reached such critical proportions" (p.47). Harris' understanding of the infusing culture and the historical experiences of African-Americans helps foster the urgency of instilling self-responsibility within African-American students.

In addition to the issues of culture and curriculum, Obiakor (1992) laid out the problems faced by African-American male youth at risk of failure in school as they confront many problems within mainstream society. African-American males are frequently misinformed, misdiagnosed, and improperly instructed (Obiakor, 1992). Problems facing at-risk young African-American males include (1) prevalence of single-parent households; (2) child abuse and neglect; (3) poverty and poor nutrition; (4) drug abuse; (5) complications of teenage pregnancy; (6) divorce and family breakdown; and (7) poor self-esteem (Obiakor, 1992). Society's response to this situation has been to blame the victims for poor progress in society. Furthermore, at-risk African-American youth face problems related to standardized tests administered by schools, negative assumptions about them by society, and a lack of culturally centered education.

New educational programs are attempting to meet the needs of African-American students. These new programs vary widely in approach, scope, content, and targeted age groups. However, the focus on helping African-American males speaks to the urgent need for manhood training and development. The support for such training is evident from the literature review.

Festus Obiakor (1991) discussed a program entitled

Project Self-Responsibility, an innovative approach to teaching at-risk African-American males to become more self-responsible, self-determined, self-reliant, and self-productive. This project consisted of 32 male subjects from three area schools who met the indicators of being educationally disadvantaged. These indicators include (1) a minority racial/ethnic group identity, (2) a poverty household, (3) a single-parent family, (4) a poorly educated mother/father/guardian, and (5) a non-English language background. Subjects were required to answer 24 open-ended questions about self-concept. The students met with trainers once every two weeks throughout the school year. An evaluation of the program indicated that no project student dropped out of school during the year and that students improved in decision-making skills, self-knowledge, responsibility, and social attitudes.

For young African-American males to perform according to an African-centered theory of manhood, certain rituals should be infused into the curriculum. The importance of infusing certain rituals serves to carry out the intentions of the culture they operate. This becomes essential in laying a foundation for a more precise self-concept than what has been displayed by African-American youth. One such ritual is to ask oneself fundamental questions of identity, such as, Who am I? Where am I going? And, Am I all I ought to be? These questions should lead to a self-discovery-leadership dialect (Tobias, 1989). Such explorations could enable youngsters to accept their strengths and weaknesses, develop self-confidence, build positive self-images, and ultimately aspire toward leadership roles.

The culturally centered African male approach should create sound development in character and social skills in young African-American males. According to Nobles (1989), the mission of manhood training is to develop each young man:

1. Something which he can do exceptionally well (competence)

2. A belief that whatever the task, he can be successful at it (confidence)

3. An awareness of his personal and moral responsibility of who he is for the future continuation of his greatness (consciousness)

The goal of manhood development derives from the philosophical assumption of the African educational process of "transformation." The notion of "transformation," going from one of not knowing to one who knows (Nobles, 1989), gives insights into how particular attitudes are governed based on an African educational process. Within this process, African-American males' attitudes develop their insight or consciousness, creating a change in behavior from their previous state.

Nobles (1989) asserts that the primary goal of manhood training and development of African-American adolescent males is to direct such youths to seek perfection within themselves. Nobles (1989) states that the foundation of such commitment is governed by African cultural precepts (e.g.., MAAT, Ancient African Principles of Initiatory Mastery, and Codes of Proper Conduct and Character) serving as an ethos or guiding principles to help shape and direct conduct for young men.

The author identified literature on the foundation for African manhood characteristics in this review. That formulation is African culture, philosophy, and worldview. Nsenga Warfield- Coppock (1990) points out that African philosophy refers to the general principles of conduct, thought, knowledge, and the nature of the universe, which serve as an entire belief system for people of African ascent. This whole belief system identifies how the survival maintenance of the group is to be carried out. Warfield-Coppock (1990) mentions that Noble's construct of ethos identifies African philosophy as survival of the tribe, oneness with nature, and responsibility to the community. This establishes how Africans view the world in which they live.

The suggestion here is that worldview shapes the thinking,

attitude, and behavior of one's existence. To understand worldview, one must be an understanding of culture. Nobles' (1986) definition of culture proposes that culture consists of ideas, behaviors, languages, traditions, customs, rituals, and practices designed for sustaining the survival maintenance of the group; culture gives people a general design for living and ways for interpreting their reality. The axiom is that nothing happens outside of culture. Therefore, it must be understood that different cultural values form different worldviews for different races. Kambon (1992) outlined some basic assumptions about culture and race as follows:

1. Each culture develops its own particular view of the world or approach to reality, which is equivalent to worldview;
2. Worldview naturally evolves from and reinforces the "survival maintenance" of the culture;
3. Culture varies with race such that different racial groups generate different cultures peculiar to their group's distinct experiential realities;
4. There are fundamental differences between the African and European Worldviews;
5. Under "normal-natural" conditions, Africans function in terms of the African Worldview and Europeans function in terms of the European worldview, and finally;
6. Any substantive deviations from these normal-natural relationships reflect unnaturalness and abnormalcy (p.2-3).

The above assumptions imply that it is normal and correct for one to operate from his /her cultural referent. For people of African ascent, an optimal functioning level can only occur by operating from African Cultural schema or standards. African and European worldviews differ. What is optimal within a European context may not have particular relevance within an African context (Kambon, 1992).

What is the operating force that establishes African manhood characteristics? To establish proper manhood characteristics and attributes for adolescents, first, we must understand how culture plays a unique role in the socialization of adolescents. Nobles' (1985) idea of cultural structure infused with Marimba Ani's (1994) scheme of the ideational infrastructure of cultural systems provides excellent insight for developing a schematic cultural theme. This author has titled the infusion "Nobles-Ani Cultural Schema."

Table 1

NOBLES - ANI CULTURAL SCHEMA by DJW

Cultural (Orientation) Manifestations

Level 3

UTAMAROHO	BEHAVIORS	ATTITUDES	VALUES
Dictates:			
The vital force or			
conscious energy		Ideas, Language, Symbols, Rituals, Inventions, Mores	
(ngolo zasikama)		Traditions, Ceremonies, Customs, Beliefs and	
Practices			
force set in motion			
by *"collective behaviors"*			
of members in a particular group			

Cultural (Template) Aspects

Level 2

UTAMAWAZO	ETHOS	WORLDVIEW	IDEOLOGY
Explains:			
Cultural structured	Set of guiding	Comprehensive	Ideational basis of
thought pattern	principles	ideas about order	conduct
by members of			
particular groups			

Cultural (Core) Factors

Level 1

ASILI	ONTOLOGY	COSMOLOGY	AXIOLOGY
Determines:			
developmental	Nature of Being	Origin/ structure	Primary
character of	(essence)	of universe	universal
"germ/seed" of a			relations
cultural essence			

Viewing this model from a step ladder approach, we will identify proper manifestations of African cultural intentions within manhood training. Ani's (1994) *Asili* (Core) is the cohered developmental "germ or seed" of cultural essence. Nobles' (1985) deep-level cultural factors are ontological, cosmological, and axiological. The *Utamawazo* (Ani, 1994) is explained as a cultural structure of "thought patterns" by members of a particular group (template). This comprises the aspects of culture (Nobles, 1985) of ethos, ideology, and worldview. Finally, *Utamaroho* (Ani, 1994) is the vital force or *ngolo zasikama* (conscious energy) source set in motion by the "collective behaviors" of members in a particular group (orientation). Nobles (1985) sees these "collective behaviors" as the overt expression of a people's culture. These expressions are cultural manifestations exhibited through behaviors, attitudes, values, practices, rituals, and customs.

All theory is the offspring of observation, experience, and reasoning (Morris, 1994). The theory driving African Manhood development is centered within the African cultural schema (Asili). Ani (1994) identifies Asili as our reference point, which explains cultural phenomena within the context of a specific cultural tradition. The traditions of African people are based on the philosophy that everyone and everything existing within the universe come from the same essence or spirit relating to each (an interconnectedness). The concept of African manhood is further developed through principles, ideas, and conduct (Utamawazo). Utamawazo, much like worldview, emphasizes how particular groups view themselves within the world. This is the thrust for which ideas about group survival are determined (Coppock, 1990). Therefore, African-American Manhood training should define and reinforce African cultural identity, consciousness, and values. The Utamaroho (spirit force) regenerates and carries out the cultural intentions specific to different cultural groups. The Utamaroho is the manifestation of the collective group by which behavior, ideas, and more are created. Within Black manhood training and development, the practice of traditional customs (i.e., reverence to ancestors), ceremonies (naming and rites of passage), and rituals (libation), are all designed to influence the consciousness and values of African-American adolescent males. This, in turn, refuels the Asili to keep the cultural schema in constant motion. The aforementioned cultural schema sets the foundation for appropriate Black Manhood Characteristics within manhood training. Therefore, what establishes African Manhood is the *Asili* (core factors), *Utamawazo* (aspects/templates), and *Utamaroho* (manifestations/orientation). This determines what attitudes, behavior, and conduct are for Black manhood.

Table 2

Comparing Cosmological *(Asili)* Schema
to Appropriate Black Manhood Characteristics

characteristics	African Worldview characteristics	African Manhood
Utamawazo	Oneness/Harmony with Nature	Balance to opposite sex
Ethos	Survival of the group	Procreation
	Inclusive/Synthesis	Synergistic
	Cooperation/Collectivity	Unity of Being
	Responsibility	Cultural traditions
Utamaroho	Corporateness/Interdependence	Consubstantiation
Values and	Spiritualism/Transcendence	Transformation
Customs	Complimentarity/Understanding	Egalitarianism
	Groupness/Sameness	Communalistic
Psycho Behavior	Commonality	Originality
Modality	Religious	Veneration of Ancestors
	Humanistic	Compassion for life

>< >< >< >< >< >< >< >< >< >< >< >< >< >< >< >< >< >< >< >< >< >< ><

Very little research exists identifying African-centered values and their influence on behavior. However, one such study has been conducted in this area. Belgrave (1994) examined the relationship between African-centered values on self-esteem, African-American identity, and drug-related attitudes in 54 fifth graders attending public school. Her measures include The Children's African Value Scale, Children's African-American Identity Scale, Rosenberg Self-Esteem Scale, and Attitudes Towards Drug Scale. The results yielded that African-centered values were the only variable significantly related to explaining drug attitudes. Furthermore, a negative correlation occurred between African-centered values and the non-African-centered self-esteem scale. This would support the idea that African-centered values can influence adaptive functioning in other areas (Belgrave, 1994).

Since little research existed on programs connecting the impact of cultural values on behavior and attitudes, the author attempted to identify studies looking at the importance of adopting and utilizing African or African-American cultural values to improve their cultural awareness and instill positive self-concept within young African-American males. In addition, literature on the empowerment of African-American males to achieve academic success supported this research topic.

Kofi Lomotey (1989) conducted a study to determine what contributed to African students' academic achievements. The results revealed that when key people such as principals, teachers, and parents display qualities of

1. a strong commitment to African students' education,

2. a deep understanding of and compassion for their students, and

3. a sincere confidence in African-American children's ability to learn, the child's expectancy of academic achievement will be enhanced

These three qualities are centered on the purpose and role of African-centered education, curriculum, and rite of passage training.

Warfield-Coppock (1992) conducted a research survey of 20 Rites of passage programs in which respondents defined and analyzed their programs' success based on their goals and objectives. Parameters of program success were based on observable aspiration changes in the initiates' attitudes, relationships, and/or behavior. The major indicators of success were: improved cultural awareness and knowledge, more responsible behaviors, improved self-esteem, self-concept, socializing with peers, sense of maleness and femaleness, improved relationships with elders, and acceptable school behavior. It has been revealed that in contemporary times young African-American males are, in a sense engaging in rituals of passage. However, these rituals involve gangs who foster anti-social or criminal behavior by offering what most young people need: friendships, a sense of belonging, and bonding. Rites of passage programs are designed to address specific problems of young African-Americans. Self-identity and culture, for example, serve a crucial role within rites of passage programming.

Lawrence Gary (1992) identified several pertinent factors in the development of young African-American males. These factors included the need for a positive home environment, a transformation of peer group influences, and establishing goals early in life. Other factors include fostering racial pride and awareness, and using African cultural exposure and instruction to foster achievement, encourage a sense of self-control, and cultivate academic motivation and stamina. The need to motivate African-American males towards success within the academic arena stands out as one of the most important factors to look at.

In further developing this argument, Bernida Thompson (1992) introduced an eight-month program to motivate African-American boys toward excellence through an actively intense African-centered lesson plan. Along with this was the implementation of a male rites program club, which reinforced their integrity and potential of being a positive African-American male. The goal was to motivate African-American middle school males to strive for academic excellence. The results confirmed that African-centered, high-energy, and high-interest activities raise African-American male students' motivation for academic excellence in school.

The HAWK Manhood Development Program

A review of a previous HAWK Demonstration Project (Goddard, Nobles, and Wilson, 1993) highlighted the importance of continued evaluation of a culturally specific curriculum. The overall goal of this project was to increase African-American youth's knowledge about their cultural awareness and its impact on drug-related attitudes, sense of self-worth, Black manhood responsibility, and character. The target population for this project consisted of 60 African-American male youth (10-14 years) in Oakland, CA. Considered to be at risk for drug involvement. This program was designed to run three District-wide sites throughout Oakland. Participants were presented with an African-centered curriculum emphasizing African cultural precepts (e.g........., MAAT, Ancient African Principles of Initiatory Mastery, and Codes of Proper Conduct and Character). Pre-post-test results revealed the efficacy of an African-centered curriculum.

The participants involved in the program exhibited increases in their sense of self-worth. Data revealed that 80% felt they were important class members compared to 75% pre-tested. Also, participants' feelings of self-worth increased in that 87% of the youth said that their friends liked their ideas compared to 74% pre-tested, while 82% expressed that their classmates thought they had good ideas compared to 74% pre-tested. Furthermore, the participant's confidence level may have increased regarding their sense of competency. Nearly all of the youth (96%) believed that they could be trusted, compared to 84% in the pre-test. Regarding the performance context, 78% of youth indicated that they work best in a group setting compared to 54% pre-tested.

Post-test data indicated that participants were likelier to hold attitudes that reflected an African-centered value orientation. Ninety-four percent (94%) of the post-test group versus eighty percent (80%) of the pre-test indicated a feeling of social responsibility towards others of their race. 100% vs. 90% felt the importance of understanding the value of being Black. 100% vs. 85% felt proud when another Black person does well. 78% vs. 71% noted that their careers should contribute to their race. 100% vs. 88% felt that they could become anything they wanted. 42% vs. 53% said that personnel gain was more important than anything else. Lastly, 94% vs. 85% expressed the importance of respecting elders because they know more about life.

Regarding household responsibilities, 85% vs. 63% felt that children should help parents care for younger siblings. 100% vs. 73% felt that a person should support a needy relative. 100% vs. 90% expressed that children should help around the house in whatever way possible. Finally, 31% vs. 61% felt that their family had very little group spirit. These data would indicate that building a strong family establishes the foundation of moral character (Goddard, Nobles, and Wilson, 1993). The prediction is that African-centered values influence a youth's over-all quality of life.

Participants also indicated greater awareness and knowledge about Black manhood's responsibility and character. Regarding their belief in the greater good, 89%, compared to 71% of the youth, indicated that family needs should be considered more important than individual needs. Similarly, 94% vs. 85% felt that a person should help his parents with the support of his younger brothers and sisters; 100% vs. 73% would extend their support to relatives in general; and 100% vs. 68% felt they had an obligation to work cooperatively with their family.

The belief in the sanctity of the family further reflects a loyalty and obedience. Here 84% vs. 73% felt that children should always obey their parents; 100% vs. 88% felt that a person should always be loyal to their family.

Negative attitudes toward women decreased in post-test data compared to pre-test data. Post-test scores favored attitudes toward women in that 26% vs. 50% believe that women cannot manage their affairs without the help of a man. 47% vs. 74% believe that women are too suspicious of what men do when they are together. 42% vs. 58% believe women are set in their ways and cannot change. Lastly, 42% vs. 55% believe women demand too much love and reassurances. These atti-tudinal dispositions reflect a change in orientation toward women that sees them as capable of self-sufficiency and mastery of their destiny, less rigid and more flexible and independent in their relations (Goddard, Nobles, and Wilson, 1993). This represents an encouraging, non-sexist attitude towards women. When coupled with the attitudes about sexual responsibility, they represent a profile that could now result in a realigning of family values and a reduction of sexual exploitation and domination of women, which, in turn, could lead to less involvement in unsafe sex practices, and a decrease in risk-taking behavior (Goddard, Nobles and Wilson, 1993).

As mentioned earlier, the premise of this research followed the guidelines, objectives, and rationale of manhood training and development set forth by Dr. Wade Nobles' HAWK Federation Program (Nobles, 1989). This study aims to evaluate to what extent the HAWK program affects African-centered cultural values and consciousness of African-American adolescent males. Cultural values and consciousness are the person's awareness of his cultural identity concerning his racial and personal identity, his purpose in life, and his path to success as an African-American. The theoretical justification lies in the plethora of problems faced by African males, forcing us to look at prevention/ intervention programs geared specifically toward their needs. Manhood training, therefore, serves as a viable option for young African-American males. Nobles' (1989) HAWK Federation intentionally creates symbols, rituals, practices, and responsibilities to instill and reinforce positive attributes of Black manhood. As such, the HAWK Federation is designed to promote and improve African-American adolescents' cultural affirmation, behavior, African-centered values, and attitudes for self-motivation and empowerment toward social and school success.

Rationale for the Study

This research proposal examined the effectiveness of the HAWK Federation Manhood Training and Development program in enhancing cultural values and consciousness in African-American adolescent males. The growing problem for African-American adolescent males has increased regarding their education, psychological well-being (mental health), and crime. Within the State of Florida, for example, overall data suggest that there is an overwhelming dissatisfaction with the public school system. Data from the State of Florida Department of Education (Statistical Briefs, 1994) revealed that the African-American population participating in Florida public schools was 24.74% (504,619). As of February 1994, Leon County school district consisted of 36.81% (10,982) African-American students compared to 69% (17,989) White students. Between grades six to nine, total population estimates stood around 9,344, of which 3,324 (35%) were African-American students. However, alarming and staggering figures identified by the Exceptional Student Report revealed that African-American students made up 72% (250 out of 346) of those labeled "educable mentally handicapped." The majority of the students labeled "trainable mentally handicapped" were African-American (53% compared to 43% Whites), while half (51%) of those labeled "emotionally handicapped" were African-American students.

Students identified as "gifted" showed alarming rates in that only 6% (147 of 2,200) of African-American students were identified as compared to 93% (2,056) of Whites. What is suggested here is that only 147 out of a population of 11,000 African-American students were excelling in school. A student performance report from a middle school in Tallahassee, Florida, indicated that African-American students performed well below the national median for 8th-grade middle school students. Overall writing scores on expository and persuasive writing skills averaged 2.4. The scores range from a low of zero to a high of 6. African-American students' average score was 2.2 on both expository and persuasive writing skills. In reading, 29% of 136 African-American students tested scored above the national median score, while 71% of White students scored above the median. For mathematics, 25% of African-American students scored above the national median score compared to 53% of Whites. One can conclude that this school is a low-performance school concerning African-American students. Most alarming is that this situation is rampant throughout the entire school district. District-wide, White students' averages were higher than African-American students (70% and 27%, respectively) in reading and mathematics. Although no figures showed a breakdown by gender within race, it can be expected that African-American males disproportionately are affected by such staggering statistics presented (see Jones, 1989). It can also be expected that students who do not perform well in school are potentially more prone to participate in juvenile delinquent acts (Nobles, 1989; Latimer, 1995; Monroe, 1995).

Leon County has the ninth-largest African-American student population. Yet, it leads the State of Florida in the increase in juvenile felony crimes - up 241% (from 351 cases to 1,196) between 1982 and 1993, compared to a statewide gain of 95% as reported in the Juvenile Justice Executive Summary report (December 1993). Leon County also ranks number one in the State in the rate of juvenile arrests per 100,000 population. The arrest rate in the calendar year 1993 was 1,372.37 per 100,00 population (2,780 arrests versus a population of 202,570). The Executive Summary report also revealed that African-American adolescents have disproportionately higher percentages of arrests than any other group. African-American youth constitute only 32% (5,900) of the juvenile population as compared to 66% (12,172) of the White population, yet, African-American adolescents were charged with 69% (1,598 intake cases) of all crimes. A 1992 study by the Tallahassee police department showed that habitual juvenile offenders committed 56% of the severe crimes in Leon County. This helped to establish an intervention program targeting serious habitual offenders known as SHOCAP. Unfortunately, the SHOCAP program run by the Tallahassee police department consists of 30 participants, all (100%) of whom are African-American adolescent males.

Similarly, their Near-SHOCAP and Monitor SHO program contained some 78% (98 of 123) African-American adolescent males. African-American adolescent males are six times more likely to be arrested for juvenile crime than White youth. The Juvenile Justice Executive Summary stated that a severe weakness lies in prevention efforts that are not successful in measuring the effectiveness of prevention/intervention programs. Mostly, they do not know which programs reduce juvenile crime or delinquent behavior.

Thus, there is a great need to conduct evaluation research on programs concentrating on enhancing African-American adolescent males' cultural values and cultural consciousness to establish which effective preventive intervention strategies motivate African-American males to strive for success. This study examined the effects of a culturally centered prevention/intervention strategy on enhancing African-American males' cultural orientation, values, and consciousness levels. This research argues that African-centered cultural values and cultural consciousness should be critical factors in understanding African-American adolescent male behavior. In this context, African-centered cultural values and consciousness refer to the African-American adolescent's awareness of his cultural identity concerning his racial and personal identity, his purpose in life, and his path to success as an African-American male. The HAWK program is designed as an African-Centered developmental, educational program affecting African-American adolescent males' attitudes, values, and behavior by facilitating their acquisition of insight into their cultural competence, self-concept, discipline, and prosocial skills as young African-American males. In evaluating the effects of the HAWK program on cultural values and consciousness, we should identify how culturally-based programs impact the cultural consciousness of African-American adolescent males. This study will also provide insight into how such programming affects attitudes toward school achievement. The research model involved in this study is summarized in the following diagram, Figure 1.

Figure 1

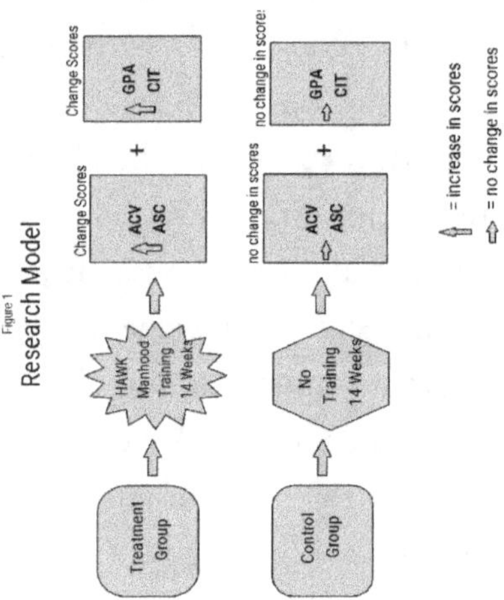

Hypotheses

The goal of this research was to evaluate the effectiveness of the HAWK Program in enhancing African-centered cultural values and consciousness in African adolescent males. If the program is successful, a positive shift on several relevant indicators should be observed. The hypotheses of the study were as follows:

H1: Participants in the HAWK program will manifest a greater increase in African-centered values than a control group as measured by an African-centered Values scale.

H2: Participants in the HAWK program will manifest a greater increase in their African self-consciousness than a control group as measured by the African Self-Consciousness scale.

H3: As African-centered values and African self-consciousness increase, academic performance will increase as measured by school grade reports.

H4: As African-centered values and African Self-consciousness increase, citizenship will increase as measured by school grade reports.

METHOD

Subjects

This study consisted of a total of 60 African-American males ranging in age from 11-14 years old. Thirty subjects were recruited and assigned to the treatment group, HAWK program participants. The second group of 30 subjects was recruited from local middle schools and comprised the control group. The subjects were similar in age and grade level, and it was suspected that the socioeconomic levels of both groups were similar. Considering the widespread underachievement of African-American students, we expect no significant difference in academic ability and performance between students recruited for the HAWK program and those selected from local middle schools. The general characteristics of youngsters participating in this study were students who would be considered at-risk for drop-out, academic underachievement, or those believed to need some type of extra help to behave more appropriately in the academic environment. Parents and school officials referred some students (e.g., counselors, advisors, and teachers), and some were recruited through informal outreach efforts. Participation in this study was voluntary based on parental consent.

Instruments

A pre-post-test interview protocol was administered to all subjects (both treatment and control groups). This consisted of the African-centered values scale and the African self-consciousness scale.

African-Centered Values Scale - This scale, developed by Nobles and Goddard (1996), is designed to assess the cultural values and attitudes of people of African ascent. The scale is comprised of 20 items responded to on a four-point Likert scale (Strongly Agree = 1 to Strongly Disagree = 4). Subjects responded to each item by checking a box from 1 to 4 according to the code. 13 items affirm an African value orientation and seven non-affirming items. An example of an affirming (positive) item is: "It is important for me to understand the importance and value of being Black." An example of a non-affirming (negative) item is: "What I do is my business and no one else's." The scores recorded on items affirming African values were scored as the reverse of their scale values. An example of a reverse scoring of an affirming African value scaled score was as follows: 1=4, 2=3, 3=2, and 4=1. The subject's score on the ACVS was computed by summing the weighted scores. All missing values were counted and then subtracted from the total scaled items. This produced the actual answered item sum which was then divided into the total sum score that produce the average mean score within each item. The average mean score was added to the sum of weighted scores to derive at the adjusted total score. Fortunately, there were no missing items within the sum scores. The theoretical range of scores is from 20 to 80 with the higher scores reflecting a stronger sense of African values. This procedure was completed for both pre and post-test scores. The derived change score was computed by subtracting the pre-test score from the post-test score. Subsequently, a median split was calculated from the frequency of scores to record negative or no-change and positive change scores. The administration time took approximately ten minutes for the subjects to complete this instrument. The reliability of the scale was determined through the split-half reliability method which generated a coefficient of r = .8910. The correlation between the ACV scale and the Child Rearing Preference Scale (CRPS) yielded a concurrent validity coefficient of .5721 (p < .001). The child Rearing Preference Scale (CRPS) assesses the extent to which parents engage in positive and adaptive behavior and respects the child as a significant person (Goddard and Nobles, forthcoming, 1995). Since the African value system is a family/child-centered system designed for the growth and development of the child, this instrument will be used to assess the rate of change in African-centered values across a three-month interval among these African-American youth.

The African Self-Consciousness Scale - This scale, developed by Baldwin and Bell (1985), is designed to assess the African-American personality construct of African self-consciousness (ASC). The ASCS scale is a 42-item personality questionnaire. The items alternate from negative to positive skewing for ASC. Odd-numbered items are negatively skewed or weighted, while even-numbered items are positively skewed or weighted. An example of an odd (negatively skewed) item is: "I have difficulty identifying with the culture of African people." An example of an even-numbered (positively skewed) item is: "Black children should be taught that they are African people at an early age." Even numbered items were scored by computing their scaled scores directly, whereas odd items were reversed before computing. For example, 1=8, 2=7, 3=6, etc. The subject's score on the ASCS is based on an average mean score per item. After reversing odd items all scored responses were summed. Then the sum of missing values was counted. Next, missing values were subtracted from the total items to make up for the number of answered responses. The answered responses were then divided into the total sum score to derive the overall mean of the scores. This procedure was completed for both pre and post-test scores. The derived change score was computed by subtracting the pre-test score from the post test score. Subsequently, a median split was conducted from the frequency of scores to record negative or no change and positive change scores. The administration of this scale took approximately twenty minutes for the subjects to complete. The correlation between the ASC scale and the Robert Williams' Black Personality Questionnaire yielded a convergent validity coefficient of r = .70, (p < .01). The test-retest reliability for the ASCS is .90. Factor analysis of the ASCS has generated a four-factor solution consistent with Baldwin's theory (Kambon, 1992). The four ASCS factors are as follows: (1) awareness and recognition of one's African identity and cultural heritage; (2) general ideological and activity prioritizing African survival, liberation, and affirmative development; (3) prioritizing self-knowledge and self-affirmation; and (4) resisting threats of anti-African forces. This instrument will be used to assess the rate of change in ASCS scores across a three-month interval among these African-American youths.

Design

This research employed a 2 x 2 pre-post-test design. The independent variables in the study consisted of two groups of subjects, the treatment group (HAWK program) and a control group, and age (11-12 and 13-14 years). The dependent variables consisted of the change scores from pre to post-test assessments on the following:

1. African-centered values scale scores;
2. African Self-Consciousness scale scores;
3. GPA, obtained from their report cards based on a four-point scale, from A = 4 to F = 0;
4. Ratings of citizenship performance obtained from report cards based on a four-point scale, from 1 = unsatisfactory to 4 = outstanding.

Procedures

Data was collected on participants in both the treatment and control groups before the treatment group was exposed to any substantive content of the HAWK program. Parental consent was obtained for both the treatment and control groups. The informed consent message explained that their sons had: 1) been selected to participate in research dealing with manhood training; 2) that their names would be kept strictly confidential; and 3) that identification numbers would be assigned to all data sets before participation in any portion of the HAWK program. Subjects in both groups were given a pre-test, which included the African-centered values scale and the African self-consciousness scale. The treatment group was tested at the Aakhet Center as a group upon arrival to the program. Subjects in the control group were tested as a group in a local school library. An adult male trainer facilitated the administration and completion of the test battery, assisting subjects when necessary. Thereafter, HAWK subjects were introduced to the program where they were told that their participation in the HAWK program would help them to become positive Black men for the 21st century. Training began after the maximum number of subjects were obtained and all pretest assessments had been collected.

In terms of actual data collection, the procedures consisted of administering both the African-centered values scale and the African Self consciousness scale at the beginning of the training period for both the treatment and control groups. Once completed, test forms were collected and identification numbers were assigned to all documents. They were subsequently referred to by ID numbers only. After completing fourteen weeks of training, both subject groups were re-tested (post-test assessment) in the same respective locations. An adult male trainer conducted the administration of both testing sessions All of the subjects completed all of the assessments within a 45-minute time frame for the per pre-post testing session. Copies of the subjects' report cards were collected at the end of the second report period for use in data analysis. These reports were provided by the subjects with their parent's consent.

RESULTS

The data analysis consisted of pre-post-test difference scores obtained on the African-Centered Values Scale (ACVS) and the African Self-Consciousness Scale (ASCS). Differences in GPA and citizenship ratings were calculated between report period one before subjects participated in the study and report period two after participation in the study, along with the age of the Subjects. The analyses consisted of chi-square, correlation, t-test, and analysis of variance. An alpha level of .05 was used for all statistical tests. Scores were computed for both the ACVS and ASCS.

In computing the scores for the ACVS, the affirmative African value items were reversed then the subject's total score was summed. The theoretical range of scores is from 20 to 80 with the higher scores reflecting a stronger sense of African-centered values. This procedure was completed for both pre and post-test scores. The change score was then computed by subtracting the pre-test scores from the post-test scores. Increased scores were indicated by a positive value, while decreased scores were indicated by a negative value. A frequency distribution was conducted to obtain a median split on change scores. A test-retest reliability coefficient was computed on the ACVS and it generated a reliability factor of r. = .9113.

The score on the ASCS is based on an average mean score across the items. This procedure was completed for both pre and post-test scores. The change score was computed by subtracting the pre-test score from the post-test score. Increased scores were indicated by a positive value, while decreased scores were indicated by a negative value. A frequency distribution was conducted to obtain a median split on the change scores. A test-retest reliability coefficient was computed on the ASCS and it generated a reliability factor of r = .8391.

A 2 X 2 Chi-Square test for independence for changes on the dependent variables ACVS, ASCS, GPA, and CIT was conducted to show how the group related to positive change in these scores.

The 30 treatment group subject's ACVS change scores ranged from -14.47 to +18. Nine subjects (30%) reflected a low change in ACVS scores and 21 (70%) reflected a high change in ACVS scores, however, a different pattern was exhibited in the 31 control group subject's ACVS change scores which ranged from -9.53 to +9. Of the control group, seventeen subjects (54.8%) reflected a low change in ACVS scores, and 14 subjects (45.2%) reflected a high change in ACVS scores. This analysis revealed that group was significantly related to positive change in ACVS scores (2 = 3.9, df=1, p< .05). Significant difference occurred for group and change scores for ASCS scores (2 = 17.9, df=1, p< .001). The HAWK group range of ASCS change scores was from -1.50 to +3.10. Their ASCS change scores consisted of seven subjects (24.1%) reflecting a low change in ASCS scores and 22 subjects (75.9%) reflecting a high change in ASCS scores, whereas a different pattern occurred for the control group in that the control group's range in ASCS change scores was from -2.52 to +1.21; 24 subjects (77.4%) reflected a low change in ASCS scores and seven subjects (22.6%) reflected a high change in ASCS scores. The range of changes in GPAs for the HAWK group was from -1.16 to +1.17. Five subjects (22.7%) reflected a low change in GPA scores and 17 subjects (77.3%) reflected a high change in GPA scores, whereas again, a different pattern was exhibited for the control group; their range of changes in GPAs was from -.83 to +.66. Twenty-six of these subjects (83.9%) reflected a low change in GPA and five subjects (16.1%) reflected a high change in GPA. Again, the group was significantly related to a positive change in GPA (2 = 20.9 df=1, p< .001). Lastly, for the HAWK group, the range in citizenship performance (CIT) change scores was from -.00 to +.73. Ten subjects (45.5%) reflected a low change in CIT and 12 subjects (54.5%) reflected a high change in CIT. For the control group, by contrast, the range of changes in CIT was from -1.00 to +.50, whereby, 20 subjects (64.5%) reflected a low change in CIT and 11 subjects (35.5%) reflected a high change in CIT. No significant differences occurred between group frequencies for change in CIT (2 = 1.9 df=1, p< .167).

The group by high/low change scores for each dependent variable comparison are summarized in Figures 2 through 5.

Figure 2

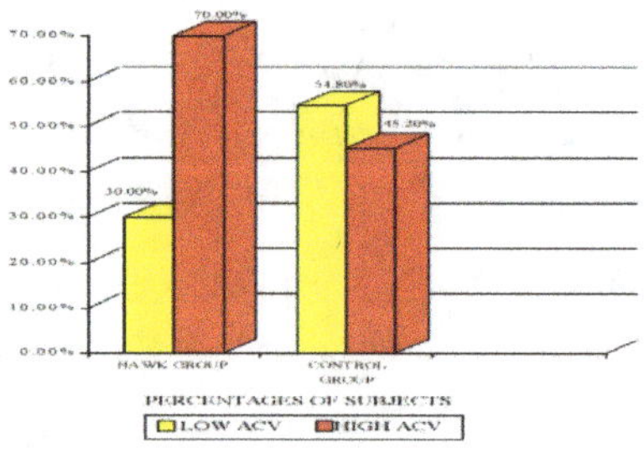

Figure 3

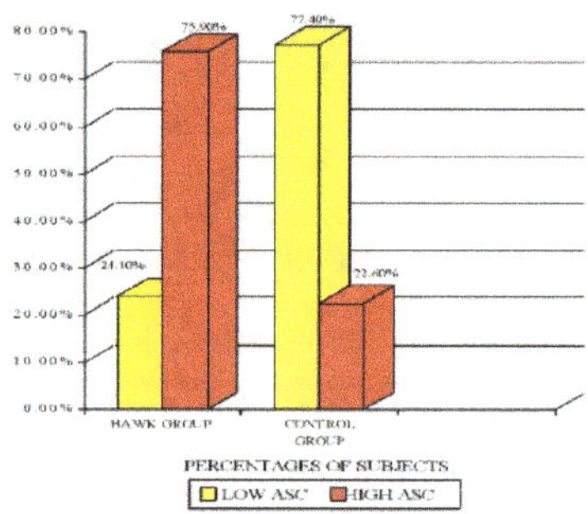

Figure 4

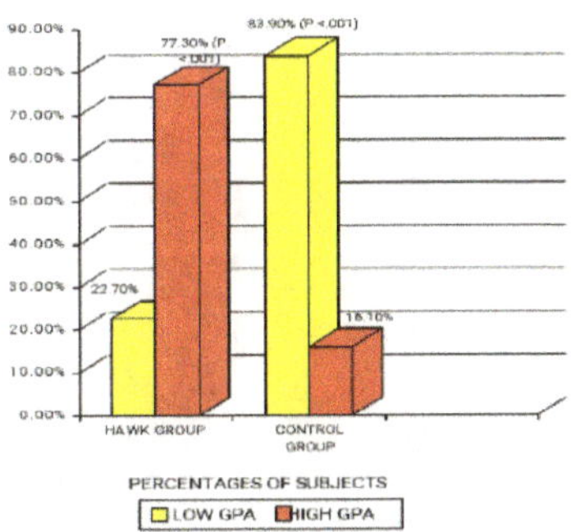

Figure 5

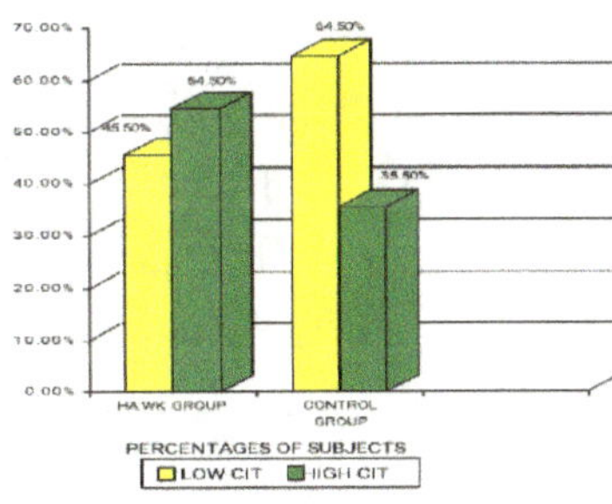

The data were analyzed using a correlation analysis to determine if any significant relationships occurred between group (control = 1, and HAWK = 2), and change scores for ACVS, ASCS, GPA, and CIT. These results are presented in Table 3.

Table 3

- - Correlation Matrix - -

	GROUP	ASCHNG	ACVCHNG	CITCHNG	GPACHNG
GROUP	1.000				
	(61)				
	P=.				
ASCHNG	.409	1.000			
	(60)	(60)			
	P=.001**	P=.			
ACVCHNG	.233	.031	1.000		
	(61)	(60)	(61)		
	P=.071	P=.816	P=.		
CITCHNG	.389	.216	.181	1.000	
	(53)	(52)	(53)	(53)	
	P=.004**	P=.123	P=.195	P=.	
GPACHNG	.463	.126	.139	.359	1.000
	(54)	(53)	(54)	(53)	(54)
	P=.001**	P=.367	P=.317	**P=.008****	p=.

(Coefficient / (Cases) / 2-tailed Significance)

The correlational analyses revealed significant positive correlations between group experience and ASCS (r =.4096, p<.001), GPA (r =.4630, p<.001), and CIT (r =.3893, p<.001) change scores. This indicates that membership in the HAWK program was significantly correlated with higher change scores on the ASCS, GPA, and CIT evaluations. Thus, while participating in the HAWK program, the subjects' level of ASC tended to increase as well as their school performance in GPA and CIT. A significant positive correlation also occurred between GPA and CIT (r =.3589, p<.008). This finding indicates that as one's GPA increased so did his CIT. While change scores for ACVS and groups did not produce a significant correlation (r =.2327, p<.071), there was a tendency towards significance evident in this relationship. No significant correlation occurred between the other variables in this study.

The t-test performed on the ACVS total pre-test scores revealed a significant difference between the HAWK Program and the control group (t (59)=2.64, p < .01). This result indicates that the two groups were not similar in ACVS scores at the start of the program. The HAWK group possessed significantly higher ACVS scores than the control group prior to manhood training. T-test analysis on the ASCS mean pre-test scores revealed no significant differences between the HAWK group and the control group (t (58)=-1.59, p < .117). This means that pre-test ASCS mean scores were similar between the groups. T-test analysis for GPA (t (52)=-.24, p< .811) and for CIT (t (51)=-.32, p< .748) were similarly not significant, indicating that the subjects were also similar on these variables prior to the HAWK program experience. This indicated that subjects in the HAWK program and control group had similar ASCS, grades, and citizenship performance scores prior to the start of the program, but were very dissimilar in ACVS scores.

To identify if the change scores within groups on ACVS, ASCS, GPA, and CIT were significant, a paired sample t-test was completed. The paired sample t-test performed for the HAWK group on ACVS scores resulted in a significant increase in scores (t (29) = 2.35, p<.03). This result indicated that the increase occurred in ACVS due to the HAWK program. The paired sample t-test performed for the HAWK group on ASCS also resulted in a significant increase in scores (t (28) = 3.28, p<.003). This result indicated that the increase occurred in ASCS due to the HAWK program as well. The paired sample t-test performed for the HAWK group on GPA (t (22) = 2.05, p<.05) and on CIT (t (21) = 4.29, p<.001), also resulted in a significant increase in scores. These results indicate that the increases that occurred in GPA and CIT were similarly due to the HAWK program.

The paired sample t-test performed for the control group on ACVS (t (30) = 1.09, p<.286), on ASCS (t (30) = .99, p<.329), and on CIT (t (30) = -.51, p<.617) were not significant, indicating that no meaningful changes occurred in these variables within the control group. The paired sample t-test performed for the control group on GPA, however, did reveal a significant difference in scores (t (30) = -3.44, p<.002). This result indicates that a negative change (decrease) in GPA occurred due to the conditions of the control group.

Two sets of two-way ANOVAs were computed for group x ACVS change score (high versus low) and group x ASCS change score (high versus low) on GPA and CIT change scores. These results are presented in Tables 4 and 5 and Figures 6 through 9.

Figure 6

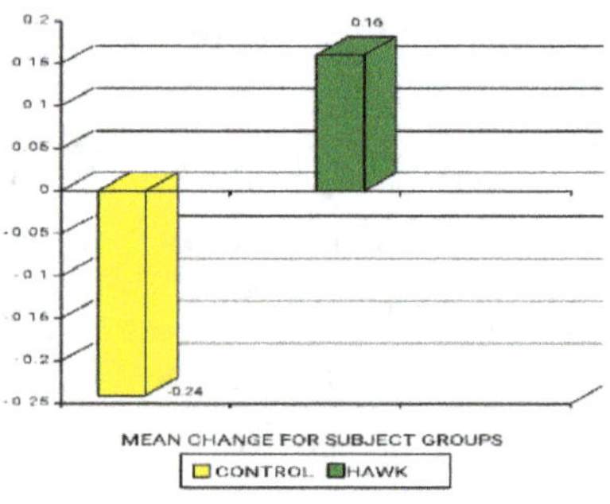

Figure 7

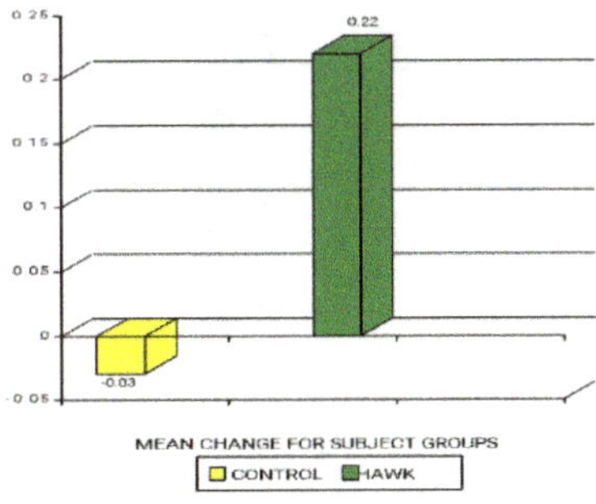

Figure 8

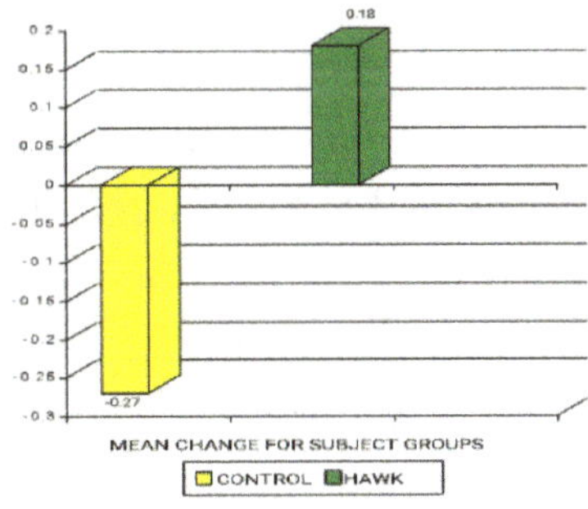

Figure 9

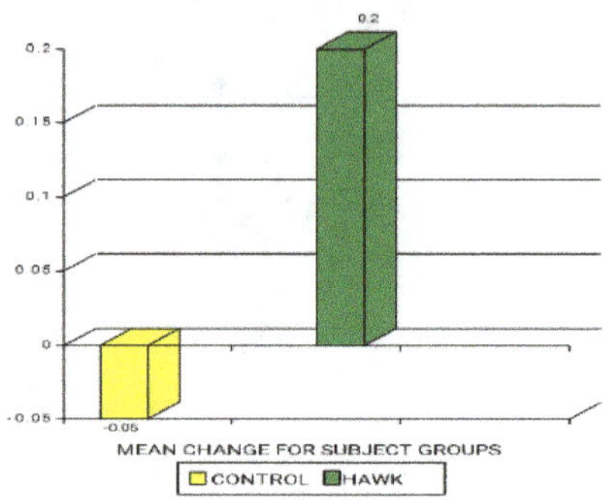

The first set of ANOVAs was conducted on group by ACVS (high versus low) on GPA and CIT change scores. Within the first set of analyses, a significant main effect occurred for group on GPA (F=13.978, df=1, p< .001). This suggests that the HAWK group (=.16) had a significantly greater increase in GPA than the control group (= -.24). In addition, a significant main effect occurred for group on CIT (F=7.085, df=1, p< .011). This indicates that the HAWK group (=.22) had a greater increase in affirmative school behavior than the control group (= -.03). No significant interaction occurred between the two independent variables in these analyses.

The second set of ANOVAs revealed similar findings. This set of two-way ANOVAs was conducted on group x ASCS change score (high versus low) on GPA and CIT change scores. A significant main effect occurred for group on GPA (F=8.208, df=1, p< .006), which suggests that the HAWK group (= .18) had a greater increase in GPA than the control group (= -.27). In addition, a significant main effect occurred for group on CIT (F=7.085, df=1, p< .011), which similarly indicates that the HAWK group (=.20) had greater increase in affirmative school behavior than the control group (= -.05). Again, there were no significant interactions between the two independent variables in these analyses.

Due to the differences within pre-test ACVS scores, a

two-way analysis of covariance was computed for group by age (older versus younger) on ACVS change scores, with ACVS total pre-test scores as the covariant. This finding is summarized in Table 6.

Table 6

Analysis of Covariance of ACVHI-LO
on Group by Age with ACV Pre-test scores

| | | F |
Source	df	ACV
Between Subjects		
Group (G)	1	.663
Age (A)	1	.946
G x A	1	**4.707***
S within group error	49	(.235)

Note. Values enclosed in parentheses represent mean square errors. ACV = African Center Value; S = subjects. *p < .05. **p < .01.

This analysis revealed a significant interaction between group and age on ACVS change scores (F=4.707, df=1.p<.034). In conducting a Tukey HSD analysis, a significant difference occurred between older subjects of the HAWK group (= 1.75) and older subjects of the control group (=1.29). This finding indicated that for the HAWK group, the older subjects obtained significantly higher ACVS change scores, while for the control group, the older subjects obtained significantly lower ACVS change scores (see Figure 10).

Figure 10

2-WAY INTERACTION BETWEEN GROUP AND AGE WITH TOTAL PRE-TEST SCORES ON ACV CHANGE SCORES

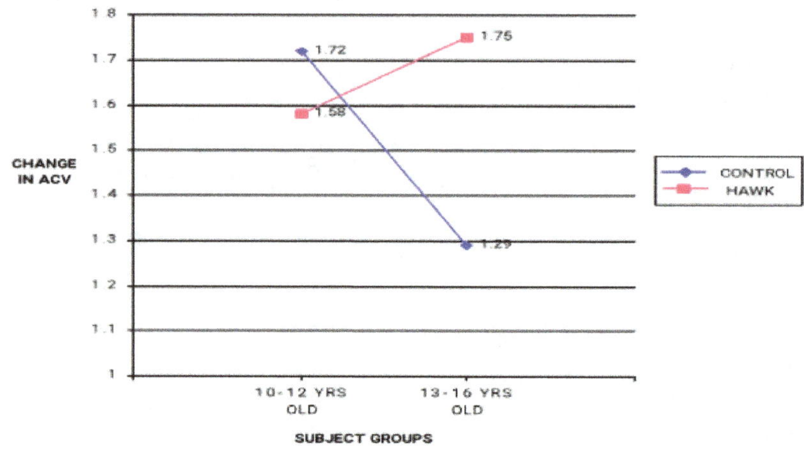

A couple of two-way ANOVAs were also computed for group by age on ACVS and ASCS changes scores. These results are presented in Table 7 and Figure 11.

Table 7

Analysis of Variance of ACVHI-LO and
ASCHI-LO on Group by Age

Source	df	F ACV	ASC
Between Subjects			
Group (G)	1	1.131	**15.322****
Age (A)	1	1.074	.408
G x A	1	**4.718***	.636
S within group error	56	(.233)	(.191)

Note. Values enclosed in parentheses represent mean square errors. ACV =
African Center Value; ASC = African self-consciousness S = subjects. *p < .
05. **p < .01.

Figure 11

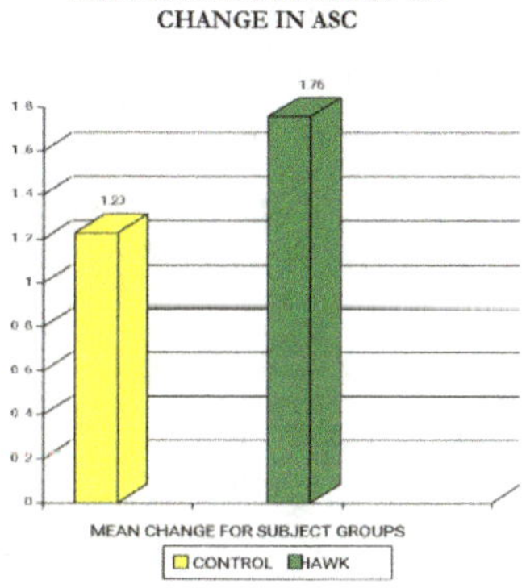

The first ANOVA conducted on group and age on
ACVS change scores yielded the same results as the CO-
ANOVA (see Figure 9 for interaction). The second two-way
ANOVA was conducted for group and age on ASCS changes
scores. A significant main effect occurred for group on ASCS
change score (F=15.322, df=1, p< .001), while there was no significant interaction between group and age. This result indicates that the HAWK group (=1.76) experienced a significantly
higher change in ASCS scores than the control group (=1.23).

DISCUSSION

A review of the results of this study indicates that two

of the four hypotheses were supported. The results confirmed that a manhood training and development program geared toward African-Americans increases African-American adolescents' African-centered values and consciousness, GPA, and citizenship performance. This study also highlighted the utility of more than one cultural assessment to tap into different phenomena, experiences, and needs of African people.

Related to Hypothesis 1, the prediction was that participants in the HAWK program would manifest a more significant increase in African-centered values than a control group as measured by an African-centered Values scale. This hypothesis was supported by group comparison, correlational analysis, and CO-ANOVA. Group comparison figures show that more HAWK group subjects had a more significant positive change in African-centered values than the control group. While not significant, the correlational analysis revealed a tendency toward a significant positive correlation between group experience (the HAWK Program) and ACVS. The CO-ANOVA revealed that the HAWK program subjects experienced significant increases in ACVS change score for the older HAWK participants than the control group's older participants. As the older HAWK subjects became more aware of the importance of values, they tended to adopt more African-centered values. In contrast, younger subjects may not fully understand the role values play. Perhaps this is due to different comprehending levels. Whatever the case, after 14 weeks of training, the older subjects in the HAWK program experienced an increase in African-centered values more so than the older subjects in the control group. For the older participants, then, the findings support the first hypothesis.

Related to Hypothesis 2, the findings supported the prediction that participants in the HAWK program would significantly increase their African self-consciousness more than a control group. Group comparison figures show that more

HAWK group subjects had a more significant positive change in African Self-consciousness than the control group subjects. The correlational analysis revealed a significant positive correlation between HAWK experience and ASCS change scores. The ANOVA revealed that the HAWK program experience had a more significant effect on the HAWK participant's ASC change scores than the control group experience had on the control group subject's scores. These findings support the effectiveness of the HAWK training program, indicating that the HAWK program participants tended to exhibit higher ASCS change scores. In contrast, the control group subjects tended to exhibit lower ASC change scores. Thus, the increase in African self-consciousness within the HAWK participants more than within the control group supported the second hypothesis of this study.

Related to Hypothesis 3, the prediction that as African-centered values and African self-consciousness increase, academic performance would increase as measured by school grade reports was not supported. ACVS and ASCS were not related to increases in GPA. Independent t-tests on pre-GPA scores revealed that GPAs were similar for both groups before implementing the HAWK program. However, increases in GPA were associated with the group experience. A paired sample t-test revealed a significant difference between pre-test and post-test scores for the HAWK program participants but not for the control group. The analysis of variance findings does support the expectation that the HAWK experience did play a significant role in effecting positive changes in GPA. The HAWK program experience enhanced academic performance in the participants, but these increases were unrelated to increases in ACVS and ASCS scores.

Related to Hypothesis 4, it was predicted that as African-centered values and African self-consciousness increase, citizenship performance would also increase as measured by school grade reports. This hypothesis was not supported. ACVS and ASCS were not related to increases in CIT. Independent t-tests on pre-CIT scores revealed that CIT was similar for both groups before implementing the HAWK program. However, increases in CIT were associated with the group experience. A paired sample t-test revealed a significant difference between pre-test and post-test scores for the HAWK program but not for the control group. Thus, the HAWK program experience also enhanced affirmative conduct performance within the school environment among the participants in this study. However, these increases were also unrelated to ACVS and ASCS scores.

The t-test analysis revealed that pre-test scores on ACVS differed between the HAWK and control groups, meaning that the two groups possessed very different African-cultural values before implementing the HAWK training. However, they possessed similar scores on the ASCS, indicating that the HAWK and the control group were more or less equivalent in their cultural consciousness prior to the training experience. The disparity between the groups on ACVS and the lack of a correlation between ACVS and ASCS suggest that the two scales are probably measuring very different dimensions of African cultural centeredness, such that one is not dependent upon the other. The question then becomes, "can someone have strong or high African-centered values and not have high African-self consciousness?" Some research suggests that the African self-consciousness scale may emphasize the strong linkage between African-centered values, African-centered behavior, and African-centered ideology commitment more than other measures like the ACVS, is perhaps more descriptive (Burlew & Smith, 1991; Myers & Sanders-Thompson, 1994). Such a difference between these measures might explain their lack of correlation. Further analysis of this relationship in future research seems warranted to clarify the issues raised by these findings.

Pre-test data suggest that young African-American males do not always have the exact needs. African-American youth come with various problems and/or issues that require immediate attention. As the findings suggest, some youth may contain higher levels of African-centered values than others, perhaps on an unconscious level. Yet, they may lack a level of conscious awareness of the values they possess. However, these findings suggest that as these African-American adolescents became more aware of their indigenous African cultural values, their conscious awareness of them probably increased as well.

Overall, the findings of this study suggest that the HAWK program acts as an effective intervention and preventive program, as noted throughout the literature review, at least in enhancing African-centered values, African Self-consciousness, and academic performance. Culturally centered programs, thus, can positively affect cultural consciousness, cultural values, and school performance among African-American adolescent males. Previous HAWK Training in Oakland, California, revealed similar results: HAWK students' GPA increased from 2.2 in the pre-test to 2.4 in the post-test. In other words, this finding establishes the consistency of the implementation of the HAWK program. It is also very likely that the behavior and attitudes of the Oakland HAWK students towards school/academics increased as a result of the program, although this data was not reported.

Furthermore, this supports Nobles' theoretical approach of inoculating African-American males with African cultural values to enhance their self-worth. The data suggest that the HAWK program's curriculum probably profoundly affects what African-American adolescents do and think. These findings lend further support for implementing such a program more widely throughout the African-American community and schools at large. This may benefit the African-American community (Chuck, 1994).

Implications of the Research

The failure to obtain a significant positive correlation between ACVS and ASCS raises the question of the relationship between ACVS and ASCS. This finding certainly appears to be theoretically inconsistent. As noted earlier, it raises the question of whether one can possess high African self-consciousness and not possess high African-centered values. Does consciousness precede values or vice versa? Or, could it be that one scale is more sensitive than the other in assessing "African-centeredness?"

Perhaps one way to bring more clarity to this issue in future research would be to look at the relationship between these variables and specific kinds of African-centered behaviors. Africentric theory would suggest that both of these constructs should be related to some form of African-centered behavior (Kambon, 1992). Maybe they tap different aspects of African-centered orientation that relate to different African-centered behaviors. Measuring these variables concerning a broad spectrum of African-centered behavioral outcomes may be critical in clarifying their relationship. Measuring these relationships to African-centered behaviors as opposed to general efficacious behavior like school performance should help to clarify this concern. The evidence suggests that these two scales appear to be consistent in tapping African-centered phenomena. However, by adding measures of African-centered behavioral outcomes, we may understand how these variables relate to behavioral outcomes having culturally common elements. Factor analysis of both measures to assess their structural relationship is also warranted and would help to shed more light on this finding. Furthermore, linking the HAWK training process with the African-centered and African-centered behavioral outcomes measures will provide a more rigorous assessment of the effectiveness of such a program. In addition, using measures like parent feedback and observing actual community and/or group involvement in practicing actual African-centered rituals could also enhance our understanding of the effectiveness of the HAWK training program.

A question may arise as to whether the content of the HAWK Program or merely the positive attention afforded the HAWK subjects relative to the control subjects accounts for the outcomes observed in this study. While this specific issue was not addressed in the paradigm of this study, future research might include the utilization of a non-Black culturally focused Black male mentoring program as a comparison (control) condition to the HAWK program. This addition would no doubt provide a more rigorous and systematic test of the effectiveness of the HAWK program.

Conclusions

The findings of this study support the need to establish and reestablish African-centered manhood training programs that further develop the African-centered values and African Self-Consciousness of African-American males. This research suggests potential benefits in return to a more traditional socialization process, e.g., initiation/rite of passage programs for African-American males (Chuck, 1994). This seems to be especially true concerning African self-consciousness.

This evaluation research also suggests that additional assessments should be added to this kind of evaluation to further explicate the value of the HAWK training program or other comparable programs. This would include measuring specific culturally centered behavioral outcomes of African-centered values and African Self-consciousness. When evaluating the effectiveness of manhood training and development, as well as utilizing a non-African culturally focused control group like a Black male mentoring program.

Further study of the HAWK program may well include

a more longitudinal approach in evaluating the long-term effects of manhood training and development. Data indicates that change scores in ACVS tended to increase significantly with older subjects. This would suggest that perhaps the institution of cohort studies involving repeated measures assessment would allow us to ascertain whether positive changes continue with time. This would help to further clarify the effectiveness of African-centered manhood training programs. Lend more robust support for the idea that cultural awareness development can enhance general efficacy, as demonstrated, and most importantly, group empowering/affirmative cultural behavior among young African-American males.

VIII

Materializing Our Conceptions: Practical Applications of Training Techniques for Developing African Critical Consciousness

We need to find it within ourselves to operate from a spirit of wholeness, a consciousness of Blackness, and forthrightness of upholding the African way of being. In today's generation, some fighters/warriors have represented the epitome of Black critical consciousness. These brothas and sistas demonstrate with great clarity operating from an African Spirit as critical conscious intellectuals, activists, and spiritual healers (Chief Oluwo Obafemi Fayemi Epega, Iyalosa Odujinmi Oyabunmi Funimole Abimbola, a.k.a. iiiYansaje T. Muse, Dr.

Mumbi), community activists (Tamika Mallory, Rizza Islam). Entertainers (Bob Marley, Sona Jobarteh), rappers (Professor Griff, KRS One, Lupe Fiasco), athletes (Colin Kapernick, Kyrie Irving, Lebron James), comedians (DL Hughley, Dave Chappell), educators (Barabara Sizemore). Psychologists (Umar Johnson) are engaging in the fight to liberate the African mind and save the future of our African children. Black Psychologists need to stand with them collectively and wholeheartedly to help save future generations. They have demonstrated keen piercing of the third eye vision consciousness, that if we came together, we could take our rightful place in this world. Their mastery and advocacy demonstrate an understanding that tells us to go back and fetch the wisdom and strength of our ancestors to help guide our future generations. How do we do this? How do we develop correct character and optimal functioning and restore our spirit? We need to RAP (Reconcile Adversarial Patternings) about it. Recognize the Divine speech in Emceeing. Operate out of our full authentic cultural character. Beseeching knowledge to edify ourselves. Zola up (Love) on our children in a way that provokes their intuitive intelligence to solve our problems.

While these may sound like soundbites, it is our job to make our reality a living, generative, and productive experience so that we can materialize our conceptions when all is said and done. This is where we are lost. White supremacy, European colonization, European imperialism, and racism against all African people have contributed to the psychological infliction placed on the cultural psyche of us Africans globally. So much to the point that we have created multiple terms leading up to the same outcome. African people have been abused psychologically to the point we function not from within our consciousness but the consciousness of colonizers. Bobby Wright states, "the only contradiction about Blacks in America is that there are no contradictions." From this, we see the following:

- Menticide - - the deliberate and systematic destruction of a group's mind with the ultimate extermination of the group (Bobby Wright, 1982).
- Conceptual incarceration - - is the use of foreign and incorrect concepts in the process of knowing, and the knower becomes a prisoner of these nonnative ideas (Wade Baba Nobles).
- Cultural Misorientation - - is the Eurocentric self-consciousness in African people (Kobi Kambon).
- Internalized oppression - - is a concept in which an oppressed group accepts the methods and incorporates the oppressive message of the oppressing group against their own best interest. It is believing, adopting, accepting, and incorporating the negative beliefs provided by the oppressor as the truth. It occurs when a dominating group preemptively displays aggression from a perceived inequality of self-worth compared to the group it wants to dominate with the intention of establishing themselves as a highly-valued/ superior group in order to achieve authority and power, and its benefits, also known as practice of cultural imperialism among many forms of oppression.
- Falsification of the African consciousness - - is European/ White supremacist establishment and control to define reality and exclude the truth and beauty of Afrikan history and culture from its collective consciousness of Afrikan peoples (Amos Wilson).
- Mental slavery - - is the condition of controlled African cognitive-intellectual functioning by the internalization of the European Worldview (Bob Marley).
- Psychological chains of slavery - - discuss how slavery captures the mind and imprisons the motivation, perception, aspiration, and identity in a web of anti-self images. Generating personal and collective self-destruction, the

slavery that feeds on the mind, invading the soul of man, destroying his loyalties to himself, and establishing allegiance to forces that destroy him (Na'im Akbar).

- Mental incarceration (Derek Wilson) - - The condition of African thought under the influence of the European Worldview and where Black social scientists can't seem to think outside of Western paradigm, pedagogy, or praxis.

These individuals rely upon European thought and ideas for understanding Black folk. They genuinely believe that Blacks and Whites, Africans and Europeans, are all the same. They accept as universal truths the thought pattern of Westerners/Europeans. They cannot fathom what it is like to think honestly from an African mindset as the result of the Yurugu virus, the experiences of the maafa, European imperialism, white colonialism, white supremacy, racism, prejudices, and discrimination. I would argue that they are more inclined to accept other groups' cultures for indoctrination before they accept African culture.

African = Black = African American

African psychology > Black Psychology = African/Black Psychology

Alien-Self Disorder, Anti-Self Disorder, Self-Destructive Disorders,

Colonialism = Cultural Imperialism = White Supremacy = Institutional Racism = European Hegemony = Racism = Racist

Conceptual Incarceration = Menticide = Mental slavery = Psychological chains of slavery = cultural misorientation = Internalized oppression

European = Colonizer = White = West = Western = nonnative

European psychology = Western Psychology

Europeanized Africans = Colonized Africans = Culturally Misoriented = internalized racism

Oppression = Cultural Oppression = Domination = Dehumanization

Scientific colonialism = Scientific racism

Mazungu = Mischeivious spirit that bounces around and cause trouble

Reflections of a Mazungu mindset displayed in the image below:

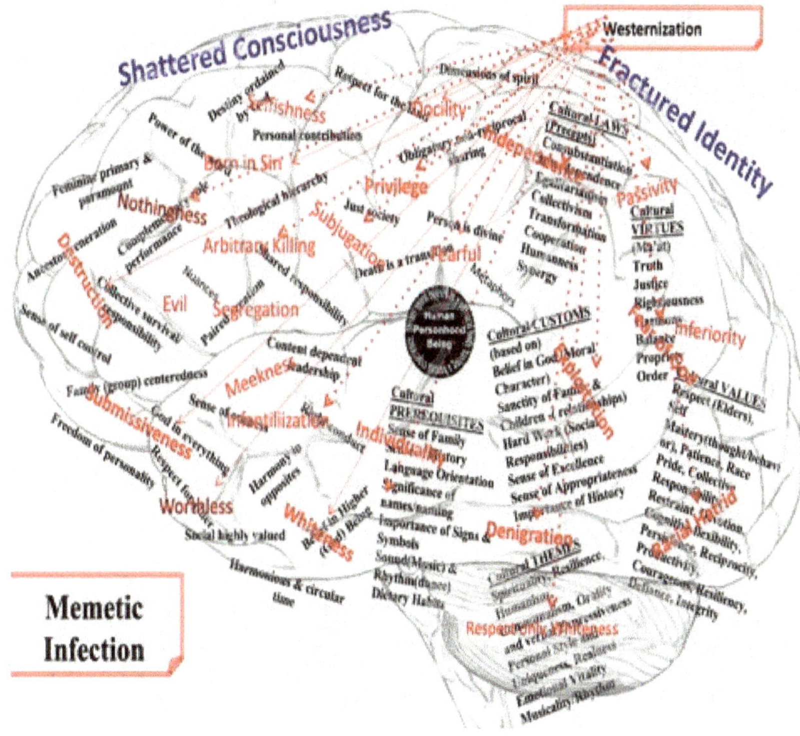

All this means is that we continue to create terms with similar themes without creating new terms from our old languages that can help us to solve our problems. Europeans do

not want us Africans to know who we are. The collective conscious connection to our spirit must be reawakened to continue our fight for liberation and freedom.

The above terminology represents culturally alienated individuals who have been infected by and infected others with the disease of destruction. Adopting nonnative ontological, alien cosmological, and foreign epistemological paradigms and praxis as their identity and thought construction demonstrate distorted consciousness. Black social scientists express this disposition in one of three ways:

1. Identification with white racists stereotypes, Black are intellectually inferior but physically gifted **(mis)Knowing**
2. Unself-conscious identification with white mainstream psychology ideology and praxis **(non)Being**
3. Intense passionate dissatisfaction with Black nationalists' ideology **(unDoing)**

The prescription for such infected persons is to implement a psychology of liberation and restoration. What methods are to be applied to liberate the minds of the infected? Black social scientists who continue to believe that APA can be our savior for human dignity should be questioned. Liberating the African community and personhood need to engage in practices designed for Awakening, heightening awareness of individual and communal implications of racist claims, Affirming, and highlighting African attributes to weaken the racists' claims, and Grounding, enhancing cultural appreciation.

Taylor and Obiechina have outlined the enhancement of black critical consciousness and deep-level thinking, and Harrison as strategies for reclaiming and restoring values to enhance the African community's quality of life and how to value formation and promotion can enhance liberating the African mind. The process for this critical conscious development is represented as follows.

We first want to Awaken within the individual a heightened awareness of the personal and communal implications of racist claims and acts by enhancing critical consciousness, communal consciousness, and transcendent consciousness. To enhance *critical consciousness* by becoming inquisitive, probing, and relentlessly understanding the causes of racism. We want to outline and identify cultural contradictions, identification of antithetical cultural insults as presented in the cultural charts (see Tables 2, 3, and 4). The following method enhances *communal consciousness* by recognizing the communal implications of their behavior. We should create an understanding of the nature of a community from the perspective of ancestors, contemporaries, and progeny (those yet to be born) and embody the position, character, and spirit of crucial actors, players, and activists who demonstrate this critical consciousness. Finally, to demonstrate *transcendent consciousness* by subjecting racist notions to transcendent value-building principles like "Initiatory Mastery, Principles of Ma'at, and Nguzo Saba." In addition, engage in routines where you explore and expose how the Oppress, Oppressor, and Liberator triad can be infected with a transcendent value orientation.

The following deep and elaborative process is the Affirming or highlighting African attributes to weaken the racist claims. One excellent book I highly recommend is J. A. Rogers's "From Superman to Man." This work perfectly demonstrates African intelligence and the culturally integrative of Africans as competent, moral, and emotional. This book also enhances our state of the conscious identity of Being, Belonging, and Becoming and demonstrates the importance of combating Nobles' Triangular Law of anti-African reality: (1) the law of (mis)knowing; (2) the law of (non)being; and (3) the law of (un)doing.

Lastly, the need for Grounding or centering the Black social scientist through enhanced cultural appreciation. Cultural appreciation requires continued systematic exposure to African history, politics, psychology, art, literature, etc., with three strategies for normalizing the perspective and values to enhance the quality of life for the African community through Discovery, Engaging, and Maintenance. Throughout *Discovery*, we learn to discover a normative and natural way of being that enhances the viability of the African community and families. The following process of *Engaging* is by providing planful opportunities to engage in activities to affirm our Discovery. The last is *the Maintenance* and development of a communal culture that supports Awakening, affirming, Grounding, Discovery, and engaging activities. We cannot allow their fear to materialize as our fear. Therefore we must utilize what we know and create new radical methods rooted in moral states and virtues to create a new genre of success. Below are some strategies to promote Black critical conscious building. These exercises stimulate restorative health through connectedness, competency, and consciousness. Through African wisdom, we establish optimal wholistic wellness and Beingness for reclaiming and restoring values to enhance the African community's quality of life and how to value formation and promotion can enhance liberating the African mind. The tactics demonstrated in this chapter will provide

- strategies of deep and elaborative processing for Awakening,
- affirming, and
- grounding for reclaiming and restoring values to techniques for Discovery, engaging, and Maintenance to enhance the quality of life for the African community.

The first is to start with a song about liberation and

appreciation of sound, rhythm, cadence and beat. The art of analyzing a song is to marinate over the lyrics and to engage in the visualization of bravery, warrior, and being God intensely fighting mental slavery.

Redemption Song Lyrics

[Verse 1]
Old pirates, yes, they rob I
Sold I to the merchant ships
Minutes after they took I
From the bottomless pit
But my hand was made strong
By the hand of the Almighty
We forward in this generation
Triumphantly

[Chorus]
Won't you help to sing
These songs of freedom?
'Cause all I ever have
Redemption songs
Redemption songs

[Verse 2]
Emancipate yourselves from mental slavery
None but ourselves can free our minds
Have no fear for atomic energy
'Cause none of them can stop the time
How long shall they kill our prophets
While we stand aside and look?
Ooh, some say it's just a part of it
We've got to fulfill the book

[Chorus]
Won't you help to sing
These songs of freedom?
'Cause all I ever have
Redemption songs
Redemption songs
Redemption songs
[Acoustic Break]

[Verse 3]
Emancipate yourselves from mental slavery
None but ourselves can free our minds
Whoa! Have no fear for atomic energy
'Cause none of them-ah can-ah stop-ah the time
How long shall they kill our prophets
While we stand aside and look?
Yes, some say it's just a part of it
We've got to fulfill the book

[Chorus]
Won't you help to sing
These songs of freedom?
'Cause all I ever have
Redemption songs

[Outro]
All I ever have
Redemption songs
These songs of freedom
Songs of freedom

Applications for development of ACV and ASC

In developing African consciousness, the synthesis between awareness of culturally deep structures and concrete conditions establishes the foundation for analyzing, interpreting, and transforming the individual and collective reality. The process to achieve these objectives of African values and consciousness includes training techniques of (1) dramatic consciousness, (2) mind modeling, (3) image and interest discussion/dialoguing, (4) culturally consistent problem solving, (5) metaphoric memory, and (6) Analogical thinking. These techniques help to build and maintain traditional African values within African American youth. The notion of preserving values instills within African American children and adolescents recognition of their Afri-sense or African self-consciousness.

Dramatic Consciousness - - Critical Consciousness

Dramatic consciousness training is designed to teach youth and upcoming Black Psychologists about the five dimensions of consciousness (e.g., self, personal, famous, historical, and mythic) unveiled to them through drama performed. For example, the youth told about the Ausarian Mythology, where Ausar, who had the power to be *one* with all things, established order, harmony, and prosperity throughout the land. Set, his youngest brother, jealous of Ausar and driven by a lust for power, assembled a band of thugs to kill Ausar. Once dead, Set and his no-gooders chopped Ausar's body into fourteen pieces and scattered them throughout the region. With the guidance of Tehuti, the mouthpiece of Ausar, Auset and Nebt-Het, Ausar's youngest sisters, collected his body parts and (re)membered him back together. With one part missing, the penis in the shape of an obelisk, Auset turned into a bird and hovered over his body, and Auset performed the first story of the immaculate conception. Heru was then born as heir to the throne. Once Heru reached the stage of manhood, he avenged his father's death through Tehuti's wisdom and power of knowing. Heru restored order, harmony, and reciprocity to the kingdom (Nefer Amen, 1990).

Within this drama, the youth's concepts and inner perceptions are built by what they witness, hear, and encounter. First, we seek their attention to what other stories have similar themes—the Lion King since everyone is familiar with that African fable. With connections made to the five dimensions of consciousness, youth then asked essential questions about the self, personal, famous, historical, and mythic realms of knowing. For African American youth, this story activates the consciousness through their understanding of thought, desire, and action. Upon manhood training, Heru demonstrated will, courage, and fierceness, yet was a disciplined and devoted warrior to a higher purpose. Within this victory, Heru's actions should inspire Black social scientists to restore our African wisdom to help solve problems of order, harmony, and reciprocity for the African mind by demonstrating whole ways to function and operate with the proper conduct. The antagonist, representing European/western/Greek philosophical tenets, was eventually subjected to his powers. Through the action of reciprocity, the laws that Set created eventually placed upon himself.

Mind Modeling - - Communal Consciousness

Another technique for establishing African-centeredness is mind modeling. Mind modeling instills within African American youth a sense of excellence and appropriateness. African American youth were asked to identify African and African-American men and women who exhibit(ed) excellence. Then, youth would be required to incorporate how these great men and women would think and respond in familiar situations. For the Black social scientists, how can you incorporate the teachings of Marcus Garvey in response to today's identity issues, drugs, and economic or educational problems in the African community? To evaluate personal situations and bring into account famous Africans and Africans in America, men, and women of excellence, to demonstrate how we can infuse the greatness of African people's thoughts, ideas, and solving of problems. Another example of a great African thinker would be Kwame Nkrumah, who philosophizes: "Capitalism...sheds its humanist stimulus under the impulse of the profit motive... The evils of capitalism can lead to alienation and unjust; in our newly independent countries [thinking self] it is not only too complicated to be workable but also alien." For the Black critical conscious social scientists, we must break away from and correct our thinking minds from the spiritless capital dogma and pedagogical paradigm. Why is it so hard for those trained to work with the mind to change their thinking? That is because we were not trained to think for ourselves.

Image and Interest Dialoguing Discussion - - Awakening

Image and interest dialoguing, a third form of an Afrocentric training technique, focuses on the youths' reality, image, and interest, in the topic of discussion. Presentations with music videos, documentaries, short movie clips, and reading of short stories and poems are all used to explicate real-life connections to the understanding of themselves within the context of the group. Take, for instance, the story of the minks (Vanzant, 1993) *January 13:*

> Pretend for a moment that you are a mink -- beautiful, valuable, precious because of the skin that covers you. Suddenly your homeland is invaded by hunters, with bats. The hunters seem kind, yet you

approach them cautiously. They pet the younglings who are innocent, less cautious. As you approach your young, the hunters attack. They beat you. You are dazed, struggling for composure. The hunters steal your skin, your heritage, the very essence of your being. They leave you to die, but you survive. Your fur grows back. Stronger. More beautiful than before. Somehow it doesn't make sense. The very thing that makes you who and what you are is the source of pain. Confused, distrustful, you hide yourself or camouflage your fur, your essence. Silently you begin to curse your fur because the hunters return again and again. You begin to understand you will never get away from being what you are. As long as you have fur, you will be hunted. The issue is: Will you curse your fur, give up and die? Or just continue to be proud but cautious mink?

Possible discussion topics from the cultural vantage point of Black social scientists include many subjects. Here we can see the use of empowerment theory, Liberation psychology, and community psychology, but what would be required to solve the problem if operating from an African-centered psychological framework? The youth would be required to give examples of familiar situations and discuss what should be deemed appropriate in responding to the issues they face.

Culturally Consistent Problem Solving - - Grounding

Regarding dealing with such issues, a fourth training technique requires the skill of culturally consistent problem-solving. The strategies or solutions include (1) the elimination and opposition to any condition or situation that prevents the positive development of self, family, and community; and (2) creating or reinforcing those situations, conditions, or agents fostering positive growth and development of self, family, and community. Eight cultural precepts have been identified in influencing people's general design for living and patterns for interpreting their reality. An example of culturally consistent problem-solving could include how the African American community would deal with the issue of COVID. Operationally, the cultural precepts are as follows. (1) Consubstantiation assumes that all things in the universe have the same essence, entails and supports the belief that COVID can affect all persons living within a community where somebody has COVID; more importantly, no one stands above the epidemic of COVID. (2) Interdependence assumes that everything in the universe is connected; youth must recognize the danger of COVID and identify how easily this disease can affect them. (3) Unicity/ Egalitarianism states that the correct relation among people is equality, harmony, and balance; therefore, youth would be required to research studies of COVID in terms of its development, transition, and transmission of disease as it relates to their community. (4) Collectivism assumes that individual effort reflects communal survival. Youth would be required to identify ways, as members of the community, they can contribute to the well-being of others in restricting the spread of COVID (e.g., teaching their family and friends about protection). (5) The precept of Transformation assumes that everything has the potential to function at a higher level; youth are required to develop the belief that everyone can lead a healthy lifestyle free from COVID and other diseases. The remaining cultural precepts are (6) Cooperation, (7) Humanness, and (8) Synergism.

In my mind this connect to the Black Mutual Aid societies that existed before we had access to insurance. The societies were social and practical. Members had access to resources in case of illness and funds for a proper burial. Mutual assistance and self-help have always been cornerstones of the African community for generations. Texts are offered as documented by W E. B. Du Bois, in 1903, called "the first wavering step of a people toward organized social life." These societies promoted education and job training, especially for newly arrived Africans, freemen, and fugitive slaves. These African societies attest to the wide-ranging efforts to liberating the African mind, illuminating and enlivenment of the African Spirit and enlivening the African character.

1. **Free African Society**, Philadelphia, 1787. Founded as a Free African Society where its goals were to pay to the "needy of this society . . . provided, this necessity is not brought on them by their own imprudence." The society was nondenominational to include free blacks of all religious sects, as no one sect had enough members to create its own mutual aid society.

2. **New York African Society for Mutual Relief**, 1808. The New York Society was formed two decades later to provide a form of health and life insurance for its members and their families. The Society persevered for more than 150 years, into the 1950s.

3. **Negro mutual benefit societies in Philadelphia**, 1831. Listed their goals and financial contributions for the relief and education of poor Africans in the city. The societies insisted their funds go to the neediest among them for basic sustenance.

4. **Phoenix Society**, New York City, 1833. The Phoenix Society's primary goal was an Educational objective and outlined achievable steps to enroll black children and adults in reading and writing classes, vocational training, community libraries, lecture series, and self-improvement

groups. They provided clothing and other material needs to children who could not, in any other way, participate.

Here we can see how Black Panther Party kept alive the spirit of African upliftment, social justice, and education with head start programs and free breakfast and lunch programs for Black children.

Metaphoric Memory

Metaphoric memory incorporates proverbs to transmit values affecting consciousness and develop cognitive competency skills. Integrating words and objects (symbolic images) with deep feelings (affective loading) to convey meaning is a practical learning style. This learning style is known as effective symbolism. Proverbs represent the fundamental principles governing behavior, and in response to the proverbs, a cunningness to confront life situations. Proverbs are used in context, with their content conveying the meaning of values and behavioral outcomes.

The following is a list of proverbs representing the African value orientation:

Value Orientation

Proverbial Representation

Unity — Two birds disputed about a kernel when a third swooped down and carried it off.

Cooperation — The strong person builds a path for the weak to walk on.

Respect — Mothers-in-law are hard of hearing.

Purpose   Before healing others, heal thyself.

Creativity   If you find no fish you have to eat bread.

Familyhood   Dine with a stranger but save your love for your family.

Responsibility   If relatives help each other, what evils can hurt them?

Since we are conscious beings and our consciousness is spirit-connected to God's consciousness as spirit Beings driven, we are to operate in a man-God conscious state. It is this totality of Being conscious of the Becoming self-consciousness that we are knowing and knowable spirits. Being, Belonging, and Becoming with God's spirit consciousness reflects us within that we learn to import attributes of critical consciousness for the transmission of African values. The following were chosen maxims for the context of thought: "height not reached in a hurry; memory reaches further than the eye, and wisdom is not in the eye, but in the head." Critical conscious social scientists would be required to analyze a proverb and report its meaning and intention as a group. Another exercise would be to lay out many different life situations (i.e., familyhood, loving, being a man or woman, character, success, natural goodness, etc.) and identify proverbs that fit. Reflective of how culture demonstrates its moral demand functioning.

Analogical Thinking

The last technique is analogical thinking. Where the thought process utilizes a *cultural reference system*. The analogical process arranges thinking as a constant, moving, and dynamic force through critical understanding. Take, for example, the development of the "Statue of Liberty." The Statue of Liberty came to be because of the critical role that Black soldiers played in the Civil War, ending African Americans being in bondage. In the mind of a French historian, Edourd de Laboulaye, chairman of the French Anti-slavery Society, who, together with a French sculptor proposed that the French Government present to the American people, through the American Abolitionist Society, the Statue of Liberty as a gift. The statue was first presented as an African woman cradling a child in her arms with broken shackles around her wrist and ankles. However, it was rejected because it would have been offensive to the Southerners, progenitors of a white supremacist. It reminded them of how Blacks won their freedom. So the statute underwent several changes to hide any connection to the freedom of African Americans. It was contrasted to the Southern States protecting vestiges of the Confederacy as an insult to Africans in America as a reminder of slavery.

A staunch Black critical conscious social scientist would recognize how the most dangerous thing in the Black community is the introduction of religion (Christianity, Islam, and Judaism as we know it) offered by the same group who oppressed them. One should ask how we can accept and adopt the oppressor's practice of oppression as a means of liberation. In addition, in studying the history of these religions we find that the languages used to write the Torah, Bible, and Quran did not even exist in the regions discussed yet we treat them as facts filled with transsubstantive errors and turn African stories into false narratives. The underlying story is that all African parables, and allegories, provoke higher spirits in the consciousness of the spirits of your ancestors. Why don't we, Black social scientists, take more significant advantage of proverbs, not just in passing?

The wisdom of African proverbs from around the continent manifests in ways of knowing, seeing, and thinking:

Wisdom creates well-being — Ghanian Proverb.

Anger and madness are brothers. — African Proverb

Do not follow a person who is running away. — Kenyan proverb

An orphaned calf licks its own back. — Kenyan proverb

Even as the archer loves the arrow that flies, he also loves the bow that remains constant in his hands. — Nigerian proverb

He who burns down his house knows why ashes cost a fortune. — African Proverb

If you build a house and a nail breaks, do you stop building or change the nail?

—Rwandan proverb

You cannot build a house for last year's summer. — Ethiopian proverb

We desire to bequeath two things to our children. The first one is roots; the other one is wings. — Sudanese proverb

Rituals

Certain rituals should be used to infuse an "elevation to divine status; deification" for young African-American males and African social scientists to perform according to an African-centered philosophical orientation. The importance of investing in certain rituals serves to carry out the intentions of the culture they operate. The technology of rituals can help reach deeper apotheosis in man's relationship to nature and mankind's place in nature. The path to development occurs through the development of virtues. The capacity of a person was determined by the degree to which he is able to overcome certain natural impediments of the body. Virtue was seen as the antidote to character flaws and only perfected through study and effort. According to George G.M. James, the following ten virtues were practiced in the Ancient Egyptian (KMT) Mystery Systems.

The Ten Virtues:

1. **Mastery of one's thoughts**

2. **Mastery of one's behavior/actions**

(Both principles are the virtue of wisdom of thought and action.)

3. **Devotion to a higher purpose**

4. **Faith in the ability of the teacher to teach the truth**

("When the student is ready, the teacher will appear.")

5. **Faith that one can know/recognize the truth**

(Which was equivalent to Prudence [wisdom], of deep insight that befitted the faculty of Seership).

6. **Faith that one can use the truth**

(Confidence in one's own ability to learn.)

7. **Free from resentment when punished**

(Which was equivalent to the virtue of Fortitude.)

8. **Free from resentment when wronged**

(Fortitude meant such courage as we would not allow adversity to turn us away from our goals.)

9. **Ability to tell right from wrong**

10. **Ability to tell the difference between the real and the unreal**

(Both principles derive the virtues of justice and temperance.)

Contemporary African-centered programs engage in ritual practices designed to assist us in advancing our spiritual connections and power. Rituals help to alleviate the emotional distance of people from themselves and others and compel us by the aspects of culture. For example, in context, the ritual of communicating to our ancestors reveals the power of Zola-ing (zoh-lah) up (loving on) from below to the heavens and from above to earth. Zola activates the 'Ngolo,' the energy of self-healing power (potential). Epigenetically, Zola is an infectious love activating the emotional molecules that move through our conscious DNA. It is the genuine yearning of our ancestors to pass their Spirit to join, unite, broaden, and swell into an unlimited source with our Spirit. Rituals restore to life the connections with the spirit world performed in traditional forms. Our ancestors provide us with a transgenerational self-healing energy pattern. Rituals on Zola require us to value and adore each other with caring and affection. Zola (Love) is self and collective cherishment designed to sustain, promote, nurture, and inspire 'perfectibility.' It is the actual act of personal and collective preservation and actualization (Kikongo).

Rituals form the context to help us remember and create a purpose for our place in the world. In addition, they serve as cultural cues to the values we consciously possess. Since rituals serve this function in transmitting African values at their deepest level of communication, they also expressed the reaffirming unity, consubstantiation, collective consciousness, and interdependence of group -- community hood, familyhood, and personhood. Rituals serve a conscious developmental function in establishing the context of social order. For African youth and Black social scientists, rituals are intended to preserve and ensure cultural integrity for our African ancestors. Rituals can be what we don't see as impacting things in the world. Still, if we maintain consistent ritual practices, we will come to know the key to understanding the essential constitutions of human healing, insight, consciousness, and power.

God who remembers,
They think we will forget. We cannot. Thank you for being a God who keeps account of every evil thing. A God who calls us toward habits of memory for both death and liberation. Forgive us for how we've discarded and diminished the evils of the past as some fractured end note in the book of American glory. Help us to remember all that made us, that the beneficiaries of injustice and exclusion would look in the mirror and be unable to perceive their reflection apart from those dark histories that have placed them in front of that particular mirror in that particular neighborhood. Help us to remember those ancestors from whom this land was taken and those whose backs were broken to build up a fortune and society that would never embrace them. How long will the arms of death and injustice see themselves as heroes? It seems that whiteness alone can never be trusted to tell its own story. Have mercy and hand us the pen.

@blackliturgies

In closing

Thus far, learning these techniques and rituals engenders within the African cosmology concept that African people's reality is connected to a more significant force (Spirit). This asili (cosmic 'seed' force) governs the group's social order and establishes "right character and conduct." Culture teaches all within society what is just through practicing ritual techniques. This discourse examined how African-centered thinking enhances Black critical consciousness from the knowledge and wisdom of traditional African values and consciousness. Africans who participate in certain collective practices based on specific African-centered training techniques are bound to find beauty and answers in our way of being. Black social scientists must make explicit use of rituals, expand Black critical consciousness, and enliven and illuminate the African Spirit when mastering acquired African-centered values.

UBUNTU

IX

DR. DEREK J. WILSON

Ubuntu Musings

Foreward by Baba Dr. Wade W. Nobles

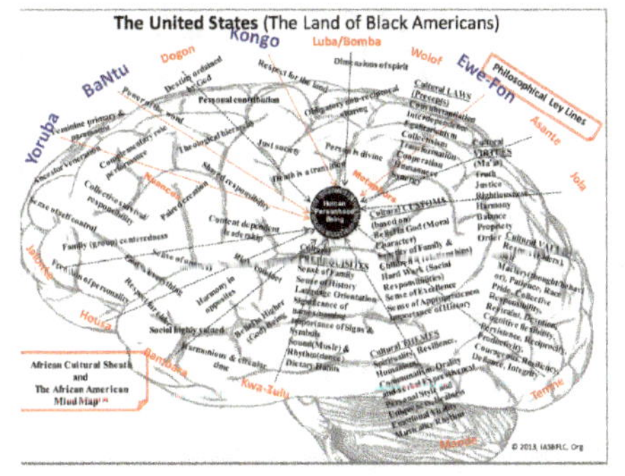

The Need for Black Critical Consciousness

VOL. 1

References

Abimbọla, M. A. M (2019). On Òyìnbó: Yorùbá Religion, Resistance, and Polyepistemic Knowledge. *The Journal of Interreligious Studies* (28)

Akbar, N. (1980). Our destiny: Authors of a scientific revolution. In J. McAdoo et al. (Eds.), *The Fifth Annual Conference on Empirical Research in Black Psychology*. Washington, DC: National Institute of Mental Health.

Akbar, N. (1989). Nigrescence and identity: Some limitations. *The Counseling Psychologist* 17 (2) 258-263.

Akbar, N. (1991). *Visions for Black Men*. Tallahassee, FL: Mind Productions & Associates, Inc.

Akbar, N. (1994). *Light from Ancient Africa*. Tallahassee, FL: Mind Productions & Associates, Inc.

Akoto, A. (1994). Notes on an Afrikan-Centered Pedagogy. In M. J. Shujaa (Eds.), *Too Much Schooling Too Little Education: A Paradox of Black Life in White Societies*. Trenton, N. J. African World Press, Inc.

Amuleru-Marshall, O. (1992). *Nurturing the Black Adolescent Male: Culture, ethnicity, and race*. Paper presented at Conference on the African American Adolescent Males.

Anderson, J. R. (1995). *Cognitive Psychology and its implications*. New York, NY. W. H. Freeman and Company.

Ani, M. (1994). *Yurugu*. New Jersey. African World Press.

Armah, A. K. (1979) Two Thousand Seasons. Chicago, IL. Third World Press, 1979

Asante, M and Asante K. W. (1989). *African Culture: The Rhythms of Unity*. Trenton, NJ: African World Press.

Ayittey, G. (1991). *Indigenous African institutions*. New York, NY: Transnational Publishers.

Baldwin, J. A. (1991). African psychology and Black personality testing. In A. G. Hilliard (Eds.) *Testing African American Students*. Chicago, IL: Third World Press.

Baldwin, J. and Bell, Y. (1985). The African Self Consciousness: An

Africentric personality questionnaire. The *Western Journal of Black Studies* 9 (2) 61-68.

Bandura, A. (1969). Social learning theory of identificatory processes. In David Goslin (Ed), *Handbook of socialization theory and research* (pp. 213-262).

Bandura, A. (1971). Analysis of modeling processes. *Psychological modeling: Conflicting theories.* Chicago, IL: Aldine-Atherton.

Bandura, A. (1986). *Social foundations of thought and action: A social cognitive theory.* Engle-wood Cliffs, NJ: Prentice-Hall.

Bandura, A. (1994). Social cognitive theory and exercise of control over HIV infection. In R. J. DiClemente and J. L. Peterson (Eds). Preventing AIDS: Theory and methods of behavioral interventions. Plenum Press: NY.

Bandura, A., and Walters, R. (1963). *Social learning and personality development.* New York: Holt, Rinehart & Winston.

Barton, L.R. (2020).*Young People. Always at the Forefront of Change.* Center for the history of psychology. https://centerhistorypsychology.wordpress.com /2020/02/20/ young -people-always-at-the-forefront-of-change

Battiste, M. (2002). *Indigenous knowledge and pedagogy in First Nations education: A literature review with recommendations.* Ottawa: Apamuwek Institute.

Belgrave, F.Z., Cherry, V. R., Cunningham. D., Walwyn, S., Letlaka-Rennert. K., Phillips, F. (1994) The influence of Africentric values, self-esteem, and Black identity on drug attitudes among African American fifth graders: A preliminary study. *Journal of Black Psychology.* 20 (2) 143-156.

Bell, Y. R. (1994). A culturally sensitive analysis of black learning style. Journal of black psychology. 20 (1) 47-61.

Bettencourt, B. A Dill, K. E., Greathouse, S. A., Charlton, K., and Mulholland, A. (1997). Evaluations of ingroup and outgroup members: The role of category-based expectancy violation. *Journal of Experimental Social Psychology* 33, 244–275.

Bhola, H. S. (1992). *Literacy, knowledge, power, and development--multiple connections.* Ann Arbor, MI. (ERIC Document Reproduction Service No. ED345587).

Biernat, M., Vescio, T.K. and Theno, S. A. (1996). Violating American Values: A "Value Congruence" Approach to Understanding Outgroup Attitudes. *Journal of Experimental Social Psychology* 32, 387–410.

Boykin, W. (1985). In McAdoo (Ed.) *The Black children: social, educational, and parental environments.* (pp.) Beverly Hills: Sage Publications.

Burlew, A. K. and Smith, L. R. (1991). Measures of racial identity: An overview and a proposed framework. Special Issue: Incorporating an African world view into psychology: II. *Journal of Black Psychology* 17 (2) 53-71.

Byrne, D., Barry, J., and Nelson, D. (1963). Relation of the revised

Repression- sensitization scale to measures of self-description. *Psychological Reports.* 13. 323-334.

Carlson E. R. (1995). Evaluating the credibility of sources: A missing link in the teaching of critical thinking. *Teaching of Psychology.* 22 (1). 39-43.

Cattaneo, L. B and Chapman A. R. (2010)The Process of Empowerment: A Model for Use in Research and Practice. *American Psychologist* 65(7):646-59

Center For Applied Cultural Studies and Educational Achievement (CACSEA). (1995). *Designing Staff Development Programs for Educators of African American Students: A resource guide for teachers, administrators, and staff developers.* Summer Institute Training. San Francisco State University.

Chen, M. and Bargh, J. A. (1997). Nonconscious behavioral confirmation processes: The self-fulfilling consequences of automatic stereotype activation attitudes. *Journal of Experimental Social Psychology* 33, 541–560.

Chioneso, N. A., Hunter, C. D., Gobin, R. L., McNeil-Smith, S., Mendenhall, R., and Neville, H. A., (2020) Community Healing and Resistance Through Storytelling: A Framework to Address Racial Trauma in Africana Communities, *Journal of Black Psychology,* Volume (46) https://doi.org/10.1177/0095798420929468.

Chuck, J. L. (1994). *The efficacy of Rites of Passage intervention and its impact on the self-esteem and vocational readiness for disadvantaged Afrikan-American adolescent males.* Dissertation Abstracts (AAC #9421270).

Cohen, R. (1969). Conceptual styles, culture conflict, and nonverbal test intelligence. *American Anthropologist.* 71, 828-856.

Cokley, K. and Garba, R. (2018) Speaking truth to power: How black/African psychology changed the discipline of psychology. *Journal of Black Psychology.* 44(8) 695 –721 DOI:10.1177/0095798418810592

Dan Hocoy, Aaron Kipnis, Helene Lorenz, Mary Watkins Liberation Psychologies: An Invitation to Dialogue retrieved 11/20/2022 https://www.pacifica.edu/degree-program/community-liberation-ecopsychology/what-is-liberation-psychology/.

Dawkins, Peter. 1988. *Arcadia, The Ancient Egyptian Mysteries & The Arcadia and the Arcadian Academy: Studies in Ancient Wisdom.* The Francis Bacon Research Trust Journal, Series I, Volume 5: London, England. Coventry Printers

Dawkins, R. (1989). The evolution of evolution ability. In E. C. Langton (Ed.), Artificial life. Santa Fe, NM: Addison-Wesley.

Diop, C. A. (1974). *The African origins of civilization: Myth or reality.* Brooklyn, NY: Lawrence Hill.xiii

Division of Public Schools' Education Information and Accountability Services (1994). *Statistical Briefs,* State of Florida Department of Education, Tallahassee, FL.

Dixon, V. J. (1976). Worldviews and research methodology. In L. M. King et al. (Eds.), *African Philosophy: Assumptions and paradigms for research on Black persons.* (pp. 51-77). Los Angeles: Fanon Center.

Downey G. "Practice without theory": a neuroanthropological perspective on embodied learning. J R Anthropol Inst. 2010;16 (Special Issue). S22–40.

Edwards, S. D., Makunga, N. V., Ngcobo, H. S. B. & Dhlomo, R. M. (2004). Ubuntu: A cultural method of mental health promotion. International Journal of Mental Health Promotion, 6(4), 17-22.

Ellen Hawley McWhirte, E. H. (1998). An Empowerment Model of Counsellor Education. *Canadian Journal of Counselling/Revue* Canadienne de counseling/1998, Vol. 32:1

Fanon, F. (1967). *Black skin, white mask.* New York: Grove Press, Inc.

Fanon, F. (1963). *The Wretched of the Earth.* New York: Grove Press, Inc.

Fiske, S.T. (1995). Social cognition. In A. Tesser (Ed.) *Advanced social psychology.* McGraw-Hill, Inc.

Foster, M. (1993). *Successful intervention with African American pupils in regular and special education.* Paper presented at the Symposium Special Education in Multicultural California: Reform and Restructure.

Freire, P.(1973) *Education for critical consciousness.* New York, NY. The Seabury Press.

Freire, P.(1985) *The politics of education: Culture, power, and liberation.* Massachusetts. Bergin and Garvey Publishers, Inc.

Freire, P.(1993) *Pedagogy of the Oppressed.* New York: Continuum.

French, B. H., Lewis, J. A., Mosley, D. V. Adames, H.Y. Chavez-Dueñas, N.Y., Chen, G.A., Neville, H. A. (2019) Toward a psychological framework of radical healing in communities of color. https://doi.org/10.1177/0011000019843506.

Gadzella, B. M., Ginther, D. W., and J. D. (1986). Differences in learning processes and academic achievement. Perceptual and Motor Skills 62 (1) 151-156.

Gary, L. E. & Booker, C. B. (1992). Empowering African-Americans to achieve academic success. *NASSP Bulletin 76* (546) p. 50-55.

Geertz, C (1973) The Interpretation of Cultures, Basic Books, pp. 123-25.

Goddard L.L. and Cavil, III, W.E. (1989). Black teenage parenting: Issues and challenges. In R. Jones (Ed.) *Black Adolescents* (pp. 373-383). Berkeley, CA. Cobb and Henry Publishers.

Goddard, L., Haggins, K. L., Nobles, W. W., Rhett-Mariscal, V., Williams-Flournoy, D. (2014) Refining the definition of an African American community-defined practice a supplemental report to the African American Population Report for the California Reducing Disparities Project: We

Ain't Crazy! Just Coping with a Crazy System: Pathways into the Black Population for Eliminating Mental Health Disparities

Goddard, L.L., Nobles, W.W. and Wilson, D.J. (1993). OSAP evaluative summary report. *HAWK federation perfected Black manhood training and development program training* (restricted document). Oakland, CA. Black Family Institute Publication.

Goddard, L.L. & Baba Nobles, W.W. (1996). The African-based childrearing opinion survey. In R. Jones (Ed.) Handbook of tests and measurements for Black populations. Hampton, VA: Cobb and Henry.

Goddard, L.L. & Nobles, W.W. (1996). The African-based childrearing opinion survey. In R. Jones (Ed.) *Handbook of test and measurements for Black populations.* Hampton, VA: Cobb and Henry.

Goddard, L.L. and Cavil, III, W.E. (1989). Black Teenage parenting: Issues and challenges. In R. Jones (Ed.) Black Adolescents. (pp. 373-383). Berkeley, CA: Cobb Henry Publishers.

Gordon, B. M. (1994). African-American cultural knowledge and liberatory education: Dilemmas, problems, and potentials in a post-modern American society. In M. J. Shujaa (Eds.), Too Much Schooling Too Little Education: A Paradox of Black Life in White Societies. Trenton, N. J. African World Press, Inc.

Grills C. and Longshore, D. (1996). Africentrism: Psychometric analyses of a self-report measure. Journal of Black Psychology. 22 (1). 86-106.

Guerry, V. (1975). Life with the Baoule'. Washington DC Three Continents Press.

Gutierrez, L (1990). *Empowerment and the Latino community: Does consciousness make a difference?* Ann Arbor, MI. (ERIC Document Reproduction Service No. ED367746).

Gyekye, Kwame (1996). *Person and Community in African Thought* http://www.galerie-inter.de/kimmerle/frameText9.htm (retrieved 11/22/2022).

Hale-Benson, J. E. (1986). *Black Children: Their roots, culture, and learning styles.* Baltimore, The John Hopkins University Press.

Harris, J. (1992). Create a culture of success for African-American students. *Social Policy 22* (3) 46-48.

Heitz, Hannah K. (2022) "Liberation Psychology: Drawing on history to work toward resistance and collective healing in the United States," *Psychology from the Margins*: Vol. 4, Article 4. Available at: https://ideaexchange.uakron.edu/psychologyfromthemargins /vol4/iss1/4

Henderson, G. (1967). Role model for lower class Negro boys. Personnel and Guidance Journal, 9, 6-10.

Hill, P. Jr. (1991). *"Forward to the past": Africentric rites of passage.* Paper presented at the conference of the 21st Century Commission on African-American Males, Washington, DC.

Hill, P. Jr. (1992). Coming of age: African American male rites of passage. Chicago, IL African American Images.

Hill, R. B. (1988). *Adolescent males responsibility in African-American families.* Paper presented at the Conference on Manhood and Fatherhood: Adolescent Male Responsibility in Black Families, Atlanta, GA.

Hilliard, A. G. (1986). Pedagogy in Ancient Kemet. In Maulanga Karenga and Jacob Carruthers (Eds.), Kemet and the African Worldview: Research, Rescue, and Restoration. Los Angeles, CA: University of Sankore Press.

Hilliard, A. G. (1991). Testing African American Students. Chicago, IL: Third World Press.

Hilliard, A. G. (1994). Misunderstanding and Testing Intelligence. In J. I. Goodlad, and P. Keating (Eds.), Access to knowledge: The Continuing Agenda for Our Nation's Schools. New York, N. Y. College Board Publications.

Hilliard, A. G. (1995). The Maroon Within Us: Selected Essays on African American Community Socialization. Baltimore, MD: Black Classic Press.

Hilliard, A. G. (2002). African Power: Affirming African Indigenous Socialization in the face of the Culture Wars. Gainesville, FL: Makare Publishing Company.

Hollins, E., and Baba Nobles, W. W. (1995). African-American cultures, social practices, and effective education. Designing Staff Development Programs for Educators of African American Students: A resource guide for teachers, administrators, and staff developers. Documented within the Summer Institute Training. San Francisco State University.

Jagers, R.J., & Mock, L.O. (1995). The communalism scale and collectivistic-individualistic tendencies: Some preliminary findings. Journal of Black Psychology, 21, (2), 153-167.

Jagers, R.J., Smith, P., Mock, L.O. and Dill, E. (1997). An Africultural social ethos: Component orientation and some social implications. Journal of Black Psychology, 23, (4), 328-343.

Jahn, J. (1961). Muntu: African culture and the western world. New York: Grover Press

James, G.G.M. (1954) Stolen Legacy: The Egyptian Origins of Western Philosophy. Published by Julian Richardson Assoc Pub

Janz, Br. (2007). African Philosophy. 10.1515/9780748629299-049.

Jeff, M. F. X., Jr. (1994). Afrocentrism and African-American male youths. In Roland Mincy (Ed.), Nurturing young Black males (pp. 99-118). Washington DC: The Urban Institute Press.

Jensen and Haynes, (1986) ch. 6.

Johnson, R. and Leighton, P.S. (1995). Black Genocide? Preliminary thoughts on the plight of America's poor black men. Journal of African American Men (1) 3-21.

Jones, R. (1989). *Black Adolescents* Berkeley, CA: Cobb and Henry Publishers.

Juvenile Crime Study Committee. (1993). *Dealing with juvenile crime in Leon County: A report to the citizens of Leon County.* 21st Century Council, Tallahassee, FL.

Kagan, J. H., Moss, H. A., and Siegal, I. E. (1963). Psychological significance of styles conceptualization. In Basic cognitive processes in children. (Society for Research in Child Development, Monograph 86). Chicago: University of Chicago Press.

Kambon, K.K.K. (1992). The African personality in America: An African-centered framework. Tallahassee, FL: Nubian Nations Publications.

Kambon, K.K.K. and Hopkins, R. (1993). An African-centered analysis of Penn's et al. 's critique of the Own-race preference assumption underlying Africentric models of personality. Journal of Black Psychology. 19 (3) 342-349.

Kaya, H. O. (2014). *Revitalizing African Indigenous Ways of Knowing and Knowledge Production* https://www.e-ir.info/2014/05/26/revitalizing-african-indigenous-ways-of-knowing-and-knowledge-production/

Kaya, H. O. & Seleti, Y. N. (2013). African indigenous knowledge systems and relevance of higher education in South Africa. *The International Education Journal: Comparative Perspectives,* 30–44 ISSN 1443-1475 www.iej-comparative.org.

Kenyatta, J. (1965). *Facing Mount Kenya.* New York, NY: Vintage Books Edition.

Kerka, S. (1986). *On second thought: Using new cognitive research in vocational education.* Ann Arbor, MI. (ERIC Document Reproduction Service No. ED272699).

Kessi, S., Suffla, S. and Seedat, M. (2022). *Decolonial Enactments in Community Psychology.* Switzerland, AG. Springer Nature.

Kirschenman, J., and Neckerman, K. M. (1991). In C. Jencks & P. E. Peterson (Eds.) "We'd love to hire them, But . . .': The meaning of race for employers," in *The urban underclass.* The Brookings Institution, Washington.

Krueger, J. (1996). Personal beliefs and cultural stereotypes about racial characteristics. *Journal of Personal and Social Psychology.* 71 (3) 536-548.

Kunjufu, K. (1985). *Countering the conspiracy to destroy Black boys.* Chicago, IL: African-American Images.

Landrine, H. and Klonoff, E.A. (1995). The African American acculturation scale II: Cross validation and short form. *Journal of Black Psychology,* 21, (2), 124-152.

Latimer, L.Y. (1995, October). Facing the fear. *Emerge* 38-41.

Lee, C. (1991). A group counseling model for developing manhood among Black males adolescents. *Journal of Health Care for the Poor and Underserved.* 2, 19-25.

Lee, C. (1992). *Empowering Young Black Males.* Ann Arbor, MI. (ERIC Document Reproduction Service No. ED354468).

Lewis, J. J., (1990). Learning processes among Black students: What academic support personnel need to know. *Journal of College Student Development.* 30(2) 179-180.

Lomotey, K. (1989). *African-American principals: School leadership and success. contributions in Afro-American and African Studies.* Ann Arbor, MI. (ERIC Document Reproduction Service No.).

Macrae, C. N., Bodenhausen, G. V., Milne, A. B., Thorn, T. M. J., and Castelli, L. (1997). On the Activation of Social Stereotypes: The Moderating Role of Processing Objectives. *Journal of Experimental Social Psychology* 33, 471–489.

Majors, R. and Billson, J.M. (1992). *Cool Pose.* New York, NY: Simon and Schuster Inc.

Martín-Baró, I. (1989). Political violence and war as causes of psychosocial trauma in El Salvador. *International Journal of Mental Health,* 18(1), 3-20. http://www.jstor.org/stable/41344526.

Martín-Baró, I. (1994) *Writings for a liberation psychology,* (A. Aron & S. Corne, Ed.). Harvard University Press.

Maurer, K.L., Park, B. And Judd C. M. (1996). Stereotypes, Prejudice, and Judgments of Group Members: The Mediating Role of Public Policy Decisions. *Journal of Experimental Social Psychology* 32, 411–436.

Mbiti, J. S. (1970). *African Religions and Philosophy.* Garden City, NJ: Anchor Books.

McCarthy, P. R. and Meier, S. (1983). Effects of race and psychological variables on college student writing. *Journal of Instructional Psychology.* 10 (3). 149-157.

McNair, J. (2004) *Culture: What It Is! The Question of Culture.* Webarchive.

Metofe, P. Wilson, D. & Graves, K (2018). The relationship among Black consciousness, self-esteem, self-efficacy and academic achievement in African American students. (Ed. James L. Conyers) in *Africana Methodology: A Social Study of Research, Triangulation and Meta-theory.* Cambridge Scholars Publishing, Newcastle upon Tyne, United Kingdom.

Meyer, B. *Voodooism in Haiti.* https://scholar.library.miami.edu/ emancipation/ religion3.htm.

Monroe, S. (1995, October). America's most feared. *Emerge* 20-28.

Moore, E. G. J. (1986). Family socialization and the IQ test of performance of traditionally and transracially adopted Black children. *Developmental Psychology.* 22 (3) 317-326.

Moore, E. G. J. (1987). Ethnic social milieu and Black children's intelligence test achievement. *Journal of Negro Education.* 86 (1) 44-52.

Moore, E. G. J. and Smith, A. W. (1985). Mathematics aptitude: Effects of coursework, household language, and ethic differences. *Urban Education.* 20 (3) 273-294.

Morrow, S.L. Gore, P. A.. JR., and Campbell, B. W. (1996). The Application of a Sociocognitive Framework to the Career Development of Lesbian Women and Gay Men. *Journal of Vocational Behavior.* 48, 136–148.

Myers, M. A. and Sanders-Thompson, V. L. (1994). Africentricity: An analysis of two culture specific instruments. *The Western Journal of Black Studies.* 18 (4) 179-184.

Myers, L. M. (1993). *Understanding an Afrocentric World View: Introduction to an Optimal Psychology.* Dubuque, IA. Kendall/Hunt Publishing Co.

Nelson-LeGall, S. and Jones, E. (1991). Classroom help seeking behavior of African-American children. *Education and Urban Society.* 24 (1) 27-40.

Nelson, T. E. Acker, M. and Manis, M. (1996). Irrepressible Stereotypes. *Journal of experimental social psychology* (32) 13-38.

Nkondo, M. (2012). *Indigenous African knowledge systems in a polyepistemic world: The capabilities approach and the translatability of knowledge systems.* Paper presented at the Southern African Regional Colloquium on Indigenous African knowledge systems: methodologies and epistemologies for research, teaching, learning, and community engagement in higher education. Howard College Campus: University of KwaZulu-Natal.

Nobles, W. W. (1976) Black People in White Insanity: An Issue for Black Community Mental Health. *Journal of Afro-American Issues,* 4 (1) pp. 21-27.

Nobles, W. W. (1976) Extended-Self: Re-Thinking the So-Called Negro Self-Concept. *Journal of Black Psychology,* 2 (2).

Nobles, W. W. (1978) Understanding Human Transformation; The Praxis of Science and Culture in *Seeking the SAKHU: Foundational Writings for an African Psychology.* Third World Press, Chicago 2006.

Nobles, W. W. (1980). Extended self: rethinking the so-called Negro self-concept. In R. Jones (Ed.) *Black Psychology.* (pp. 99-105). New York Harper and Row.

Nobles, W. W. (1985). *Africanity and the Black Family: the development of a theoretical model.* Oakland, CA. Black Family Institute Publication.

Nobles, W. W. (1986). *African Psychology: Towards its reclamation, reascension, & revitalization.* Oakland, CA. Black Family Institute Publication.

Nobles, W. W. (1986). *The KM Ebit Husia.* Oakland, CA. Black Family Institute Publication.

Nobles, W. W. (1989a). *Towards an understanding of the philosophical bases of racism.* Oakland, CA. Institute for the Advanced Study of Black Family, Life, and Culture, Inc. unpublished document.

Nobles, W. W. (1989b) *The HAWK federation and the development of Black adolescent males: Towards a solution to the crises of America's young Black men. Testimony before the Select Committee on Children, Youth, and Families.* Congressional Hearings on America's Young Black Men: Isolated and In Trouble. Washington, D. C. (ERIC Document Reproduction Service No. ED340789).

Nobles, W. W. (1991). Psychometrics and African American reality: A question of cultural antimony. In A. G. Hilliard (Eds.) Testing African American Students. Chicago, IL: Third World Press.

Nobles, W. W. (2012) *To Be African or Not to Be: The Question of Identity or Authenticity-Some Preliminary Thoughts* retrieved 2/20/2020 http:// www.ayanetwork.com/aya/wal/african%20to%20be%20or%20not%20wade%20onobles.pdf

Nobles, W. W. (2013) Shattered Consciousness, Fractured Identity: Black Psychology and the Restoration of the African Psyche. *Journal of Black Psychology* 39(3) 232–242.

Nobles, W. W. (2015). From Black Psychology to *Sakhu Djaer*: Implications for the Further Development of a Pan African Black Psychology. *Journal of Black Psychology* 2015, Vol. 41(5) 399–414.

Nobles, W. W. and Goddard L. L. (1984). *Understanding the Black Family: A Guide for Scholarship and Research.* Oakland, CA. Black Family Institute Publication.

Nobles, W.W., Goddard L.L. and Cavil III, W. E. (1990). *HAWK Federation perfected Black manhood training and development program training procedures guide.* (restricted Document). Oakland, CA. Institute for the Advanced Study of Black Family Life and Culture.

Nobles, W.W. and Goddard (1992). *An African-Centered Model of Prevention for African-American youth at high risk.* In CSAP Technical report #6, Rockville, MD: U.S. Department of Health and Human Services.

Nobles, W.W., & Nobles Adeleke, Z. (2011) *NSaka Sunsum (Touching the Spirit): A Pedagogy and Process of Black Educational Excellence.* Multicultural Learning and Teaching. · January 2011 DOI: 10.2202/2161-2412.1076

Nunn, K.B. (2019) *"Essentially Black": Legal Theory and the Morality of Conscious Racial Identity,* 97 Neb. L. Rev. 287, available athttps://scholarship.law .ufl.edu/facultypub/832/

Obiakor, F. E. and Alawiye, O. (1990). *Development of accurate self-concept in Black children.* ERIC Digest. Ann Arbor Michigan.

Obiakor, F. E. (1992). *At-Risk youngsters: Methods that work.* Presented at the Annual Conference of the Tennessee Association on Young Children. Nashville, TN.

Obiakor, F. E. and Fowler, W. R. (1991). *African-American males experiencing school failure: Alternative self-concept model for special educators.* Presented at the Council For Exceptional Children's Topical Conference on At-Risk Children and Youth. New Orleans, LA.

Osei-Tutu, A., Vivian A. Dzokoto, V. A., Affram, A. A., Adams, G., Norberg, J., and Doosje, B. (2020) Cultural models of well-being implicit in four Ghanaian languages. *Cultural Psychology* https://doi.org/10.3389/fpsyg.2020.01798.

Oshodi, J. E. (2004). *Back then and right now in the history of Psychology: A history of human psychology in African perspectives for the new millennium.* Bloomington, IN: Author House

Perkins, E. (1986). Harvesting a new generation. Chicago, IL: Third World Press.

Piper-Mandy, E. and Rowe, T. D. (2010). Educating African-Centered Psychologists: Towards a Comprehensive Paradigm.*The Journal of Pan African Studies*, 3(8).

Powell. F. (1991). African centered education: What is it? And why do we need It? Ann Arbor, MI.(ERIC Document Reproduction Service No. ED344832).

Prilleltensky, I. (2003). Understanding, resisting, and overcoming oppression: Toward psychopolitical validity. *American Journal of Community Psychology*, 31(1-2), 195-201. https://doi.org/10.1023/A:1023043108210

Prilleltensky, I. (2008).The role of power in wellness, oppression, and liberation: The promise of psychopolitical validity. *Journal of Community Psychology*, 36(2), 116–136.

Pritchard, R. (1990). The effects of cultural schemata on reading processing strategies. *Reading Research Quarterly* 25 (4) 272-293.

Reynolds, R. E., Taylor, M. A., Steffensen, M. S., Shirley, L. L., Anderson, R. C. (1982). Cultural schemata and reading comprehension. *Reading Research Quarterly* 17 (3) 353-360.

Richards, D.M. (1980). Let the circle be unbroken. Trenton, NJ. The Red Sea Press

Ryan C.S., Judd, C.M and Park, B. (1996) Effects of Racial Stereotypes on Judgments of Individuals: The Moderating Role of Perceived Group Variability. *Journal of Experimental Social Psychology* 32, 71-103.

Schmeck, R. R., Ribich, F., & Ramanaiah, N. V. (1977). Development of a self-report inventory for assessing individual differences in learning processes. *Applied Psychological Measurement* 1 (3) 413-431.

Shade, B. J. (1991). African American patterns of cognition. In R. Jones (Eds.) *Black Psychology*, Third Edition. Berkeley, CA: Cobb and Henry.

Shor, I. (1992). *Empowering Education: critical teaching for social change.* Chicago, The University of Chicago Press.

Som'e, M. P. (1993). *Ritual: Power, healing, and community.* Portland, OR: Swan Raven & Co.

Spencer, M. B. (1991). *Adolescent African-American male self-esteem: Suggestions for mentoring program content. Mentoring program structures for young minority males.* Conference paper series. Urban Institute, Washington DC: (ERIC document #ED359313).

Steele, S.M. and Aronson, J. (1995). Stereotype threat and the intellectual test performance of african americans. *Journal of Personality and Social Psychology.* 69 (5) 797-811.

T'Shaka, O. (1995). *Return to the African mother principle of male and female equality.* Vol. 1. Oakland, CA. Pan African Publishers and Distributors.

Taylor O. L. and Lee, D. L. (1991). Standardized tests and African-American children: Communication and language issues. In A. G. Hilliard (Eds.) *Testing African American Students.* Chicago, IL: Third World Press.

Taylor, J., Obiechina, C. & Harrison, S. (1998). Toward a psychology of liberation and restoration: Answering the challenge of cultural alienation. In R.L. Jones (Ed.). *African American Mental Health.* Hampton, VA: Cobb & Henry.

Taylor, R. L. (1989). Black youth role models and the social construction of identity. In R. Jones (Ed.). *Black Adolescents* (pp. 155-174). Berkeley, CA. Cobb and Henry Publishers.

Thompson, B. (1992). Motivating African American middle school boys toward excellence through high interest and activity. Nova University: (ERIC document #ED357991).

Tobias, R. (1989). Educating Black Urban adolescents: Issues and programs. In R. Jones (Ed.) *Black Adolescents* (pp. 207-227). Berkeley, CA. Cobb and Henry Publishers.

Toldson, I. L. and Pasteur. A. B. (1982). Rhythm: A psycho-philosophical perspective on Black behavior. Journal of Non-White Concerns in Personnel Guidance 10 (3) 82-93.

Turner, V. (1969). *The Ritual Process: Structure and Anti-Structure.* Hawthorne, NY: Aldine De Gruyter Van der Walt, L. J. (2020). Interpretivism-Constructivism as a Research Method in the Humanities and Social Sciences – More to It Than Meets the Eye. *International Journal of Philosophy and Theology*, 8 (1), 59-68. https://doi.org/10.15640/ijpt.v8n1a5

Vanzant, I. (1993). Acts of faith: Daily meditation for people of color. New York, NY: Fireside.

Warfield-Coppock, N. (1990). *Africentric theory and application, volume I: Adolescents rites of passage.* Washington, DC. Baobab Associates.

Warfield-Coppock, N. (1990). *Africentric theory and application, volume I: Adolescents rites of passage.* Washington, DC. Baobab Associates.

Warfield-Coppock, N. (1992). The rites of passage movement: A resurgence of African-centered practices for socializing African American youth. *Journal of Negro Education* 61 (4) 472-81.

Warfield-Coppock, N. (1994). The rites of passage: Extending education into the African American community. In M. J. Shujaa (Eds.), *Too Much Schooling Too Little Education: A Paradox of Black Life in White Societies.* Trenton, NJ: African World Press, Inc.

Watts, R. J. (1992). Racial identity and preferences for social change strategies among African Americans. *Journal of Black Psychology.* 18 (2) 1-18.

Watts, R. J. and Abdul-Adil, J. (in press). Psychological aspects of oppression and sociopolitical development. In R. Newby and T. Manley (Eds.) *The poverty of inclusion, innovation, and interventions: The Dilemma of the African American underclass.* Rutgers, NJ: Rutgers University Press.

Weffort, F. (1967). in the preface of *Educacao como Practica da Liberdade.* Rio de Janeiro.

Westman, A. S. (1993). Learning styles are content specific and probably influenced by content areas studied. *Psychological Reports.* 73 (2) 512-514.

Williams, C. (1987). *The destruction of Black civilization: Great issues of a race from 4500 B.C. to 2000 A.D.* Chicago, IL: Third World Press.

Williams, V. & Wilson, D. (2016) White Racial Framing and its impact on African-American Male Mental Health in 2nd Volume of the African American Male series, *Counseling African American Males: Effective Therapeutic Interventions and Approaches.* (Ed. William Ross) Information Age Publishing

Willis, M. G. (1992). Learning styles of African American children: A review of the literature and interventions. *Journal of Black Psychology.* 16 (1) 47-61.

Wilson, A. (1990). *Black on black violence.* New York, NY: African World InfoSystems.

Wilson, A. (1991). *Understanding Black Adolescent male violence.* New York, NY: African World InfoSystems.

Wilson, D. (1995). *Evaluation of Black manhood training and development: the importance of a culturally consistent curriculum.* (Thesis:restricted document).

Wilson, D. (2001). Evaluation of a Black Manhood Training and Development Program: The Importance of a Culturally Consistent Curriculum. *African American Male Research, 5(2).* April/May 2000.

Wilson, D. (2012). Competency, connectedness, and consciousness: Mental Health Model. In *"We ain't crazy! Just coping with a crazy system": Pathways into the Black population for eliminating mental health disparities* (Eds.) V. D. Woods, N. J. King, S. M. Hanna and C. Murray (pp. 159-161).

Wilson, D. (2017) Education/Certification: Its importance to an African American Holistic Wellness Hub. In *Research and Planning Design Initiative Report Supplement: Technical Support Full Thematic Briefing Papers.* (Eds. Nobles, Goddard and Watson) African American Wellness Hub ACBHCS.

Wilson, D. (2020). African Cultural Psychology. *Alternation,* 27(1) 85 – 112 DOI https://doi.org/10.29086/2519-5476/2020/v27n1a6

Wilson, D. & Williams, V. (2013) "Ubuntu: A Model of Positive Mental Health for African Americans". *Psychology Journal,* 10(2): 80-100 *www.psychologicalpublishing.com*

Wilson, D. & Williams, V. (2014) Mental Illness Defined: Sociological Perspectives in *Cultural Sociology of Mental Illness:* An A-to-Z Guide (Ed. Andrew Scull) January 2014, (pp. 518-521) *SAGE* Publications, Inc.

Wilson, D. Muhammad Ali, AKA "The Greatest" Demonstration of Ubuntu In book: Muhammad Ali in Africana Cultural Memory (Edited by James L. Conyers Jr. & Christel N. Temple) *Anthem Africana Studies* Hardcover – January 2022, Publisher: Anthem Press. ISBN:9781785277207 https://www.researchgate.net/publication/349028993_Muhammad_Ali_AKA_The_Greatest_Demonstration_of_Ubuntu

Wilson, D., Asby, A. & Bryant, C. (2020). Evaluation of the relationship among moral foundations, criminal justice, and perceptions of terrorism in African American College Students attending HBCU. In *Blacks in Higher Education: A review of Social Science Research, Vol 8* (Ed. James L. Conyers Jr.) Routledge Taylor and Francis Group, UK.

Wilson, D., Boyd, E., & Moore, P., (2008). Psychological disorder in juvenile offenders and the impact of placement. *The Journal of Knowledge and Best Practices in Juvenile Justice and Psychology,* 2(1).

Wilson, D., Foster, J., Anderson, S., & Mance, G. (2009). Racial socialization moderating effect between poverty stress and psychological symptoms for African American youth. *Journal of Black Psychology* 2009 35,102-124.

Wilson, D., Moore, P. & Bland, M. M. (2008). The impact of culturally enriched extracurricular program on academic and social performance for African American adolescent males. *Journal of the Alliance of Black School Educators* 7(2).

Wilson, D., Moore, P., Boyd, E. L., Easley, J., & Russell, A. (2008). The identification of cultural factors that impact well-being among African American college students. *Psychology Journal.* 5(2).

Wilson, D., Olubadewo, S. & Williams, V. (2016) Ubuntu: Framework for Black College Male Positive Mental Health: 2nd Volume of the African American Male series, *Counseling African American Males: Effective Therapeutic Interventions and Approaches.* (Ed. William Ross) Information Age Publishing.

Oba T. Woodyard and Cecile A. Gadson (2018) Emerging Black Scholars: Critical Reflections on the Impact of the Association of Black Psychologists. *Journal of Black Psychology* 44(8) 772–790

Appendixes

Appendix #1

Table 1

Ani/Baba Nobles Cultural Schema

Cultural Manifestation (Orientation)

surface level 3   Utamaroho

Behaviors Attitudes Values   Praxis Pedagogy

Ideas, Language, Symbols, Rituals, Inventions, Mores

Traditions, Ceremonies, Customs, Beliefs and Practices

Dictates:

The vital force or conscious energy (ngolo zasikama) force set in motion by *"collective behaviors"* of members in a particular group

Cultural Aspects (Templates)

deep level 2   **Utamawazo**

Ethos	**Worldview**	**Ideology**	**Paradigm**
Set of guiding principles	Comprehensive ideas about order	Ideational basis of conduct	philosophical and theoretical framework

Explains: Cultural structured thought framework by members of particular groups

Cultural Factors (Core)

deep level 1   Asili

Ontology   Cosmology   Axiology

Nature of Being   Origin/structure   Primary universal
  (essence)   of the universe   relations

Determines: The cultural essence of the inertia character or "germ/
 seed"

Epistemology

Theory of knowledge, ways of knowing

Praxis - practice, as distinguished from theory.

Paradigm - a typical example or pattern of something; a model.

Pedagogy - the method and practice of teaching, especially as an
academic subject or theoretical concept.

Appendix #2
Table 2
African Worldview vs. European Worldview

	African Worldview	**European Worldview**
Mind	Right Brain functioning and mid brain analysis. Characterized by spiritual concepts such as love, affection and sharing. The mid brain is characterized by equal balances or rational thought and creative thought.	Left brain functioning Characterized by egotism individualism. Rationalizes, intellectualizes and is non-creative.
Time	Time is based on the beginning and ending of an event. Time is composed of the seen and unseen Time is fixed by the event or to nature. (e.g., the seasons start according to nature's unseen clock).	Time is a fixed, abstract, measurable duration. The seasons start according to fixed calendar
Economics	Based on abundance sharing of goods, talent, labor, child rearing and knowledge with society.	Economics is based upon of scarcity or the creation of shortages. Thus only an elite few can gain access to goods, talent and knowledge.

Table #3

WORLD VIEW COSMOLOGICAL SCHEMAS

African	Ethos/Basic Reality Orientation	European
Life is Spirit		Life is Material
Known through A 6th Sense		Known Through the 5 Senses
Spiritual force Animates All Matter		Physical Laws Act On Matter
Survival Thrust Is For The Group		Survival Thrust of the Fittest

Philosophical Values and Customs

African		European
Interdependence	vs.	Independence - Competition
- Group Rights		- Individual Rights
Di-Unital & Wholistic	vs.	Dichotomous & Exclusive Logic
Cyclical-Rhythmic		Linear Discrete Time Concept
Time Concept Eternity		Finite Measurements of Components
Is Immeasurable		
Death Is Transformative Birth		Birth and Death Are Final
Value Is Fundamental in Being		Value Is Based on Doing – Material
Nature/Divine Order Is Power		Power Is Derived Through Control/Aggression
Emphasis On Social Technology		Emphasis on Material Technology
Harmony Among Peoples		Seeks Domination of Peoples

Psycho- Behavioral Modalities

Collectivism - Extended Family	Individualism - Nuclear Family
sociability	do "your own thing"
interdependence	emotionally distant from in-groups
family integrity	self-reliance
collectivism	hedonism
Eldership Placed At The Top	Youth Placed At Top
(Wisdom)	(Strength)
All Children Are Raised	Unwanted Children
By All Adults	Are Aborted
Differences Are Synergistic	Differences Are Prioritized
(Compliments)	(Unrelated)
Sexes Are Equally Divine	Sexism Fundamental Between Sex
All Elements Are	Superiority/Inferiority
Equally Necessary	Defines Need

Mode of Production

Territorial States (Federation)	Nation States (City-State)
Stronger Responsive to Weaker	Stronger Exploits Weak
Development from within	Development From External
	Exploitation
Trade by need	Trade by Greed
Acceptance of Cultural Pluralism	Cultural Monism/
	Supremacy Domination
Solidarity	unique/uniqueness
submit to the authority of group	be "the best" at others expense
sacrifice for the group	emotional distance from in-group

Table 4
Historical Environment for African Youth
(Perkins' African American Roots to the Present)

	Environmental Characteristics	**Behavior Outcomes**
PRE-MAAFA		
AFRICAN ROOTS	-supportive environment	-highly discipline
	-stable family unit	-positive self-concept
	-close kinship bonds	-prosocial
	-supportive institutions	-cultural competence
	-well-defined roles	-self-appreciation
	-RITES OF PASSAGE	
MAAFA		
CAPTIVITY AND	-death of 90-100 million	-resistant or suppressed behavior
	-uprooted kinship bonds	-psychological scars
	-physical punishment	-damaged self concept
SLAVERY	-suppression of culture	-suppressed behavior
	-hostile environment	-adaptive behavior
	-suppression of family	-self-diffusion
	-distortion of images	-cultural incompetence
	-disruption of Rites of Passage	-confused self-concept
		-depreciated character
SO-CALLED EMANCIPATION		-dependent behavior
	-hostile environment	-institutional racism
	-colonized education	
	- " " culture	
	scientific colonialism	
MAAFA	-ghetto-colony	-ambivalent behavior
PRESENT	-street institution	-reactionary behavior
	-cultural confusion	-aberrant values

If you don't understand White Supremacy then all that you think you know will only confuse you!

Appendix #5
America's stereotypes (Popular Consciousness) regarding Black men.

Black men are superior athletically

Black men are possessive

Black men are lustful

Black men are materialistic

Black men have a childlike attraction to material wealth

Black men control their emotions and suppress their fears

Black men are sexually aggressive and denigrating

Black men are non-monogamous

Black men are violent

Black men do poorly in school

Black men can't work effectively together and are competitive

Black men are loyal to white people

Black men are overly dependent upon white people

Black men are lazy

Black men are pragmatic

Black men want to live off of the woman

Black men won't support their children

Black men are insecure

Black men are irresponsible

Black men are untrustworthy

Black men are docile

Black men are paranoid

Black men disrespect and won't protect their women

Black men are independent of attitudes and opinions of others, i.e., non-conforming

About the Author

Dr. Wilson is a Husband, Father, an African Centered Psychologist, and Educator. He continues to inspire his audience with his unusually profound idea about Blackness, consciousness, health, and thinking as a black man. He is convinced that Black Consciousness is African Consciousness, and this consciousness is the world's greatest power. The power to ignite, inform, and inspire the minds of revolutionists. Dr. Derek Wilson is a man on a mission: to improve mental health for people of African descent. He established the working idea of a positive mental health model for African people as *connectedness*, *competency*, *and consciousness*.